JACK THE RIPPER
UNMASKED

JACK THE RIPPER

UNMASKED

THE REAL IDENTITY OF THE WORLD'S MOST INFAMOUS KILLER IS REVEALED AT LAST

WILLIAM BEADLE

JOHN BLAKE

Published by John Blake Publishing Ltd,
3 Bramber Court, 2 Bramber Road,
London W14 9PB, England

www.johnblakepublishing.co.uk

First published in hardback in 2009

ISBN: 978-1-84454-688-6

British Library Cataloguing-in-Publication Data:

A catalogue record for this book is available from the British Library.

Design by www.envydesign.co.uk

Printed in the UK by CPI William Clowes Beccles NR34 7TL

1 3 5 7 9 10 8 6 4 2

Papers used by John Blake Publishing are natural, recyclable products made from wood grown in sustainable forests. The manufacturing processes conform to the environmental regulations of the country of origin.

My four years of research for this book took me to many different places, some of which were more pleasant to deal with than others. Those who stood out as kind, helpful and patient were the Records Offices of Scotland and Worcestershire, the Newspaper Library at Colindale, the Family Record Centre and the London Metropolitan Archives. I would also like to thank my friend Dave Cuthbertson, whose help was invaluable and who on one occasion found in an afternoon the answers to questions that had been bedevilling me for months. Likewise, the other members of the Whitechapel (1888) Society for all their warmth and friendship. Finally, my fellow Ripper authors who, irrespective of whether they agree with me, have always been supportive.

This book is dedicated to my greatest friend, John Finbar Lehane, a good man in every sense of the word, stalwart, honest, upright, his friendship is beyond the wealth of this world.

James Berry, the executioner who hanged William Bury on 24 April 1889.
Reproduced by kind permission Getty Images.

CONTENTS

CHAPTER ONE

HELL'S TEETH

She was only a little woman, no more than five foot tall, and she had clearly seen better days. Her clothes, a black skirt and jacket, were old and dirty and the crêpe bonnet she wore only emphasised the fact that she was a woman of the streets and dosshouses. The human being inside them was fighting a losing battle for her life because, at 47, she had a disease of the lungs that was well advanced and made her feel constantly unwell. On the previous day, she had told a friend, 'It's no use my giving way. I must pull myself together and go out and get some money, or I shall have no lodgings.'

But, as dawn came up on Saturday, 8 September 1888, she had neither money nor lodgings. Instead, she had walked the grimy collection of mean little thoroughfares between Commercial Street and Brick Lane in London's East End for hour after hour, going round and round the same dark, dispiriting places like the circle of the suicides in Dante's inferno.

Five thirty found her in Hanbury Street with at last the prospect of earning some money, by renting out her disease-ravaged little body to a young man for whatever use he might want to make of it for a few minutes.

The bargain was swiftly struck: 'Will you?' he asked. 'Yes,' she

1

replied, and then they disappeared through the passage of 29 Hanbury Street into its backyard.

A few minutes later, the man re-emerged and scurried away. The woman did not. Instead, she lay on her back in the yard with her now sightless eyes staring into empty space. She had first been strangled and then her throat cut in two jagged lines from ear to ear. Below that, her abdomen was sundered up the middle with the small intestines and part of her belly wall draped across her right shoulder. Two more flaps of belly wall and her pubic area lay in a pool of blood above her left shoulder. The uterus and parts of her bladder and vagina had been cut out and taken away.

The dead woman's name was Annie Chapman and she was the third fatal victim of the Victorian serial killer known to history as 'Jack the Ripper'.

Legend has it that Jack the Ripper was the world's first serial killer. It is more accurate to say that he was history's first *notorious* multicide. There were others before him who accounted for many more victims, and over a longer period of time, than he did.

The term 'viper in the bosom of the family' might have been invented for either Gersina Gottfried or Helene Jegado, two women born in Germany and France respectively in the latter part of the 18th century.

Blue-eyed, blonde and attractive, Gottfried poisoned her way through two families, including her own, and diverse other persons, killing in excess of 30 people by her own count. Ostensibly, her motives were financial and to remove individuals who stood in her way, but Gottfried admitted that she derived pleasure from killing; it gave her a feeling akin to a sexual orgasm. She was executed in 1828.

Helene Jegado used arsenic as a means of avenging herself on a world that didn't care about her. Killing people was her rationale for living, her one escape from a bleak existence that began in an orphanage and continued first as an insignificant little housemaid, and then as a nun, Sister Helene. She was thrown out of the convent for murdering a fellow nun and went back to destroying her employers and fellow servants instead – 'Wherever I go, people die,' she whined. Nobody suspected such a pitiful creature till 1851. Then she was finally apprehended and sent to meet her final employer, Madame Guillotine. Jegado's final death toll is unknown but it was probably somewhere in the region of 40.[1]

As the 19th century wore on, so Gottfried's and Jegado's male counterparts began to appear. The latter was followed in France by Charles Avinmain[2] and Eusebuis Pieydagnelle, both butchers by trade. They practised their craft on their victims. Italian Vincenz Verzeni strangled two women and tore out their entrails,[3] while Jesse Pomeroy provided America with its first flowering of the demon seed. Hair-lipped, one-eyed and mentally retarded, Pomeroy murdered two children in Boston in 1874. He was only 14 at that time, but had commenced his deluge of atrocities two years previously with a series of vicious assaults on other boys.[4]

Arguably, John Williams, dubbed the 'Ratcliffe Highway Murderer', has some claim to be regarded as Britain's first known serial murderer. In December 1811, Williams was arrested for the wholesale slaughter of two families living in and off of the Ratcliffe Highway, a short distance away from Berner Street, where the Ripper struck down Elizabeth Stride almost 80 years later. The Highway (as it is now called) also runs parallel to Pennington Street, where another Ripper victim, Mary Kelly, apparently lived for a while.

The Ratcliffe Highway murders caused widespread fear and panic similar to the Ripper's reign of terror, partly due to the horrendous violence that attended them, and partly due to the seeming lack of motive, as if they were the work of a homicidal demon lighting his own hell fires, a point made with remarkable prescience by the writer Thomas De Quincey in 1827:

there mingled also in the thoughts of reflecting persons an
undercurrent of fearful expectation for the immediate
future. All perils, especially malignant, are recurrent. A
murderer, who is such by passion and by wolfish craving
for bloodshed as a mode of unnatural luxury, cannot
relapse into inertia.[5]

Little is known about John Williams, who committed suicide before
he could be brought to trial. He was young (27) and handsome in a
feminine sort of way. He was a merchant seaman by trade, and his last
captain had given him a bad character as a result of Williams's
impersonating an officer and taking part in a mutiny. Ashore, he was
a womanising drunk with a violent temper who was frequently
involved in fights. He may have been well educated and liked to pose
as a gentleman.

Williams resided within easy walking distance of the crimes and
appears to have known members of both families. The evidence
against him was at best circumstantial and there is a suspicion that he
may either have been set up by the real killer or have had an
accomplice who offloaded all the blame on him. But the fact remains
that there were no further outrages after Williams was detained.[6]

The two sets of killings, amounting to seven victims in total – one
a three-month-old baby – were ritualistically barbaric and, echoing
De Quincey, one has the impression that their perpetrator was
engaged in an orgiastic killing frenzy. It is this dimension that
separates the serial killer from other types of murderer. Brian
Marriner, in his book *A Century of Sex Killers*, provides us with these
graphic illustrations of the multicide going about his work:

> [Peter] Kurten tore out dogs' intestines. Mullins did the
> same with the girls he killed. Vacher disembowelled his
> victims as did Jack the Ripper. [Hamilton] Fish butchered

his; Ed Gein cut them up and hung them out to cure like animal carcasses. [Ed] Kemper preferred his women headless – that way there was no face to gaze at him; no eyes to observe him.[7]

What is interesting here is the way Marriner almost casually tosses the Ripper into the pot as just another example. This is correct. Although 'Jack' eternally holds our fascination, he was in fact simply one of the first of many who have stalked along the same path since. His allure lies in the fact that, officially, he was never caught. Unofficially, he was, and hanged the following spring, a fact known to at least some at Scotland Yard. This work is a biography of the man who was Jack the Ripper.

The essence of understanding him is to understand serial killers, why they are what they are and do what they do. Brian Marriner calls them 'zombies', by which he means men caught up in the throes of their own death agonies as they roam the city streets looking for victims.

Panic spreads in their wake, sometimes with dire consequences. During the hysteria caused by the Ratcliffe Highway murders, a young solicitor's clerk named Mellish was shot in the face and left blind by a man he chased, thinking he was the murderer.[8] In April 1889, 21-year-old Annie Masters drowned herself in Regent's Canal after a fortune teller predicated that she would fall victim to Jack the Ripper.[9] What is distressing is the utter futility of such incidents. Mellish was blinded on the day that John Williams was taken into custody; Jack the Ripper was awaiting execution in the death cell when Annie Masters took her own life.

Some serial killers derive a sense of power from the fear they cause; others, such as the Ripper, do not and shrink from their own infamy. Either way, it is a by-product of their own self-destruction, for the multicide is killing himself just as surely as he does his victims; it is the end of a long and harrowing journey, which often begins in the cradle.

The basic key to anybody's personality is their self-image, built up from earliest memories through into adulthood. The end product of how we see ourselves is the esteem in which we hold ourselves.

A person of low self-esteem will not thrive in the workplace, no matter how bright they are. They will not be able to forge relationships other than with those whom they see as being as weak and inadequate as they are themselves. Glad confident morning never comes and their sexuality will be bound up with their own imagined worthlessness. A poor self-image is often accompanied by feelings that sex is something unclean or unwholesome.

An American study of 36 sexually motivated killers found that 86 per cent came from stable economic backgrounds and that 80 per cent of the offenders possessed average or above-average intelligence. But closer scrutiny of their childhoods revealed that in all cases the family unity significantly malfunctioned in one way or more. Failings included alcohol or drug abuse, sexual difficulties, insanity and criminal behaviour. Seventy-four per cent of the offenders themselves reported being psychologically abused in childhood, while 42 per cent had been subjected to physical or sexual abuse.[10]

The initiators of the study, John Douglas and Robert Ressler, then supervisory special agents of the FBI's Behavioral Science Unit, and Ann Burgess, professor of psychiatric nursing at the University of Pennsylvania, found a common theme of disturbing sexual development running through the childhoods of their case studies, closely linked to their unsatisfactory family backgrounds. Sixty-one per cent fantasised about rape, 71 per cent indulged in voyeurism and 72 per cent were turned on by fetishism. More than a third engaged in acts of sadism against animals. Other consistent behavioural traits included chronic lying and theft.[11] Helene Jegado was a petty thief as well as a murderer.

Burgess, Douglas and Ressler's respondents generally performed badly in school and, later, the workplace, including military service.

Almost half dropped out of high school altogether, and others achieved only poor grades. In employment, 80 per cent either had no job or exhibited difficulties in holding one down, and only 42 per cent of those who did military service were able to gain an honourable discharge.[12]

To compensate for his poor performance, the putative serial murderer will seek refuge in increasingly violent fantasies. Burgess, Douglas and Ressler chart this development through from childhood. The following example is in the words of one of the killers they interviewed:

> 'I was eight years old having nightmares, that's when I went off into the morbid fantasy and that's when the death trip started. The devil was sharing my bedroom with me, he was living in the furnace. The furnace was there battling away in the corner with an eerie glow in the middle of the night.'

The powerful imagery deployed here, along with the cohesive use of language, suggests that this particular individual might have made a writer had his formative years been different. Unhappily, his poor self-image did not allow him to see the possibilities inherent within himself. Instead, by adolescence, 'I knew that I was going to be killing, that it was going to end up like that. The fantasies were too strong. They were going on far too long and were too elaborate.'

Eventually, the fantasies will create an inner pressure, which can be released only by turning them into violent reality. This is what happened to our narrator when he reached adulthood. Here he describes the aftermath of his first two homicides:

> 'It was almost like a black comedy of errors, the first two killings . . . It was terrible because I made three fatal errors in the first twenty-four hours. I should have been busted .

. . I saw how loose I was and I tightened it up and when it happened again and again I got tighter and tighter and there weren't any more slips.'[13]

In some instances, killing may commence during adolescence – Jesse Pomeroy for example. On this side of the Atlantic, in Wales, Harold Jones strangled two little girls when he was 15 in 1921. At the other extreme, John Christie was 45 when he committed his first murder and in the US Hamilton 'Albert' Fish is supposed to have been even older than that (47) before his homicidal tendencies developed.[14]

More often than not, the multicide's fantasy world floats in a sea of alcohol or drugs. Here in Britain, an estimated 12,000 crimes a week are linked to alcohol and the British Medical Association estimates that 60–70 per cent of homicides, 75 per cent of stabbings, 70 per cent of beatings and 50 per cent of fights and domestic violence are drink-related in one way or another.[15] According to Joel Norris, author of *Serial Killers: The Growing Menace*, the majority of serial murderers have drink or drug problems.[16] Burgess, Douglas and Ressler's study emphasises this. Of 118 murders that they examined, 49 per cent had been committed while the perpetrator was under the influence of alcohol and in 35 per cent narcotics were a factor. In some instances, the propensity to kill developed with intake. In 30 per cent of cases the killer had been drinking more than usual, and in 12.5 per cent drug consumption was higher than the subject's normal usage.[17]

An example cited was that of a soldier who beat two men to death and then murdered a woman during a prolonged alcoholic binge. Another offender claimed that drink made him feel like Superman.[18]

However, the point has to be made that, while drink may exacerbate an existing problem, it does not create something that is not already there. In the case of the soldier, he was having problems in the service and felt that he was being browbeaten by his sergeant. Drink released these resentments. His fantasy world then took over and he killed the two men as surrogates for the sergeant. But it did not end there. When he awoke the following morning, the woman lay dead alongside him, killed with a broomstick that had been thrust into her vagina with such force that it had penetrated her lungs. Once unlocked, the demon inside him had taken over and gone to the very core of his problems, sexual inadequacy caused by a deep-rooted hatred of women. We shall see this mirrored in the Ripper murders.

Burgess, Douglas and Ressler divide multicides into two basic categories: organised and disorganised. In fact, the two categories often overlap, so much so that in some cases the offender fits into a middle category classified as 'mixed'.[19]

The basic difference between an 'organised' and 'disorganised' multicide is explained by the descriptive terms used. An organised killer plans his crimes, selects his victims according to type, takes care not to leave clues scattered around at the crime scene and conceals the victims' bodies. A notable example of this category was Ted Bundy, who was, next to Jack the Ripper, history's most notorious serial murderer. Handsome and charming, Bundy made full use of these attributes to engage his victims in conversation, after which he would knock them unconscious and drive them out to the murder sites, where he raped and killed them. He then left the bodies in the wilds to be devoured by animals. Some of the women Bundy killed have never been found.

The disorganised killer, on the other hand, commits his crimes on impulse, launching what investigators call 'blitz' attacks to subdue and retain control of his victims. Their bodies are left at the scenes of the crimes.[20] This type of offender is prone to mutilation murders, the purposes being to dehumanise the victim and attain sexual satisfaction. In these instances, penetration of the body by natural means is rare. The killer achieves his release through masturbation. Some do this directly over the body, others while next to it.[21] On the available evidence, the Ripper probably did the latter.[22]

Broadly, Jack the Ripper fits the classification of a disorganised killer. But it is not as simple as that, and serial killers do not always slot neatly into little pigeonholes. Robert Ressler in his autobiography, *Whoever Fights Monsters*, notes that, in almost a quarter of the cases he studied, organised multicides made no attempt to hide the body; while, more specifically, Ed Kemper, a highly organised murderer, engaged in mutilation; and Herbert Mullen, otherwise a bastion of the disorganised variety, used a car to pick up hitchhikers, normally a characteristic of organised slayers.[23] The last of these is particularly apposite, because Jack the Ripper also travelled to and from his killing ground by transport: a horse and cart.

John Douglas, who has built up a comprehensive profile of the Ripper over a 20-year period, describes him as basically a disorganised killer, but with some aspects pointing towards a mixed offender present at the crime scenes.[24] We can build on this separately by making a number of definite points arising from what we know about the Ripper. He took from his victims both keepsakes and body parts, a classic 'mixed' bag of organised and disorganised traits (see Chapter 11), no weapons were found at his London murder sites and he was of neat and tidy appearance, characteristics more usually associated with organised offenders.

In addition to these established facts, 'Jack' was a heavy drinker, suffered from stress factors that precipitated his crimes, moved away from the area after 1888 and was married: all, again, tenets of the organised, rather than disorganised, multicide – although in respect of his marital status this was largely a sham.

The man who will unfold before us had received a better education than somebody of his origins could have expected in the 19th century, but, echoing John Douglas again, he was not intelligent enough to take advantage of it (see the next chapter). This, in an oblique sort of way, somehow seems to sum up his offender classification: fundamentally disorganised, but with organised elements in his makeup.

At this point it will be instructive to look at what Burgess, Douglas and Ressler describe as a 'motivational model', a sexual murderer who encapsulates their research. I have chosen to use the same example as they do because there are some striking parallels between this individual and the man who committed the Ripper murders.

The authors call the subject 'Warren' to protect his anonymity under the terms of his participation in their programme.

Warren was born in Mobile, Alabama, in spring 1947.[25] As with the Ripper, though for different reasons, the first months of his life were traumatic. Warren was a premature baby who spent the first nine days of his life in an incubator and was subsequently hospitalised again in the summer, during which, according to family legend, he 'died' and was brought back to life, giving rise to a belief on his part in later life that he was somehow special. Judging from remarks made immediately prior to his death, Jack the Ripper seems to have held a similar view of himself.

Warren's childhood is best described as a confused mess. Up to the age of seven, he slept in the same bed as his mother and thereafter for another eight years in the same room, apparently to shield her from the advances of his alcoholic father. During this time, the father shared a bedroom with Warren's elder sister.

His mother and maternal grandmother, both strict disciplinarians, regularly beat Warren. He believed that outsiders viewed him as a 'freak' and thought of himself as a dog who got petted only if he jumped through the right hoops. The self-image on display here is about as low as it gets. The family environment might stand as a prototype for that put forward by Dr Alice Miller, a Swiss psychoanalyst who believes that harsh and unfeeling discipline imposed on children, allegedly for their own good, destroys their self-worth and desensitises them, leaving them walking time bombs ready to go off as adults.[26]

Both at school and at home, Warren showed a tendency to wander off into a fantasy world. What he says happened to him at the age of 12 may or may not be part of that world. As Warren tells it, he was pounced upon by two women who forced him to engage in oral sex on one of them while the other held a knife to his throat. Beforehand they had tried and failed to bring him to an erection.

In all probability, this was a fantasy, but one that charts the way in which his mind was developing because at around the same time he began to spy on his sister in the bathroom and developed a fetish for female underwear and a compulsion to masturbate. Like the Ripper, he was the youngest of four children and was deprived of his two eldest siblings (in Warren's case, brothers) as role models because they had left home. Jack, as we will observe, lost the kinship of his brother and sisters in very much more traumatic circumstances.

In adolescence, Warren began to show a propensity for violence. The women in his family, including his sister, encouraged him to hit his father, but on occasions he also turned on his mother and struck her over trivial matters. At 14 he began to run with a street gang and became uncontrollable.

Worse inevitably followed. In April 1963, he was charged with attacking and robbing an elderly blind woman and sexually assaulting her 14-year-old niece. While these indictments were pending, he shot dead a second old woman; she had made the mistake of remonstrating with him about his behaviour. In retrospect, it seems clear that he was, in effect, killing his tyrannical grandmother through her.

Arrested again, this time for murder, he escaped prosecution when his father provided him with an alibi.[27] He did not own up to this crime till 1976. The other charges pending against him were dismissed, on a technicality.

Warren completed his education and acquired a girlfriend of sorts, a 13-year-old with whom he maintained a platonic relationship. On the surface he showed no interest in sex. Beneath was a different matter: ugly fantasies were festering. They came into flower on an

October evening in 1965, a month after he had joined the army, when he attacked and almost killed a 19-year-old woman, choking her and battering her about the head with a large metal ashtray. She was a stranger to him and the assault was entirely unprovoked.

Warren was convicted of attempted murder and sentenced to 20 years' hard labour. He served only seven and a half. During his time in prison, his mother campaigned indefatigably on his behalf. Theirs was a deeply ambiguous relationship and central to the way he had developed in life. She simultaneously both succoured and emasculated him while he in turn loved and hated her in equal measure. The same core problems are evident with Jack the Ripper. He never really knew his mother but hated her and killed both her and his sister over and over again.

Warren was released late in 1973 despite the warnings of a psychiatrist that he posed a clear and present danger to women (this was a minority opinion). He went to work in a shipbuilding yard and began his first proper relationship with a woman, a divorcee four years his senior who had a child.

History here was repeating itself, albeit unknown. The man who was Jack the Ripper evinced no outward interest in women up to his late twenties, when he took up with the woman who became his wife. She also was several years older than he was and had once had a child. There was, however, one difference: despite warning signs, the Ripper's soon-to-be wife continued with the relationship – Warren's girlfriend did not. Noting some things about him that she did not like – including, probably, his apparent lack of interest in sex – she split with him.

Almost immediately he began to pay suit to another divorcee, this time with four children, and married her after a seven-month courtship. At this point, Warren's wife seems to have been too preoccupied with her ex-husband and his affairs really to take stock of the new man in her life. Symbolically, in taking on a woman with four children, Warren had married his mother. Serial killers, in their fantasies, often relive the abuse they have suffered, only with themselves as the aggressor.[28] Warren was reliving his relationship with his mother, but with himself as his father.

At the beginning of 1975, Warren's wife became pregnant and the deep ambiguities evident in his relationship with his mother began to be visited on her. When she became depressed over a matter concerning her ex-husband and mentioned suicide, Warren forced her to write a suicide note and then made an apparently serious attempt to smother her with a pillow.[29] The police were contacted but took no action.

Here we have another Ripper parallel. Only days after his marriage, Jack made an attempt to cut his wife's throat.

Warren's behaviour continued to give cause for concern. He threatened to smash his wife's skull in after he had been drinking and on another occasion brutally battered a pet rabbit to death, drenching himself in blood. He also bought a gun, to protect her, he said, against burglars and assaults.[30]

Ripper parallels mount. John Douglas believes that Jack carried his knife basically for protection, a paranoid way of thinking resulting from his poor self-image.[31] The man who was Jack never went out without at least one knife and even slept with one under his pillow!

In October, Warren's baby daughter was born. On 11 November, he and his wife bought petrol at a local convenience store. After dropping her off, he returned and, when the coast was clear, attacked the shop assistant, a 27-year-old woman. After beating her, he shot her through the head. Surprisingly, in view of his past record, nobody associated him with the murder.

The fallout from these events manifested itself through increasing anxieties. There is evidence that Warren's paranoia deepened, that he lost interest in sex and had trouble sleeping. Disruptive sleeping patterns are sometimes indicative of damage to the hypothalamus, the area of the brain that regulates the emotions. One of the causes of this type of damage is childhood beatings. If Warren did have this condition, he may also have been suffering from hormonal imbalance.[32]

Given his past history, Warren's aversion to sex was not so much newly found as rediscovered. Despite it, his wife found herself pregnant with his second child the following April. This coincided with another murder, again a female convenience-store assistant, but this time in her forties. Warren abducted her and drove to a derelict farm, where he raped and killed her, shooting her in the face before finishing the job with a hammer blow to the head.

The body was discovered three days later and could have come straight out of Whitechapel in 1888, so gruesomely reminiscent was the scene. In the interim, Warren had returned and dragged the corpse into the empty farmhouse, where he ripped open the abdomen, made incisions to the inner and outer thighs of both legs and cut off her breasts. With shades of Ripper victim Liz Stride, the woman was found with something clutched in her hand, some dead vines.

Once again, Warren was not suspected.

His fourth and final murder occurred on his daughter's first birthday that October. After driving his mother home from a family party for the child, Warren kidnapped yet another convenience-store assistant, a woman of 24, and drove her to a dirt road where he raped her before leading her into a wooded area. Here, he made her sit down and then shot her.

He went back next day intending to mutilate the corpse but was put off by some boys walking in the woods. A day later he returned again and pulled the body further into the woods. He then seems to have gone back to his truck, because the landowner had seen him and went to investigate. When the man reached the spot, he found an unmutilated corpse but no sign of anyone else. But, while the landowner was away summoning the police, Warren, oblivious to the fact that he had been noticed, turned up again and this time eviscerated the remains, cutting off the left breast, partially severing the right and making a 4-inch (10cm) incision into the woman's stomach, interestingly enough almost exactly the length of wound that the Ripper made into the abdomen of his last victim (see Chapter 11).

Warren then left the area, apparently taking the cut-off breast with him,[33] but he now made a fatal mistake by going back to the scene for the third time that day, only to discover that it was swarming with police. He drove off but was trapped by a road block and surrendered.

I have dwelled at some length on Warren's comings and goings at this murder site to demonstrate another Ripper comparison. Both here and in his penultimate crime, Warren made somewhat desultory attempts to conceal the body, which is paralleled to some extent by Jack's rather febrile bid to clean up his final crime scene, which included putting the body into a trunk. Both killers then overreached themselves, Warren in returning once too often to the murder locale, Jack in gambling that he could fool the police, a classic illustration of the point that, as we shall see, John Douglas makes in his profile of the Ripper: he was lucky, not clever.

But the most telling and chilling comparison is that both men actually did go back to the body and inflicted further mutilating injuries on it, a trait found only in sexual serial killers.

Warren was sentenced to be executed.[34] A pre-trial psychiatric examination concluded that he had a schizoid personality accompanied by 'marked' paranoia. He had, said one examiner, murdered and mutilated his victims in order to prevent his own destruction. If that sounds insane, it is because it is: although adjudged legally sane, Warren was in fact as mad as a hatter. This is a fundamental contradiction at the heart of serial murder that is unlikely to be resolved.

The triggering force for Warren's behaviour in 1975 and 1976 was anxiety associated with the conceptions and birth of his children. His behaviour towards his wife became highly erratic as soon as she became pregnant. Shortly after the birth, he committed the first of his murders during this period. He killed the second victim when his wife conceived again, and the third on his daughter's first birthday.

The pregnancies and childbirths caused Warren to relive his own childhood fears. As a result, the pressures inside him, and the sexual fantasies that they generated, built up to the point where they had to be released through murder.

We shall see that family memories going back to his own infancy caused Jack the Ripper to kill and mutilate anybody who brought them to mind.

Warren's victims were of a certain type who reminded him of family members. The woman in 1963 was reminiscent of his grandmother. In 1975–76, his victims were rather heavily built females who resembled either his wife or his mother, although for practical purposes the distinction did not exist anyway, as in his mind his wife and mother were one and the same person.[35]

Jack the Ripper slaughtered women who in his mind were his mother and sister.

Like his behavioural antecedent, Warren displayed a mixture of organised and disorganised tendencies. His care in selecting his victims and the use he made of his truck were redolent of an organised killer, the mutilations a disorganised one, although, as Douglas and his colleagues point out, there was an element of planning inherent in his going back to commit them.

Lastly, history almost repeats itself in the trials of both Jack and Warren. In the case of the first, in 1889, the jury were sent out a second time after the judge was unhappy with their first verdict (see Chapter 12). Warren, in fact, had two trials. In the original, the judge directed the jury that if they brought in a guilty verdict the form of their verdict should read, 'We find the defendant guilty of murder', whereas he was on trial for rape and 'intentional killing'. This was considered to be a reversible error and Warren had to be retried. One sometimes feels that the legal process is becoming as insane as some of the people it tries![36]

I have gone into Warren's history step by step for two reasons. One is that this is how the story of Jack the Ripper will unfold in the succeeding chapters. Warren's story is in essence his; there are so many similarities between the two that at times they seem indistinguishable from one another. The second is that both Warren and Jack are representatives of a syndrome of evil. So too are Ted Bundy, Peter Kurten, Bobby Joe Long, Henry Lee Lucas, Peter Sutcliffe, John Christie and many others whose names will become familiar as the story progresses. They sound like the 'and all' who accompanied Uncle Tom Cobley to Widecombe Fair in the song of that name, but *their* song is of death, and many innocents have been massacred to ensure their inclusion in it. No two of these individuals are ever exactly alike; no one fits precisely their profiles or categories. The only absolute about serial killers is that there are no absolutes. But, as we have already seen with Warren and will do again with Jack, they fit into the same overall pattern of origin, development and behaviour.

Because Warren was apprehended before his death list had too many names on it (although four are obviously four too many), he never reached the state of weary self-disgust symptomatic of many multicides during the countdown to capture.

Ted Bundy is a prime example of the latter. He deliberately fled to Florida, then the state that most enacted the death penalty. Earlier, he had asked which state he was most likely to be executed in. Now of course it could be argued that he cunningly thought it would be the last place where the police were likely to seek him, but the preponderance of evidence points to his becoming tired of the life he was leading and the repetitive horrors attending it. Subconsciously he wanted to stop, but his surface consciousness would not countenance it. The war within him produced a final killing spree in which, observes Robert Ressler, he was no longer planning his crimes. The picture that Ressler paints is of a man under extreme stress, coming apart at the seams and embarking on a death ride to nowhere except the execution chamber.[37]

After his capture, Bundy evinced a wide variety of shifting moods. First he made a partial confession, then he withdrew it, followed by a period of aloofness. Next he authorised his lawyers to pursue a plea bargain that would guarantee that he would not be executed. When the state accepted this, he abruptly changed his mind again, sacked his defence team and decided to represent himself and plead not guilty. His first biographer, Richard W Larsen, asks whether this was not in fact a subconscious act of suicide.[38]

On 24 July 1979, Bundy was found guilty of two murders and three assaults and sentenced to death. Now the pendulum swung again and he confessed to 30 murders, claiming insanity. Subsequently, he tried to use his confessions to stave off execution, arguing that he needed time to recall the details of his crimes.

At one point he even gave a series of interviews to detectives investigating the Green River murders, offering them an insight into the killer's mind![39] His attempts to avoid execution reached a crescendo over the weekend prior to it with agents and police officers scurrying back and forth to the Florida state prison while Bundy in effect held court. Ressler, in his autobiography, makes no attempt to hide his disgust at this abysmal creature's machinations.[40]

It is a stratagem that is becoming increasingly familiar with convicted multicides. Henry Lee Lucas became a past master at twisting and turning to avoid the executioner, confessing to more and more murders to buy time and then recanting them after the danger had passed. He at one time or another confessed to more than 200 homicides. The real total will never reliably be established. Like Bundy, Lucas had come to the end of the road, in his case following the murder of his 13-year-old 'partner', Frieda Powell, the one person whom he seems to have felt something for. But, also like Bundy, he later regained enough of his equilibrium to want to avoid execution.

However, no 20th-century serial killer invented these tactics. Although Bundy and Lucas were unaware of it, they were following a trail cognitively mapped out for them by Jack the Ripper a century earlier. Not successfully: the Ripper went to the gallows in 1889; one hundred years later, bar three months exactly, Ted Bundy followed him, keeping his appointment with the electric chair on 24 January 1989.

Serial offenders are the most difficult of all criminals to catch. The first question a police officer seeks to answer when confronted with a routine murder is that of who has the motive, the opportunity and the means. The multicide is different because there is no rational motive and with opportunity and means the detective is not investigating a small group of people but a huge, amorphous mass of them, from whom he will have to select the likeliest suspects before he can work backwards to try to trace their movements on the days of the crimes. It is time-consuming and often soul-destroying, especially when set against the backcloth of a frightened populace demanding action.

The difficulties facing the police in finding out whether Ted Bundy had been in a particular place at a particular time were enormous and few have appreciated how diligently and effectively they performed this thankless task. In a serial-murder case, suspects have to be systematically eliminated till only the right one remains. That, at least, is the theory. In practice, most are caught by chance, or when they give themselves away. Meanwhile, the police must carry on with endless enquiries. Weeks of shredding tyre treads and shoe leather may leave a likely suspect unavailable for one of the crimes; then they have to begin all over again. Worse, by dropping a suspect, they may inadvertently have given up on the real culprit after all. The murder he did not commit might have been the work of an imitator.

Something comparable to this happened during the hunt for the 'Yorkshire Ripper'. The police were misled into believing that the killer was from the Northeast by a taped recording from a hoaxer whose rare blood group matched that of the murderer of a prostitute named Joan Harrison. Meanwhile, Peter Sutcliffe's name kept popping up in the case, only to be ignored because he came from Bradford. Not till Sutcliffe confessed did it become clear that Harrison had been killed by an imitator.

Some believe that not all the murders attributed to Jack the Ripper were committed by him. Although I take a more traditional view, they could be right. As we shall see, Jack was available for all the crimes laid at his door, but in the final analysis only he knew which were his.

Obviously anything that enables the police to gain a clearer perspective on the murderer and pare down the list of suspects is a godsend. According to its adherents, this is what offender profiling is supposed to do. The process is defined for us by Douglas and Ressler's FBI colleague Roy Hazelwood as designed to focus not on an individual but on a type of individual. Profiles are based on a comprehensive survey of autopsy reports, scene-of-crime analysis, photographs, maps, witness statements and investigative feedbacks. From these, the compiler, using a combination of factual evidence and psychological evaluation, draws up a picture of the offender's likely motives, background and characteristics.[41]

One such profile has already passed into criminal folklore. In 1986, Professor David Canter, a consultant in criminal psychology and now head of the Behavioural Science Unit at Liverpool University, was asked by the police to prepare a profile of two men who had carried out a series of rapes and murders in North London. After researching all the available evidence, Canter drew up a 17-point profile, which matched a suspect named John Duffy in 13 of the categories. In 1988, Duffy was convicted of two of the murders and five of the rapes.

However, as Canter himself makes clear, profiling is not a panacea for solving crime. He himself was surprised at how accurately his profile fitted Duffy[42] and it did not assist in catching Duffy's accomplice, David Mulcahy, who was finally convicted in December 2000. Specifically, Canter points out that profiling is not a substitute for factual evidence and that good police work will continue to be paramount in catching criminals. Duffy was tried and convicted on overwhelming circumstantial evidence; the profile only signposted the way to him.

Another leading criminal psychologist, Paul Britton, records how one profile failed to distinguish between two separate series of rapes. Another indicated that the murder of a prostitute was a disorganised impulse crime committed by an individual residing more than a mile away, whereas it turned out to be the premeditated act of three men living close by.[43]

On the other hand, if West Yorkshire Police had listened to Robert Ressler and John Douglas, they would not have made fools of themselves over the aforementioned hoax tape in the Yorkshire Ripper investigation. The two FBI agents, who were lecturing at Bramshill Police College, were invited to listen to the tape and concluded that it was phoney. The real killer, they said, was not an individual who would court publicity. Their own off-the-cuff profile turned out to be remarkably accurate when Peter Sutcliffe was arrested.[44]

On a subsequent visit to Britain, Douglas was being interviewed on ITV's *This Morning* when news began to come in of the 1996 Dunblane massacre in Scotland, in which a former scout leader killed 15 children and an adult before killing himself (a 16th child died later in hospital). Asked for an on-the-spot profile of the killer, Douglas assessed him as a white, single male, an antisocial loner in his mid-thirties to late forties with no interest in women who was taking revenge on the community for some grievance he was nursing.

Specifically, Douglas opined that he was likely to be somebody who had worked in a voluntary position with children, a scoutmaster, for example, who had recently been removed from it following complaints by parents. He would have written letters to the local authorities, or newspapers, claiming he had been unfairly treated. Finally, he was obsessed with guns.[45]

The only thing missing from this remarkable piece of analysis was the name: Thomas Hamilton!

So, while profiling is not perfect – an art not a science – in the right hands, it can be an important tool in determining the sort of man the offender is and his likely motives.

With this in mind, let us look at the profile of Jack the Ripper.

NOTES

1. Wilfred Gregg and Brian Lane, *The Encyclopaedia of Serial Killers* (pbk), pp. 195–6 and 228–9.

2. Robin Odell, *Jack the Ripper in Fact and Fiction* (hbk), p. 233.

3. Brian Marriner, *A Century of Sex Killers* (pbk), pp. 6–7 and 73.

4. Colin Wilson, *A Criminal History of Mankind* (pbk), p. 507.

5. Thomas De Quincey, *On Murder as a Fine Art*.

6. For a comprehensive and objective account of the case see *The Maul and the Pear Tree* by T A Critchley and P D James. The authors conclude that Williams may have been framed by the real killer(s) and there are certainly some disturbing questions raised by the way in which the evidence came to light.

7. Marriner, op. cit., p. 83.

8. Critchley and James, op. cit., pp. 89–90.

9. *The Midland Wednesday News*, 1 May 1889.

10. Ann Burgess, John Douglas and Robert Ressler, *Sexual Homicide: Patterns and Motives* (pbk), pp. 16–24.

11. Ibid., pp. 24–30.

12. Ibid., p. 31.

13. Ibid., p. 42.

14. *The Encyclopaedia of Serial Killers*, pp. 171–3.

15. W D S McLay (ed.), *Clinical Forensic Medicine*, 2nd edn (pbk), p. 177.

16. Joel Norris, *Serial Killers: The Growing Menace* (pbk), pp. 68–9.

17. Burgess, Douglas and Ressler, op. cit., p. 52.

18. Ibid., pp. 52–3.

19. For mixed offenders, see Robert Ressler (with Tom Shachtman), *Whoever Fights Monsters* (pbk), pp. 180–211.

20. Burgess, Douglas and Ressler, op. cit., pp. 121–133.

21. Ibid., p. 55.

22. In only one case, that of Catharine Eddowes, is there definite evidence of semen tests being carried out, both in the body and on her clothing. These were negative. The actual autopsy reports on Martha Tabram, Mary Ann Nichols, Annie Chapman and Elizabeth Stride are missing, so the possibility of tests cannot be excluded, particularly in Chapman's case. Dr Bagster Phillips conducted the PM on both Chapman and Alice Mackenzie, an imitation murder the following year, and in Mackenzie's case he did check for semen in the body (his report has survived). It is therefore conceivable that he examined what was left of Chapman's vaginal channel and clothes for traces. The autopsy reports on Mary Kelly and the final victim are available and make no mention of any tests.

23. Ressler (with Shachtman), op. cit., pp. 180–1 and 206–7.

24. John Douglas and Mark Olshaker, *The Cases that Haunt Us* (hbk), p. 38.

25. Ressler (with Shachtman), op. cit., p. 123.

26. Norris, op. cit., pp. 259–60.

27. Ressler (with Shachtman), op. cit., p. 124.

28. Ibid., p. 134.

29. The chronology of events in Warren's life in Burgess, Douglas and Ressler's *Sexual Homicide* (p. 76) states that his wife complained he had attempted to strangle her with a rope, which would provide yet another match with the Ripper. However, in both the text of *Sexual Homicide* and separately in Ressler's *Whoever Fights Monsters*, it is stated that the incident was an attempt at suffocation with a pillow, so I have taken the text as accurate and the chronology as inaccurate.

30. Burgess, Douglas and Ressler, op. cit., p. 47.

31. Douglas and Olshaker, op. cit., p. 65.

32. Norris, op. cit., pp. 243–4.

33. Burgess, Douglas and Ressler, op. cit., p. 88, records it as 'missing'.

34. At the time *Sexual Homicide* was published in 1988, Warren's case was being appealed. Ressler, writing four years later, does not update the situation, so it is unclear whether or not the execution was carried out.

35. Burgess, Douglas, Ressler, op. cit., pp. 94–5.

36. For the full account of the case, see Burgess, Douglas, Ressler, op. cit., pp. 69–96.

37. *Serial Killers – Ted Bundy*, Channel Five, 1999.

38. Richard Larsen, *Bundy: The Deliberate Stranger* (pbk), p. 300.

39. Robert Keppel, *The Riverman* (hbk), pp. 186–286.

40. Ressler (with Shachtman), op. cit., pp. 101–5.

41. *The Secret Identity of Jack the Ripper*, television documentary, 1988.

42. David Canter, *Criminal Shadows* (pbk), p. 52.

43. Paul Britton, *The Jigsaw Man* (pbk), pp. 155–6.

44. Ressler (with Shachtman), op. cit., pp. 258–63. Ressler is, however, incorrect in stating that the hoaxer was subsequently identified by the time he came to write *Whoever Fights Monsters*. The culprit was only arrested in 2005.

45. John Douglas and Mark Olshaker, *The Anatomy of Motive* (pbk), pp. 13–20.

CHAPTER TWO

UNSUB

If the FBI had been hunting Jack the Ripper, they would have referred to him simply as 'unsub', meaning 'unknown subject', the bureau's standard term for an unnamed offender. It is perhaps a more appropriate name than Jack the Ripper, for 'unsub' depersonalises him in the way he depersonalised his victims. Certainly, the term is far more in keeping with the real man behind the mask than the suspects culled from the ranks of the rich and famous.

John Douglas, whom we met in the previous chapter, has been profiling the Ripper since 1981. During the 1980s, Douglas managed the FBI's criminal profiling and consultation programme and before he retired in 1995 was chief of the bureau's Investigative Support Unit based at Quantico, Virginia. He was technical adviser for the Oscar-winning film *The Silence of the Lambs* (the character of Agent Jack Crawford is based on him). In 1988, along with fellow agent Roy Hazelwood, an expert in analysing 'lust' murderers, Douglas compiled and presented on screen a profile of the Ripper for the television documentary *The Secret Identity of Jack the Ripper*.

Douglas's profile had actually commenced seven years earlier, when he was consultant to the 'Ripper Project', a 1981 inquiry into the Ripper murders held at the Centre of Forensic Sciences in the

University of Kansas, Wichita. A group of profilers and other experts met to compile a profile of the killer. Prominent among them was John Douglas, then Supervising Agent at the FBI's Behavioral Science Unit (now the Investigative Support Unit). Douglas subsequently refined the profile for the documentary *The Secret Identity of Jack the Ripper* and more latterly in his book *The Cases That Haunt Us*. To prevent duplication I have treated both sets of research as one and also added subsequent observations. Douglas's and Hazelwood's conclusions were as follows.

- Origin: white, working-class male.
- Age at time of crimes: almost certainly (though not exclusively) in the 28–36 bracket.
- Childhood: likely to have come from a broken home where the father was either weak or absent and the mother a heavy drinker who was sexually promiscuous. Brought up without a stable adult role model present and abused either physically or sexually by a domineering female.
- Probably had a minor physical defect, a scar or speech impediment, for example, which added to his psychological problems.
- While still a child, may have committed acts of arson, or engaged in cruelty to animals. Such activities would have made him feel powerful and dominant and taught him how to avoid detection and punishment.
- In common with other sexual killers, deviant fantasies stemming from a hatred and fear of women would have commenced in childhood, growing apace with his development to include visions of domination and mutilation. As he grew older, his fears would have been enhanced by worries about the sexual power which women possessed. In this way, sexual feeling would eventually have become bound up with the need to dominate and control women and assuage his fears by ritualistically mutilating them. To this John

Douglas adds a second dimension, believing that part of the mutilation may have originated from a morbid curiosity about female sex organs that was not fulfilled by sexual experience.

- Intelligence: Jack was of no more than average intelligence and evaded capture by a combination of luck and previous experience rather than cohesive planning.
- Abode: he lived and, if employed, worked in the vicinity of his crimes and had a good knowledge of the area. His first murder may have been close to a workplace.
- Occupation: either jobless or situated in a menial position involving little or no contact with the public.
- He would not have been employed in a profession.

Douglas and Hazelwood were emphatic about the last point – and he was certainly not a doctor, one of the most enduring myths about the Ripper. His crimes disclosed no surgical skills, although John Douglas accepts that he may have had some anatomical knowledge. This aspect needs to be seen in the perspective in which Douglas places it in his book *Mindhunter*. Here he makes the point that, in his experience, all a serial killer needs to disembowel a victim is the will to do it.[1] Roy Hazelwood adds that a doctor would have been inclined to kill in a less personal way.

Possibly Jack did work in the health industry, but as a low-level technician, a medical assistant or a hospital orderly, for instance. Alternatively, he may have been a butcher. Any of these functions would have enabled him to indulge his destructive tendencies.

He would have preferred to work alone and his job would not have entailed working at weekends or public holidays (when most of the crimes were committed).

- Marital status: single. His fear and hatred of women made him feel intimidated by them and unable to relate to them.

- Partner: in the unlikely event that he did have a partner she would have been older than he was and the relationship would have been short-lived.

At this point we should also bring in Robert Keppel who also profiles Ripper-type murderers in his book *Signature Killers* (Keppel terms them 'anger–retaliation' killers). He remarks, 'If he has a relationship, there will have generally been *a history of long-term spousal abuse*'[2] (my emphasis).

- Appearance: neat and orderly.[3]
- Habits: nocturnal.
- Personality: a quiet, shy loner, perceived as obedient and slightly withdrawn and introverted, who drank in the local pubs and was probably drinking prior to his murders. He was unlikely to engage in conversation without alcohol to prop him up.

Most of his sexual relationships would have been with prostitutes and he may have contracted venereal disease from one, further fuelling his loathing of women. He was not seeking any particular sort of victim (prostitutes required minimal social skills), and his behaviour was not influenced by the victim's looks, or any perception of her as being a vulnerable type of person.

His poor self-image was likely to induce a paranoid type of thinking, leading to his carrying knives for self-protection. At times, his inner tensions would result in bouts of erratic behaviour, causing neighbours to summon the police.

The police were likely to have interviewed him, possibly more than once, in connection with the crimes, but they would have discarded him as a suspect because he did not fit their image of the killer as a bloodthirsty ghoul.

- Scene-of-crime behaviour: it was not the taking of his victims' lives that was of importance to the Ripper but the mutilations that he inflicted upon them.

The Ripper's removal of his victims' organs was an attempt to neuter or de-sex them so that there was no longer anything to be feared. By taking these away with him, he was symbolising his possession of the victims even after death. Douglas believes that he may even have eaten the organs to satisfy his curiosity about the female body.

The ritualistic element of the murders, such as the way in which he laid the corpses out, denoted an obsessive need to control the victim or the crime scene, and the rings removed from one of the victim's fingers could have been stolen as trophies.

Although random facial mutilation is common to this type of crime, it may also suggest that the killer knew victims Catharine Eddowes and Mary Kelly and was deliberately attempting to dehumanise them. The killer would have been bothered by any of the victims' blood splattering on to him.

He saw the women he murdered simply as scum polluting the streets and believed he was justified in killing them.

- Post-crime behaviour: Jack was likely to have returned to the crime scenes or visited the victims' graves as symbols of his control over them.

The profilers rejected the idea that the murderer had authored any of the Jack the Ripper correspondence. In Roy Hazelwood's opinion, the unsub would have shunned publicity lest it draw attention to him. John Douglas thinks it conceivable that one particularly chilling letter may have emanated from him, but that in general Jack lacked the sort of criminal personality needed to inject himself into the police's running of the case.

The Ripper was unlikely to have ceased killing of his own accord but would not have committed suicide.[4]

It is easy to misuse offender profiles. For example, a theoretical case can be constructed against someone on minor points alone. If we take the unsub's profile, seven of the categories add up to a respectably dressed young bachelor of average intelligence, either unemployed or working in a menial job and living in the East End of London. About a quarter of its male population would have fitted this description in 1888.

So we need to trawl in the profile's deeper and darker waters to pinpoint a genuine suspect. We are looking for somebody who is mentally ill but not noticeably so, who knows that what he is doing is wrong but needs to do it and is capable of functioning routinely in society from day to day without ever being a properly integrated part of it. We shall see that one particular man emerges very clearly. He does not fit the FBI's hypothesis in every category or detail, nor would we expect him to. Echoing Professor David Canter, no profile is ever going to be 100 per cent accurate.

One major difficulty is that a large and important segment of the unsub's childhood is missing. The first year of his life was almost unbelievably traumatic, but then he disappears from view for the next 15. That they cannot have been happy years we shall see from the adult they fashioned. And the unsub's conspicuous silence about his upbringing is eloquent testimony to a childhood too harrowing for words. Even the woman he married was told no more than that he had been raised by a relative. Who and how he never said, never spoke about.

Which brings us to a major point of conflict between the unsub and his profile, although not one as serious as it appears at first sight. He was married throughout most of the last year of his life. However, the best thing that can be said about the relationship is that they went through the ceremony and thereafter resided together. Professor

Canter believes that the Ripper may have been married but that it would not have been a normal relationship.5 It was, as we shall see, anything but normal. John Douglas opines that any marriage would have been with somebody older than the Ripper was and that it would not have lasted long. This too is spot on – morbidly so. And we shall see that Keppel is right about his behaviour to his wife.

Another significant departure from the profile – as opposed to matters of detail or emphasis – is that the unsub's selection of victims was not quite as arbitrary as John Douglas believes. Something about these particular women did trigger off their murders.

To avoid repetition, we will see how 'unsub' gels with the profile as the story unfolds. With this in mind, we can now give him his proper name.

NOTES

1. John Douglas and Mark Olshaker, *Mindhunter* (pbk), p. 367.

2. Robert D Keppel, *Signature Killers*, p. 104.

3. In the TV documentary *The Secret Identity of Jack the Ripper*, expert John Douglas describes the killer's appearance as dishevelled, which conflicts with the testimony of witnesses who saw him. In *The Cases that Haunt Us*, he corrects this to fairly neat and orderly.

4. The profile outlined here is a composite of *The Ripper Project*, *The Secret Identity of Jack the Ripper* and *The Cases that Haunt Us*.

5. Phillip Sugden, *The Complete History of Jack the Ripper*, 1st edn (hbk), p. 471.

CHAPTER THREE

THE BABY FROM HELL

On Tuesday morning a shocking accident occurred at Muckley's Hill near Halesowen by which a man named James Berry, of this town, lost his life. Berry, has been in the employ of Mr Joscelyne, fishmonger, for the last five years, and went to Birmingham with a horse and spring cart to fetch a load of fish. On his return, the horse appeared to become unmanageable in descending the hill. Berry was sitting on a basket of fish and jumped off the cart into the road, where he fell down. The cart wheel passed over the whole length of Berry's body, frightfully mutilating his chest. Death was instantaneous.[1]

This death, on a lonely country road in the spring of 1860, was to spawn the most notorious series of murders the world has ever known. Here, among green fields and rutted wagon tracks, was fashioned the myth of Jack the Ripper.

The man who became the myth was born in the market town of Stourbridge in the spring of 1859, although he himself seems to have grown up believing that he originated from Stourport, a few miles away.

Stourbridge is situated on the northeastern border of

33

Worcestershire, 10 miles south of the centre of Wolverhampton and 14 due west of Birmingham. In 1859, it was the focal point of the parish of old Swinford, dominating the surrounding villages of Lye and Lye Waste, Wollaston, Wollescote and Upper Swinford, and the hamlets of Amblecote and the delightfully named Careless Green.

The impression is of a sedate rural community, unchanged for a century and likely to stay that way for another. It is an illusion. Jack the Ripper was born into a community that was changing fast. Rich deposits of fireclay in the soil had created a sprawling complex of clay, glass and brick works. The town boasted a tannery and a brewery, and there was an iron foundry owned by the local MP, William Orme Forster, symbolising the way in which the Industrial Revolution was taking over his constituency. The produce of all this enterprise was shipped to the great manufacturing cities of the Northwest along the manmade canal that snaked its way through the heart of the budding conurbation.[2]

It was presumably because prospects were brighter in Stourbridge than nearby Dudley or Kinver that Joseph Henley and his family were induced to settle there in the 1830s. A cooper by trade, Henley had been born in Dudley around the turn of the century.[3] On 26 August 1823, he married Jane Evans at the local parish church.[4] It is unclear whether Jane was born in Dudley or in Wales.[5]

By the time they arrived in Stourbridge, Joseph and Jane's union had been blessed five times: Penelope (*circa* 1824), William Edward (1826), Mary Jane (1830), Edward (1832) and Elizabeth (1834).[6] After they ensconced themselves in their new home in Talbot Back Lane, two more daughters, Sarah and Jane, came along to complete the family lineup.[7]

The third child, Mary Jane, grew up to be a cheerful, even-tempered young woman with dark hair, dark-grey eyes and a fresh complexion.[8] Precisely when and how she met Henry Bury we do not know, but by autumn 1851 the young couple were engaged to be married. To avoid confusion, it needs to be made clear that there are two ways of spelling his surname, Bury and Berry, both of which appear in official documents. Bury, who listed his age as 24 and his occupation as a servant, lived and worked in Stourbridge High Street for a fishmonger named Thomas Davies.[9] In the 1851 Census he gives his birthplace as Stourbridge, and on his marriage certificate his father is listed as 'Samuel Berry – labourer'. Beyond this the trail grows cold. Several extant documents, his death certificate and burial record, the marriage certificate of his youngest son and the birth certificate of his other son, Joseph Henry, establish that his full name was actually William Henry, but according to the parish records no William or Henry Bury or Berry was born in Old Swinford during the relevant period. He seems to have had an aversion to using 'William', but dislike of a first name is not uncommon: one of the Ripper victims, Annie Chapman, was christened 'Eliza Ann' but discarded 'Eliza'.

'William' was as usual omitted from the record when he married Mary Jane at Dudley parish church on 12 October 1851. Their first child, Elizabeth Ann, was born at their new home, Giles Hill, Stourbridge, just under eight months later, 6 June 1852, which suggests that the couple may have helped Careless Green live up to its name prior to tying the knot! Henry describes himself as a wagoner on the birth certificate,[10] but two years onwards, at the time of Joseph Henry's birth, he was a fruiterer and the family had decamped to Wolverhampton, where they lived in Stafford Street.[11] Things clearly failed to work out there, because the following year they returned to Stourbridge and Henry was back at his old job working for the fishmonger at 154 Upper High Street, although by now it was owned not by Thomas Davis but a couple named Joscelyne. A third child, Mary Jane, was born on 29 January 1857. At this point there is nothing to distinguish the Burys from millions of other working-class families of that era. We know nothing of their day-to-day lives. There is a hint that Henry was fond of a drink: on regular trips to Birmingham to pick up fish he traditionally stopped off at the Shenstone Hotel in Halesowen on the way back.[12] Mary Jane also earned money, by dressmaking, and at this point in their lives the family were living with the Henleys in Hill Street, Stourbridge.[13]

Plainly, they were not comfortably off. The Burys and the Henleys were at the base of the social pyramid that was Victorian England, struggling along and making ends meet with little or nothing to spare for luxuries; but they were coping. Nobody could have foreseen the awful series of tragedies that were about to engulf them.

The catalyst was the birth of their fourth and final child on 25 May 1859. He was a boy, called William Henry after his father, who proudly promoted himself to the exalted rank of fishmonger on the birth certificate. Mary Jane was not so pleased. Whether it was the prospect of another mouth to feed or some sense of grim foreboding, the normally happy young woman sank into a state of postnatal depression from which she never recovered.

She might have emerged from it but for the events of 7 September. On that day seven-year-old Elizabeth Ann collapsed in an epileptic fit at their Hill Street home. One of the family ran for a doctor but the convulsions continued unabated till she died two hours later.[14]

The family grieved through the winter, but spring produced another tragedy. On 10 April 1860, the last morning of his life, William Bury Sr set out with Joscelyne's horse and cart on his normal run to Birmingham to collect fish. This time, however, he would not return, at least not alive. On Muckley's Hill, nearing Halesowen and the welcoming arms of the Shenstone, Bury suddenly lost control of the horse. Why and how we shall never know; perhaps he had already had a drink in Birmingham that had made him drowsy. An eyewitness, whose name is not recorded for posterity, saw him get down from the wagon to see to the horse. Reaching the ground, he fell over and, before the witness could intervene, the horse had careered off, pulling a heavy cartwheel lengthways along Bury's body. He died instantly, his torso ripped asunder as the wheel passed over it. The horse and cart continued on into Halesowen, where the horse came to a dutiful halt outside the hotel, oblivious to the disaster it had caused, happily ignorant of three now fatherless children and the ailing wife whose fate had also been sealed on Muckley's Hill.[15]

The *Brierly Hill & Stourbridge Gazette* of Saturday, 14 April incorrectly gives Bury's first name as 'James'. By gruesome irony, the namesake to this error, executioner James Berry, would hang his son almost exactly 29 years later.

The sad confusion over names is repeated on William's death certificate this time, with his surname incorrectly recorded as 'Perry'. [16] According to the *Family History Monthly* magazine, copying errors are common on 19th-century documents, but equally the confusion may have arisen from the extraordinary number of Perrys living in the parish of Old Swinford at this time. The local nailing industry seemingly employed as many of them as there were nails.[17] Not till he was laid to rest on 15 April was William Henry Bury finally accorded his correct name in full.[18]

The effect on Mary Jane was devastating. In less than a year she had lost her firstborn and her husband, the family's principal breadwinner. She was already suffering from acute depression, and her condition now degenerated to the point where hospitalisation was the only option. On 7 May, she was committed to the forbidding, grim-fronted institution known as Powick lunatic asylum. Twenty years on, the young Edward Elgar attempted to lift the gloom there by conducting the asylum's band. By then, however, Mary Jane Bury was long dead.

Her admission records note that she was 'Melancholy, crying on every occasion when spoken to and [with] a disinclination to do any kind of work or leave her bed. [She was] very feeble and exhausted.'[19]

Mary Jane had no previous history of depression. This was her first bout and it was attributed to 'loss of husband', although it had lasted 11 months, which means that she had actually had it since little William Henry's birth.

Deep depression is a cruel malady that I have witnessed at first hand. Today we have effective drug therapies to combat it. In Victorian times, the remedies were tonics and hot baths. Not surprisingly, Mary Jane did not recover. The asylum records note that in June 1862 her condition was very much the same as on admission.

By February 1864, she was growing progressively worse and persistent diarrhoea had set in. The impression one gets is that nobody really cared very much. She was simply left to die in her own excrement, which she did on 30 March.[20] By then not very much remained of the hopeful young bride of 12 years earlier.

Following Mary Jane's incarceration, the children were farmed out to various members of her family, though six-year-old Joseph disappears from view completely at this point. The 1861 Census records that little Mary Jane was living with her aunt Jane in Chapel Street, Stourbridge, Jane having married a blacksmith named George Rudge and produced a child of her own. Her father, Joseph Henley, also appears to have lived with the Rudges till his death from bronchitis and heart and liver disease on 21 March 1861.[21] By 1871 Mary Jane had moved on to the All Saints district of Birmingham, where the Census finds her residing with another Joseph Henley, and family, at 97 Albion Street. Aged 43, which would make his year of birth 1828, this Joseph was presumably another Henley son, though he does not appear with them in the first National census in 1841 or that of 1851. Nor does he feature in the Mormon Index's record of the family.

We lose track of little Mary Jane after 1871. According to William, both she and her elder brother Joseph Henry were dead by spring 1889, but when and how we are not told.[22] William himself was taken to Dudley, where in 1861 he was staying with his uncle, Edward

Henley, Edward's wife Ann and their little girl of the same age, Abigail. By 1871, Edward and his brood had decamped to Saint Vincent Street, Ladywood in Birmingham, but William was no longer with them, at least at the time the Census was taken. Instead, he was back in the Stourbridge area, in Old Swinford, where he was a scholar at the Bluecoate School in Hagley Lane. The *Dundee Advertiser* would state that Bury and his siblings had received an education 'beyond his circumstances in life' paid for by a seemingly affluent woman, but the source of the newspaper's information was almost certainly Bury himself and is likely to have been one of his many embellishments. The Bluecoate School appears to have been attached to the local hospital. The matron, Caroline James, is described as the 'Matron of [the] Hospital School' and the Census likewise records the housemaid as being a hospital employee. There also appears to have been just a solitary schoolmaster for Bluecoate's 115 pupils, which hardly endorses it as a prime educational establishment. Aside from his school attendance, we do not know what circumstances Bury was living under at this point.

What we do know is that Bury never spoke of his childhood, except for fleeting references to a so-called well-to-do uncle in Stourbridge and a cousin of whom he claimed to have a photograph. The *Dundee Advertiser* records him as a native of Wolverhampton,[23] but Bury himself twice gave Stourport, a few miles away from Stourbridge, as his birthplace.[24] His silence speaks volumes of how unhappy his upbringing must have been. The *Dundee Advertiser* is again presumably quoting information provided by Bury himself when it states that his father died three months after his birth. The death in question was of course Elizabeth Ann's, but William could never bring himself to mention his eldest sister. We shall soon see why this was. The problem of attempting to piece together an individual's childhood without the necessary documentation is that we are forced to rely on speculation. What we can be certain of is that

Bury's infancy was hideously traumatic and that the person who emerged into adult life was a full-blooded psychopath, addicted to drink, lies and theft and with a violent hatred of women. All in all, we are not going to be too wide of the mark in depicting the intervening years as baleful and dysfunctional.

Like that of Shakespeare's monster king, Richard III, Jack the Ripper's fate was sealed in his own nativity, or at least within a very short time of it.

His mother's postnatal depression makes one wonder how much she actually wanted this fourth baby. Another child was obviously a burden on limited financial resources and cramped living conditions. Joel Norris, a consultant psychologist, makes the point that anxiety and tension during the pregnancy are transmitted to the foetus via the hormonal secretions and may result in damage to the unborn child's brain. Norris goes on to say,

> Even if the child is not damaged at birth, the mother's anxieties may result in a colicky, unhappy baby who becomes the object of mistreatment and abuse by a mother who was unhappy about being pregnant. Such mistreatment is also a factor in the development of a violence prone individual.[25]

Even without actual mistreatment, depressive illness may impair the bonding process. 'Depriving a new-born baby of fundamental sensory input – especially tactile stimulation – some think is tantamount to condemning the new-born to a life of psychological pain and violence,' Norris writes.[26]

Children, even when tiny babies, can sense and feel rejection, but they will not of course be aware that there may be something wrong with the person responsible for it.

Sad though this may be, it is not an uncommon situation and, while there may be emotional, even neurological, harm to the child, it does not mean that he or she is destined to become a serial offender of some kind. It is impossible to say why some survive a blighted childhood and others do not. The rule of thumb is that, whereas not every abused child will grow up to be a serial killer, every serial killer has been abused in some way as a child.

The second crucial factor in determining why William Bury became Jack the Ripper was undoubtedly the death of his eldest sister three months after he was born. We know that he kept this buried deep within himself, refusing even to acknowledge the fact. There were specific reasons for this.

Those who took on the job of raising the little boy knew that his birth had heralded a series of disasters that had all but wiped out his immediate family. People were no longer burned alive as witches but superstition lingered, etched deep into the collective psyches of rural communities and carried with their inhabitants even when they migrated to the burgeoning towns and cities to live and work. Traditions die hard with such folk. In a celebrated case in Ireland, in 1895, Bridget Cleary, a young Tipperary woman, was sprinkled with urine, force-fed herbs and finally set on fire by members of her family, who believed that an evil fairy had taken possession of her.[27] Nearer to home, in Warwickshire, which neighbours Worcestershire, a simpleton named John Haywood murdered 80-year-old Ann Turner in 1875 because he had been told she was a witch; and, as late as 1945, Charles Walton, a farm labourer, was hacked to death in a manner that convinced locals that his death was linked to witchcraft. The killer was never apprehended.[28] In their 2006 book *The Dagenham Murder*, about the unsolved murder of Police Constable George Clark in 1846, authors Kathryn Abnett, Linda Rhodes and Lee Shelden reinforce the above examples by listing accusations of witchcraft from Bethnal Green in East London out to the Essex countryside around the time of Bury's birth. In one instance, a large crowd of people descended on the home of a woman named Mole after it was claimed that she had bewitched a pig into climbing a tree and eating cherries!

It does not require any great feat of imagination to see that little William Bury's relatives would have regarded him with deep suspicion. Mary Jane Sr had been a cheerful, industrious young woman but her personality had changed fundamentally with William's birth, and now she was entombed within the forbidding walls of a lunatic asylum. Her husband was an experienced wagoner yet he had managed to lose control of a horse. Elizabeth Ann had died from a never-ending series of convulsions – epilepsy, said the doctors – but the symptoms were the same as in demonic possession. You have only to go back to France in the 1950s to discover a local bakery being exorcised after an outbreak of ergot poisoning.[29] William Henry Bury was not exorcised (at least as far as we know), but there can be no doubt that he was regarded as the baby from hell.

A child thus stigmatised would have grown up a virtual outcast, deprived of love and affection and shunned as something repellent. That something along these lines did in fact happen is clear from the self-image Bury displayed as an adult. A boyhood of anguish and ostracism produced a misfit. To those who did not know him, Bury appeared to be a diligent, churchgoing young clerk, but closer contact revealed a pathological liar who drank and stole his way through life and enjoyed inflicting violence on those he perceived as weaker than himself.

Bury's schooling educated him to a certain level of competence.[30] He worked as a clerk for several years and his surviving letters reveal a good, clear hand and are well put together. There is also evidence that he read a lot, and, as his crimes show, he had the capacity to research how to avoid extensive staining from his victims' blood after an unhappy experience with his first murder. But this was the ceiling. He had been taught to function efficiently, but within his limits and that is reflected by the fact that he did not plan his crimes overall. They were committed mainly out in the open on the spur of the moment, inspired by sudden squalls of lust-inspired rage.

A clerk, or something similar, was all he was ever going to be. When Bury later opened a shop selling meat for cats, it quickly folded and he ended up as a glorified hawker, peddling sawdust and silversand. Ultimately, his limitations would prove his undoing.

However, his education would have enabled him to see beyond simple superstition and understand that his sister had died of epilepsy and not demonic possession. But this would prove to be a case of 'out of the frying pan, into the fire'.

Dr Richard Lechtenberg, in his 1999 book *Epilepsy and the Family*, reveals that the siblings of somebody with epilepsy will develop an inordinate fear (his words) of becoming afflicted with it themselves.[31] Lechtenberg also records that up to recently epilepsy itself carried with it a wholly unwarranted social stigma. He cites a survey of the public's attitude towards the illness that appeared in a British medical journal revealing that epileptics were seen as antisocial mental defectives with criminal propensities who needed to be locked away for society's good.[32] And this survey was carried out *after* World War II!

The most cursory of glances through the Powick asylum records shows that a hundred years earlier the medical profession itself apparently shared this opinion. In short order, I came across the cases of Elizabeth Kinsey, a domestic servant from Abergavenny, whose condition was diagnosed as 'manic epilepsy' and who was said to become 'quarrelsome and vicious' during frequent attacks, and Elizabeth Rushton, a congenital imbecile whose problems were likewise attributed to epilepsy.[33] I had no wish to read on.

The young William Bury would therefore, on the one hand, have been persecuted by superstition and, on the other, terrorised by the truth! The upshot was a deep and abiding hatred for the mother who had first rejected him and then left him in the care of others. Equally, he hated the sister who he dreaded might have passed on to him a terrible illness, and for whose death, along with his father's and his mother's illness, he was held responsible by people who treated him like a leper. It was more than enough to twist and distort the mind of any growing boy. Whether he was in the room when Elizabeth Ann collapsed and died her awful death we do not know, but it brings to mind the multicide in the Douglas, Ressler and Burgess study who thought that the devil lived in the furnace in his room. Whether Bury saw his sister's death agonies or not, he would have been made aware that the devil had lived inside Elizabeth Ann that day and that he was that devil.

To his mind, his mother must have believed the same. Why else would she reject him? His father might have protected him but he was gone too and he was blamed for that as well. William Bury never revealed the details of his father's death. Had he done so years later in Dundee, the similarities with the Ripper's crimes would have been only too obvious. The cartwheel had passed along the whole length of Bury Sr's body, tearing it apart in the process. Logically, it would also have shredded his genitalia and disfigured his features. These dreadful images, lurking just below the surface of his son's mind, were to be reproduced over and over again in the streets and hovels of East London – and in Dundee, too.

Sexually, the Ripper's victims were opened up and neutered, just as Bury's father was. This in turn implies that he was himself psychologically castrated, at least in terms of relationships with women whom he considered respectable. His self-image allowed him to copulate only with prostitutes, women whom he perceived to be as dirty and degraded as he was. In fact, he married one, though not for love. Even with prostitutes he would have been able to perform only by fantasising about acts of extreme violence, and it is likely that, by early 1888, stress was causing his behaviour to become ever more extreme.

What happened in the spring of that year turned him irrevocably towards murder. He contracted venereal disease and prostitutes now joined his mother and sister in the chamber of his mind reserved for those he hated the most, those who had done harm to him. Thereafter, he could no longer engage in sex with them except through the 'safe' mechanism of his knife, allowing his warped fantasies to flow down its blade. Even here it is doubtful that he was any longer able to achieve an orgasm during the acts themselves. On the evidence of the only crime in which the victim and her clothing were definitely checked for sperm traces, he had failed to reach a climax. Robert Keppel explains that such a killer is liable to be

> hardwired so perversely that in the neural circuitry of his brain sex becomes violence and violence becomes sex, in such a way that the killer never reaches climax at all, or if he does it's much later and in private. Many times in cases like these, the fury expanded in carrying out violence is the only physical or psychological release the killer experiences.

William Bury habitually carried knives around with him and even slept with one under his pillow, a powerful interlocking of paranoia and symbolism representing impotence, sadistic sexual fantasies and an inordinate fear of being attacked himself. Such a mixture, says Keppel, typifies knife-toting multicides.[34]

Whether Bury hated his father alongside his mother and sister is difficult to assess. Sexual homicides traditionally slake their thirsts on the gender towards which their sexual desires are expressed. However, in some perverse way Bury may have believed that the women in his family had driven his father to an early death and then saddled him with the responsibility. In London, Bury drove a horse and cart in his work, as his father had done. The memories, and the images stemming from them, that this provoked may have helped in pushing him towards the edge, reminiscent of Chapter 1's 'Warren', who murdered to prevent his own destruction, i.e. Bury had to kill those he held responsible for his sufferings, otherwise they would destroy him as they had his father. Their sexuality had to be obliterated to satisfy his fantasies. Perched atop his horse and cart, William Bury was a diminutive incarnation of hate-filled lust.

If this all sounds insane, it is because Jack the Ripper *was* insane. Not in the legal sense: he understood right from wrong perfectly well. Nor in a way that would draw attention to him: serial killers need to appear relatively normal in order to escape detection, a point we examined in the preceding chapter. But the Ripper's *behaviour* towards his victims, and the motivation behind it, were anything but normal.

Which brings us on to what is likely to be a controversial issue. Multicidal behaviour is triggered by a variety of factors often as irrational as the thought processes of the killer himself. Joel Norris, for example, mentions the case of a Florida murderer whose homicidal instincts were ostensibly sparked by the fact that his victims had red hair. What makes sense to the multicide does not make sense to us. People who remind him of hated family members tend to be right at the top of the list when it comes to turning on the tap of hatred. Another example is a killer named Carroll Cole. What he termed 'loose women' provoked his fury because he associated them with his mother: 'I think I kill her through them,' he told his captors.[35] Arthur Shawcross, who, uniquely, began as a paedophile multicide and later changed his victimology to prostitutes, told psychiatrists that the little girl and the women he killed were surrogates for his sister and mother.[36] Cole and Shawcross, however, pale into insignificance beside Edward Kemper and Henry Lee Lucas, two men who made bizarre art forms out of their oedipal hate complexes. Females whose voices sounded like their mothers' were, in Lucas's words, 'as good as dead'. Joel Norris very neatly articulates this phenomenon:

As in dreams in which people replace people and identities become confused, the delusional or hallucinatory state of the serial killer confuses individuals from the killers past, such as parents or siblings, with the victim who has just crossed his path . . . the victim before him has no identity whatsoever except for the identity his mind has already imposed.[37]

With this, and the examples we have looked at, in mind, let us look at the so-called 'canonical' victims of Jack the Ripper, i.e. the five women who most (though not all) Ripperologists are generally agreed upon were his victims. When we look at them, we see that all five bore a first or middle name associated with Bury's mother and sister, *Mary Ann* Nichols, *Annie* Chapman, *Elizabeth* Stride, Catharine Eddowes who on the night of her death was using the name *Mary Ann* Kelly and, lastly, *Mary Jane* Kelly. To these we can plausibly add possible victims *Annie* Millwood and Catherine Mylett who was going by the name *Elizabeth* Davis.

It is fair to make the point that there are two other possibles, plus the final victim, who do not accord to 'Elizabeth', 'Ann' or 'Mary', but, as will be seen, there were other, specific, factors associated with the assaults on them that made it a necessity for him to attack them.

Obviously, we have to look at this scenario carefully. Mary, Ann(e) and Elizabeth were the three most common female given names in Victorian England. But so frequent as to make it likely that all the canonical victims would have them by chance? To test this, I carried out two surveys, one at the Family Records Centre, the other with the 1881 Census. The first analysis, of three pages of the death index for September 1888, showed 526 female names. Of these, 59 were Marys, 38 Ann(e)s and 33 Elizabeths, an aggregate of 130, or 24 per cent of the total.[38] The second, of inmates at the Mile End Old Town Infirmary on 1881 Census night, produced a much higher proportion, 150 out of 359, amounting to 42 per cent.

This suggests that the three names were particularly prevalent in London. But, even using this higher figure, only two of the five victims should have been a Mary, Ann(e) or Elizabeth. For argument's sake, let us say one of each; we are still left with the statistical fact that not all of the canonical victims should have had these given names. One, Eddowes, actually did not, but this would appear to reiterate the point that, because she used 'Mary Ann', she became a victim through it.

There is no evidence that any of the 'canonical' victims operated under 'work' names, other than Eddowes's, alas, lethal alias. But a problem does arise with Mary Ann Nichols. She had been in the East End less than a month prior to her death, and her friends knew her only as 'Polly'.[39] However, this was an intimate name, signifying friendship and affection, and prostitutes do not share intimacies with clients. Sex is business.

Names were in fact all William Bury did have to recall his mother and sister. Unlike Warren, who murdered women who physically resembled his mother, and Kemper's and Lucas's aural reminders, Bury was too young when he lost his family to remember what his mother and sister looked like, or how their voices sounded. But he did know their names.

Also important were the timings of Elizabeth Ann and Mary Jane Bury's deaths, the 7th and 30th of the month. Crime historian Don Rumbelow had commented that the Ripper seemed to have been working to some internal clock.[40] When we look at the dates on which the canonical victims were murdered we find that Annie Chapman and Mary Kelly were killed on the 8th and 9th respectively – the end of the first week of the month just like Elizabeth Ann Bury – and that Elizabeth Stride and Catharine Eddowes died on the 30th and Mary Ann Nichols the 31st, dovetailing with Mary Jane Bury on the 30th, the end of the month.

Bury's final victim was his wife Ellen, who he murdered sometime between 5 and 10 February 1889. Exactly when, we cannot be sure, but on the available evidence the night of the 8th/9th is the likeliest date. Among those who may also have been Ripper victims, Martha Tabram was murdered in the early hours of 7 August 1888, Ada Wilson was attacked on the night of 28/29 March 1888 and Annie Millwood was stabbed on 25 February 25 1888. As February is a short month, the 25th arguably counts as being towards the end of it. Catherine Mylett does rather disrupt the pattern, the 20th, but she is the most dubious of the possibles.

So were the murders linked to the periods of the month when Elizabeth Ann and Mary Jane perished? I believe that could very well be the case.

Joel Norris recounts the story of Bobby Joe Long, a Florida serial rapist and murderer who suffered from a congenital disorder that in puberty caused him to grow breasts and develop a form of menstrual cycle. An operation corrected the physical problems but thereafter he experienced what Norris terms a 'lunar protomenstrual cycle' in which he committed his rapes and murders loosely in accordance with the cycle of the moon.[41]

Jack the Ripper was not of course a moon murderer, and we have no evidence of problems similar to Long's occurring in William Bury's background, but the important point here is the so-called 'protomenstrual cycle', which I believe existed in Bury in a purely emotional form, causing the pressures inside him to build up to a greater degree at those times of the month than others. Warren provides support for this. Each of his three 1975–76 homicides were related to times when he came under maximum pressure due to matters related to the conception and birth of his children.

The case against William Bury does not hang by whether we accept these theories about how and when he was motivated to kill. What they do provide is answers that have hitherto been lacking to questions connected with his crimes. Was there something other than prostitution that linked the victims? Yes, but nobody could ever have guessed what it was without knowing the Ripper's background. Why did he strike at these times of the month? To know that you have to understand the forces that drove him.

William Henry Bury emerges from the long hiatus of his childhood in 1875, sometime after his 16th birthday. Here we have almost the finished article, a short (5ft 3½in), swarthy young man with broad shoulders and a barrel chest who in the main dressed as respectably as his finances permitted, 'shabby genteel' or 'clerkly', as witnesses who later saw him with his victims testified. He had a moustache, which in contrast to his complexion, was fair, and, by the time he arrived in Dundee in 1889, a beard and side whiskers. Significantly, in profile he could be mistaken for being Jewish:

> In his own clothes he was a fairly decent looking man but in prison garb . . . he strikes one as being weak minded. Bury is of fresh complexion, his hair is dark brown, his moustache and whiskers being a shade lighter. He has a somewhat timid and excitable appearance. Viewed from the side he presents features somewhat of the Jewish or Semite type. He has dark but not heavy eyebrows and his eyes are keen and sharp. His nose is long and prominent, his cheeks thin, and his beard sparse and straggling . . . he appeared a diminutive and insignificant creature.[42]

Each eye sees things differently. The journalist who composed this description of Bury describes his complexion as fresh. Others saw it as dark – a neighbour in fact actually referred to him as a 'black man'.[43] Whether or not he had a pleasing countenance was likewise a matter of opinion. 'Rather a good looking young man with sharp features', wrote another reporter, but a colleague from the same newspaper was not nearly so impressed: 'His face was not repulsive but neither was it a pleasant face'.[44]

Man gazes on the outward manifestation but sees not the inner. Joseph Merrick, the 'Elephant Man', was physically repulsive but possessed a gentle innocence and nobility of spirit that all who came into contact with him attested to. William Bury, outwardly normal and presentable to some, had Merrick's deformities festering away inside him.

The near-adult Bury was the alter ego of Dickens's David Copperfield, and would be the villain, not the hero, of his own life. His self-image had already cast him in that role. Childhood had made him into what Professor David Canter describes as an alienated outsider, unable to socialise and integrate, especially with women, and possessed of a penchant for theft and lies, which quickly become apparent to those he worked with. The *Midland Evening News* would later describe his canards as 'so clumsily constructed as to be obvious to the densest intellect'.[45]

This inability to think through the consequences of his falsehoods would one day cost Bury his life. The netherworld in which he dwelled, containing as it did the ugly sexual fantasies that he carried forward to the streets and alleys of East London, was also to be fuelled by prodigious quantities of alcohol as he grew older.

One thing conspicuous by its absence is any mention of romance in the young William Bury's life.

His first known job was at a warehouse in Horseley Fields, East Wolverhampton. Here he was employed as a client by the factor (manager) a Mr Bissell. He appears to have done his work satisfactorily for he was still there in 1881; the Census gives his occupation as 'factor's clerk'.

Bury was lodging with a man named William Hicklin in Paternoster Row,[46] sharing the accommodation with Hicklin and three members of the landlord's family, his brother-in-law William Belchre and Belchre's wife Elizabeth and Hicklin's stepson Charles.[47]

Sometime in the early 1880s, Bury borrowed money at the warehouse on the pretext of needing a loan to pay off some debts, and promptly skedaddled, as the saying goes. He next turned up at a lockmaker's in nearby Lord Street looking for work. The owner, a Mr Osborne, checked his references and discovered the outstanding loan. His first instinct seems to have been to tell Bury to look elsewhere, but, according to the *Midland Evening News* of 12 February 1889, 'He [Bury] told such a pitiable story about having no home and no friends, and made such promises about mending his ways, that he was engaged.'

This was not destined to be one of Mr Osborne's better decisions. Bury remained with him for about 18 months. He worked well under supervision but when left to his own devices the wheels came off. On one occasion he smashed a window after being teased by workmates (though not on the premises), and he was much given to what was then termed as 'irregular habits'. The *Midland Evening News*, again, provides us with a potted description of what these were:

> His addiction to stating falsehoods is said to have been a continual habit. They say he had a most plausible address [manner] and was capable of inventing the most extravagant and apparently truthful stories which he told with an air of the most innocent sincerity. He was in their opinion a hopeless and confirmed 'ne'er do well', a fellow whom it was quite useless to try to help. In drink he was wholly incapable of controlling himself and when sober had not the least compunction in deceiving his best friends.[48]

From the sound of it, the 'friends' of William Bury were a very small club with a very high turnover. In 1884 or 1885, Osborne finally sacked him for theft. Thereafter, 'constant employment and a settled life appear to have been the bane of Bury's life'.[49]

Bury, as he is depicted here, has all the hallmarks of a serial killer in the making. He lies, cheats and steals (he was lucky not to have been prosecuted), violence simmers away just below the surface and he lives inside himself in a world of fantasy.

Details of his movements over the next few years are somewhat patchy. We catch fleeting glimpses of him in Wolverhampton working in a wine vault in North Street, and later a brass foundry owned by a man called Whitehouse. There is anecdotal evidence of his tramping to Dewsbury in Yorkshire and being arrested for vagrancy there. But the next definite sighting we have comes in 1887 from a Richard Swatman.

The 1881 Census lists only one Richard Swatman in Wolverhampton, a 22-year-old brass-foundry worker. Swatman is identified by the *Midland Wednesday News* of 13 February 1889 as being subsequently employed with Bury at Osborne & Co. and he was obviously the workmate there who supplied the Wolverhampton press with their background data on him, along with Bissell, a publican named James Dodd – whom we shall meet later – and another publican, a man named Wakeman, who kept the Summer House Inn in St Mark's Street.

Swatman had not seen Bury for some time when he encountered him, in the Snow Hill district of Birmingham. Bury was hawking key rings and pencils in the street and looking 'very shabby'. Swatman treated him to a drink in a liquor vault called Redpaths in the high street.[50]

Not long afterwards, this insignificant little man who was to run the streets of East London with blood and terror arrived on his killing ground. According to what the police later told Bury's executioner, James Berry, he initially earned his living there by cutting up horsemeat and selling it as cat food. Berry recorded:

He opened a shop . . . and people who knew him used to see him at work with his long knives. They spoke of the skilful way in which he handled them and according to the Detectives, it was with long weapons similar to what Bury used in his business that the Whitechapel murders were committed.[51]

Opinion is divided as to whether Jack the Ripper possessed the sorts of skills which would be derived from such an occupation, but having them was certainly not a disadvantage when Bury turned his hand to butchering human carcasses the following year.

The butcher's trade, as John Douglas points out, would have allowed Bury to give vent to his fantasies. In the same vein, criminologist Colin Wilson mentions the case of Eusebuis Pieydagnelle – referred to in Chapter 1 – who satisfied his bloodlust on animals as an apprentice butcher but turned to humans when this outlet was closed off to him by his father, who insisted that he read for the law instead.[52]

Ominously, for a number of London prostitutes, Bury's cat-meat shop did not last long. That October he presented himself for work at the premises of one James Martin in Bow. The end run to an evil destiny had commenced.

NOTES

1. *Brierley Hill and Stourbridge Advertiser*, 14 April 1860.
2. *Kelly's Birmingham Post Office Directory*, 1865.
3. The 1841 and 1851 Censuses suggest he was born in 1800 or 1801, but the age given on his death certificate puts it several years earlier, 1795 or 1796.
4. Mormon International Genealogical Index.
5. According to the 1851 Census, she was born in Montgomery in 1797 or 1798, but the Mormon International Genealogical Index records her baptism in Dudley on 13 December 1801, a year more in line with her age given on the 1841 Census (40). However the Mormon Index could have the wrong Jane Evans. The surname was reasonably common in Dudley in the 19th century.

6. Mormon International Genealogical Index.

7. 1841 and 1851 Censuses.

8. Powick Asylum Admission Records Casebook No. 5, 1858–May 1860, file ref. BA 10127, general ref. 499.9.

9. 1851 Census.

10. Misspelled with an extra *e*, 'Berrey', on the birth certificate.

11. 1 July 1854.

12. *Brierley Hill and Stourbridge Advertiser*, 14 April 1860.

13. Powick asylum records.

14. Death certificate.

15. The *Brierley Hill and Stourbridge Advertiser* mistakenly says two; the asylum record correctly notes three.

16. The death certificate lists the forenames as William Henry and records the coroner's verdict of 'accidentally killed on the hill, Halesowen', 10 April 1860.

17. 1851 and 1861 Censuses. The 1851 Census does in fact record a 'William Henry Perrey', a 34-year-old chainmaker, who lived in Lye with his widowed mother. He also appears in the 1861 Census.

18. Old Swinford Parish Burial Register.

19. The records describe her illness as 'melancholia', the 19th-century term for clinical depression.

20. Asylum records. Powick's interest in her seems not to have extended to notifying the authorities of her death. I have not been able to locate a certificate.

21. Death certificate.

22. Reprieve petition on behalf of William Henry Bury, 1 April 1889.

23. 25 April 1889.

24. 1881 Census, and statement of Mrs Elizabeth Haynes to the London Police, 14 February 1889.

25. Joel Norris, *Serial Killers: The Growing Menace* (pbk), pp. 317–8.

26. Ibid., p. 271.

27. See Angela Bourke, *The Burning of Bridget Cleary*.

28. Stephen Knight and Bernard Taylor, *Perfect Murder* (hbk), pp. 241–51.

29. *Bewitched*, Channel 4 documentary, 2000.

30. In fact, the tutor to the Bury children may have been a family member. Here the possible connection with Stourport becomes important. The Lower Mitton parish records register the baptisms of the twin sons of James Bury, schoolmaster, in October 1816, and the 1871 Census for Lye records that the village school there was being taught by Thomas Berry (*sic*) and his wife, both certificated teachers. Thomas originated from Stourport and was possibly descended from James Bury. He may have been the cousin of whom William Bury kept a photograph, and he and his wife could have been his teachers. But this is entirely speculative.

31. Dr Richard Lechtenberg, *Epilepsy and the Family*, 2nd edn, p. 160.

32. Ibid., p. 16.

33. Casebook No 9, 1863.

34. Robert D Keppel, *Signature Killers*, pp. 18 and 128.

35. Wilfred Gregg and Brian Lane, *The Encyclopaedia of Serial Killers* (pbk), pp. 107–8.

36. Jack Olson, *The Misbegotten Son* (hbk), p. 480.

37. Norris, op. cit., p. 275.

38. 'Fer–Fir', p. 87; 'Kee–Kon', p. 147; and 'Moo–Mor', p. 179. The sample pages were selected at random.

39. *Daily Telegraph*, 3 September 1888; *East London Observer*, 8 September, 1888; Phillip Sugden, *The Complete History of Jack the Ripper*, 1st edn (hbk), p. 46.

40. *The Secret Identity of Jack the Ripper*, television documentary, 1988.

41. Norris, op. cit., pp. 186–202.

42. *Dundee Courier*, 12 February 1889.

43. *Dundee Advertiser*, 12 February 1889.

44. Ibid., 12 February and 29 March 1889.

45. 24 April 1889.

46. The *Midland Evening News* of 12 February 1889 records a workmate of Bury's saying that he lodged with 'Mrs' Hicklin in Pipers Row, which is very close to Bilston Street, where Ripper victim Catharine Eddowes lived for a while with an aunt. This appears to be an error, especially as the workmate was ostensibly from Bury's next job, *circa* 1882. However, there is no trace of Paternoster Row in the Wolverhampton Census prior to 1881. So it is always possible that Bury and the Hicklins lived in Pipers Row at some point in the 1870s (they were not there in 1871).

47. 1881 Census.

48. 12 February 1889.

49. Ibid.

50. *Midland Wednesday News*, 13 February 1889.

51. Justin Atholl, *The Reluctant Hangman*, p. 71; *Weekly News*, 12 February 1927.

52. Colin Wilson, *The Mammoth Book of Murder*, revised edn (2000), pp. 402–3.

CHAPTER FOUR
THE KRAKEN

The East End of London is the hell of poverty. Like an enormous black, motionless, giant Kraken, the poverty of London lies there in lurking silence and encircles with its mighty tentacles the life and wealth of the city and of the West End.

. . . the region my hansom was now penetrating was one unending slum.

The above two descriptions of the East End of London – one by J H Mackay in a book entitled *The Anarchists* (1891), the second from the rather more famous pen of Jack London, *People of the Abyss* (1903) – perfectly illustrate the satanic cauldron into which William Bury had now descended. London's East End was the apogee of despair, the nadir of hope and aspiration.

Of the eight women whose names were to be linked in death with Jack the Ripper during 1888 – Emma Smith, Martha Tabram, Mary Ann Nichols, Annie Chapman, Elizabeth Stride, Catharine Eddowes, Mary Kelly and Catherine Mylett – only the last-named was born and raised in London's East End. The others originated either from other parts of London or outside the metropolis, in one case Sweden (Stride). They migrated into the filthy, rat-infested hovels and lodging houses of Whitechapel and Spitalfields – the 'evil quarter of a mile' as it was known – because it was the end of the road. Crushed by poverty and despair and ensnared by the drink dependency that it fostered, they found that this was the last place in which they could continue to function.

Jack London had endured an impoverished San Francisco childhood, and as a young man had crisscrossed America riding the rails as a hobo. But not even this harsh acclimatisation could prepare him for the depths of poverty he found in East London. After a few days of posing as a down-and-out, he was pleased to escape back to a hot bath and a comfortable bed. Behind him he left a variety of characters whom he brought vividly to life in *The People of the Abyss*: the venerable ex-serviceman who had won the Victoria Cross and was now reduced to dragging his aged body from one workhouse to the next; at the other end of the age scale the teenage socialist already a battle-hardened veteran of the war against oppression ('Three of us walked down Mile End Road, and one was a hero'); the little shoemaker from the sweatshop, his teeth 'coal black and rotten' from the friction of the brads that flew out of his mouth, 'like from a machine', and who was unwarrantably proud of a body the writer found 'gnarled and twisted out of all decency': 'I'm a 'earty man, not like the other chaps in my shop.'

Who, thought London, could be less 'hearty' than this poor specimen? Yet disabusal lay just around the corner in the shapes of the underclass of the underclass, hovering with dreadful anticipation of the end to come in the long chilly shadows of Christ Church, Spitalfields, 'a mass of miserable and distorted humanity', riddled and raddled with disease and covered in sores. They were, London remarked with feeling, 'a sight I never wish to see again'.[1]

After these ghastly images, it was almost a relief when he fell in again with two more members of the walking wounded. One of them, a carter in his late fifties, had operated a hand-to-mouth business with his son. Then disease – the ever-present scourge of the poor – struck, cutting down the son with smallpox, after which the carter himself had been hospitalised with fever for three months: 'He came out weak, debilitated, no strong young son to stand by him, his little business gone glimmering, and not a farthing,' wrote London.[2]

His other companion in misery had lost his three daughters to scarlet fever within the space of a fortnight. Now 65, he had been tramping the streets for five days when London met up with him, the Carter three. They were just two out of 35,000 homeless people in the capital. As London walked with them:

> From the slimy, spittle-drenched sidewalk, they were picking up bits of orange peel, apple skin and grape stems and they were eating them . . . and this in the heart of the greatest empire the world has ever seen.[3]

London contrasted this existence with that of the upper classes:

> Five hundred hereditary peers own one fifth of England; and they, and the officers and servants under the king, and those who go to compose the powers that be, yearly spend in wasteful luxury £370 million, which is 32 per cent of the total wealth produced by all the toilers of the country.[4]

While the 500 lived in opulence, an estimated 450,000 Londoners existed in the direst poverty. Their literary gladiator observed poignantly, 'I should not like to hear them all talk at once. I wonder if God hears them?'[5]

It was hardly a coincidence that the word 'unemployment' first made its appearance in the Oxford Dictionary in 1888.[6] Recession was biting deeply and its effects were particularly hard felt in the East End, where a large section of the workforce derived its income from the docks. The situation was exacerbated not only by immigrants from abroad but also by an influx of unemployed farm labourers from Essex and East Anglia who had lost their livelihoods due to a combination of mechanisation and the severe winter of 1887–88. William J Fishman, in his comprehensive study of conditions in the area, *East End 1888*, recounts how a clerical position advertised by Poplar Council at a salary of 30 shillings a week drew 80 applicants, including shopkeepers, clerks about to be made redundant from the docks and even members of the professions.[7]

A community already stagnating under its own inertia and degradation became a bottleneck for the dispossessed and the desperate. Social reformers, such as the novelist Margaret Harkness and outspoken East London clergymen like the Reverends W E Kendall and F W Newlands, saw the storm clouds of revolution gathering and heard the sound of the tumbrels creaking ominously into motion beneath them.[8] But the Ripper murders, when they came, would not only focus attention on the plight of the East End's poor, but also act as a lightning conductor as much as a vehicle of reform, diverting hatred into fear and channelling the pent-up feelings of the downtrodden *away* from economic grievances. To quote Earl Grey 50 years earlier, it was 'not revolution but the reverse'. Socialism did not benefit from William Bury's little bloodbath.

This was despite an embarrassment of riches for the cause. Thirty-five per cent of the populace of London's east quarter lived on or below the poverty line in conditions that almost defy description.[9] As one reads the available material on the subject, the same words occur over and over again like a mallet pounding into the senses: filth, rags, slums, hunger, cruelty, destitute, degraded, vicious, horrors, outcasts, squalid, distress, callous, insanitary and so on, till the brain starts to reel like a punch-drunk fighter's.

Statistics – cold as ice in their grim, impersonal way – tell us that Stepney had the worst mortality rate for infants under the age of one, at almost one in four; St George in the East had the greatest proportion of casual labourers, at 9.5 per cent, and the highest birthrate, at 39.8 per 1,000; while Bethnal Green came second in both birth and infant mortality, at 39.1 per 1,000 and 18 per cent. Bethnal Green also had the second largest population (behind Poplar), but cantered into overall first place by dint of coming top in the death rate, at 26.5 per 1,000, and the equally melancholic category of most fatalities from contagious and epidemic diseases, an unhappy distinction emphasised by the fact that it was not just first in percentage terms but actual figures as well: 562 out of more than 130,000 persons as opposed to Poplar's 475 from a population in excess of 182,000. Bethnal Green was thus the place you would least want to live and where you were least likely to live.[10]

But let us get away from sardonic statistics! These are real lives and real people. Not that the then Archbishop of Canterbury was much impressed by them. Opening the Oxford Hall in Victoria Park Square on 18 February 1888, he declared that it made his 'blood run cold to think of the many early marriages' and advised the inhabitants of Bethnal Green to practise restraint, just as the upper classes did. Unless he was uniquely innocent, he could not have failed to know that the aristocracy's idea of practising restraint was a nightly trawl of the fleshpots. Half a century earlier, Flora Tristan, a French feminist, recorded her observations of the English 'gentry' at play, on this occasion in a South London gin palace:

[T]his is where the cream of the Aristocracy gather. At first the young Noblemen recline on the sofas . . . then, when they have drunk enough . . . the very honourable members of parliament . . . proceed to set up their private boudoir.

One of the favourite sports is to ply a woman with drink till she falls dead drunk upon the floor, then to make her swallow a draught compounded of vinegar, mustard and pepper, this invariably throws the poor creature into horrible convulsions and her spasms and contortions provoke the honourable company to gales of laughter and infinite amusement.

Another diversion . . . is to empty the contents of the nearest glass upon the women as they lie insensible on the ground. I have seen satin dresses of no recognisable colour, only a confused mass of stains; wine, brandy, beer, tea, coffee, cream etc daubed all over them in a thousand fantastic shapes – the handiwork of debauchery.[11]

Fishman writes of men from the upper classes being drawn to the East End by the lure of easy sex, pubs and music halls.[12] Typical of the last of these was Wilton's near the Royal Mint in Wapping, a frequent target for reformers because its upstairs rooms were used as a high-class brothel. It was establishments such as this that the radical socialist periodical *Justice* was complaining about when it spoke of 'society Popinjays' gratifying their passions by 'ruining the daughters of the working class', using them as sexual substitutes for women from their own echelons of society.[13] Wilton's was eventually forced to close during the furore caused by the Ripper; the building still stands today, forlornly boarded up against intrusion by the outside world.[14]

The girls who catered for upper-class tastes, however, were very different from the sad little women whom William Bury destroyed. The latter reflected his own self-image: vagrants, cast adrift from their families and scraping an existence any way they could – by prostitution when all else failed.

They belonged to a vast underbody of East End society, some indigenous to the area, others not, whom, poverty had effectively criminalised. The Old Nichol gang lived in sunless, dilapidated cottages originally built below street level, situated in an area between Shoreditch High Street and Brick Lane (Spitalfields) known as 'the Jago', from which they sallied forth to engage in burglary and mugging.[15] Their speciality was robbing street prostitutes of their pittance earnings. Members of the gang were almost certainly responsible for one of the murders attributed to the Ripper (Emma Smith)

The Ripper seems to have forced the Old Nichol into temporarily operating in less blue-serge environs. In the spring of 1889, there are reports of organised teams of pickpockets and muggers at work in Stepney Green and Mile End. Angry residents complained that police officers were actually in league with the 'Mile End Moochers', as one newspaper dubbed the gangs. Not so, declared one ex-detective: the fault lay with the courts, who were too lenient.[16]

Doubtless, this individual would have been considerably heartened by the punishment meted out to a starving street urchin named James Cadderley, who wept piteously as he received 12 strokes of the birch for stealing a loaf of bread.[17] The barbarity of such sentences only compounded the conditions that caused youngsters like Cadderley to steal in the first place.

The finished products of the East End street academies could be found infesting the pubs and dosshouses in the area. Many of the latter were simply gambling dens and brothels, summed up by an East End magistrate as 'unwholesome, unhealthy and dangerous to the community . . . where the police dare not enter and the criminal hides all day'.[18] This view was reiterated by the social reformer Charles Booth. The inhabitant of the dosshouse was merely a 'loafer' who, 'lives without labour and is the major recruit to the criminal or semi-criminal classes'.[19] This, however, was not a view that found favour with H M Hyndman, the Marxist leader of the Social Democratic Federation and editor of *Justice*, who thought that such terms more aptly described the middle and upper classes, whom his organisation held responsible for the condition of the poor.[20]

Among the poorest of the poor were the East End Jews, who had traditionally settled there after emigrating from continental Europe. During the second half of the 19th century, their numbers were swelled by Jews fleeing from persecution in Russia and Poland. By 1888, an estimated 40,000 people of Hebrew origin were congregated in the parishes of Whitechapel, St George in the East, Mile End and Bethnal Green, producing a simmering tension between Jews and non-Jews in the area.[21]

East End legerdemain, fuelled by anti-Semitic demagogues such as the writer Arnold White, held that immigrants were 'colonising' Britain,[22] and driving down living standards through working for lower wages than their indigenous counterparts. Such accusations were widely believed, even by socialists such as Hyndman.[23] In fact, they were largely mythical. In 1886, the year in which 19th-century emigration and immigration each peaked, 396,494 people left Britain and only 30 per cent of that number, 119,013, arrived. In both cases, 71 per cent were of British or Irish origin, which meant that more than three times as many persons of foreign extraction left Britain as came into it.

On the economic front, gentile employers refused to hire Jewish labour, which left the latter with no other option than to work for their co-religionists at rock-bottom wages. Despite this, their jobs were often less secure than those of gentile workers. A prime example was the boot-and-shoe industry, which by the 1880s was gravitating from the Jewish-dominated sweatshops of East London to factory production in provincial towns such as Northampton.[24]

Such realities were, unfortunately, beyond the grasp of those who made the Jews scapegoats for homelessness and unemployment in the East End. Anti-Semitism even permeated the courts. In September 1888, an East London magistrate named Saunders told a Polish plaintiff that he was 'taking the bread out of the mouths of Englishmen'.[25]

The situation was not helped by a well-publicised case the previous year in which a young Polish Jew, Israel Lipski, was executed for the murder of Miriam Angel, a Jewess he was allegedly smitten with.[26] 'Lipski' subsequently became a term of abuse shouted at Jews in the street, including on one occasion by the Ripper! Ironically, the first two women to be murdered in the East End during the year of his reign of terror were, like Miriam Angel, also Jewish immigrants, one the victim of a jealous husband (the so-called 'Othello syndrome'), the other a female found dead in a tunnel leading to St Mary's railway station in Whitechapel.[27] Nobody mentioned these crimes during the near state of pogrom that existed in the East End at the height of the Ripper murders.

The reality was that there was no difference in the living standards of poor Jews and gentiles alike, with one exception: the former were not as prone to pouring vast quantities of cheap liquor down their throats as the latter. Here the Kraken softened up its victims, allowing them a brief respite from their ills so that the hopelessness of their situation might be made even clearer to them in the morning through their empty pockets. 'The Public House is the Elysian Field of the poor toiler,' wrote William C Preston in 1883.[28] And how! Newlands counted almost 2,000 people going into a pub during a three-hour spell one Saturday night; over the same period, 1,538 entered another hostelry.[29] Not surprisingly, the police cells overflowed with inebriates: in 1889, there were 2,309 arrests for drunkenness in the Whitechapel Police district alone.[30]

Newlands and others concluded that poverty derived from intemperance and not the other way around. In fact, it was a dreadful vicious circle: poverty begot the necessity to drink in order to blot out its realities and drink then compounded the poverty. Children born into such circumstances grew up knowing no other way of life. They became desensitised by their environment at an early age: J H Mackay recounts how he came across a group of youngsters amusing themselves with the death agonies of a cat whose eyes they had gouged out.[31]

The surroundings themselves were also an important contributory factor in producing drunkenness and violence. A contemporary journal, *The Nineteenth Century*, makes the interesting psychological point that such behaviour was more prevalent in areas surrounded by walls or water on three sides leaving only a single entrance. Many parts of the East End were hemmed in by railway embankments, canals or the River Thames.[32]

This ties in with the results of modern-day experiments with mice. Placed in cramped and overcrowded conditions – adjectives synonymous with Victorian slums – the mice's behaviour degenerated into violence, with gangs forming to mug and rape the more docile of the species, while in turn dominant mice emerged to lead the gangs, rather, in human terms, as the Krays did in East London.

William Bury, however, was not a dominant individual; life had never fitted him to play first fiddle in the orchestra. He was an anomalous, anonymous creature who slotted easily into the drink culture of the East End without ever being part of the poor man's camaraderie that it fostered. But in London he was not a slum dweller and he was always at least a half a jump ahead of the direst poverty. He gravitated towards Poplar, largest of the East London districts, and in particular the parishes of Mile End and Bow, which in 1888 could be termed upper-working-class. The district was boosted by large open squares and Georgian houses, and, while it also had its share of brothels and prostitutes, most of its citizens were hardworking and respectable. Residents even made wills worth publishing: John Ashbridge of Mile End and Harry Perry of Bow both left in excess of £30,000, around £2 million on today's values.[33] It was natural that Bury, a little man with large pretensions, should eventually seek work and lodgings here.

But it was the 'evil quarter of a mile', Whitechapel and its surrounds, that fired his fantasies – and his fears. J H Mackay never met William Bury, or heard his name, but in an extraordinary passage in *The Anarchists* he vividly brings him to life against the backdrop of one of the rooms in his charnel house, Spitalfields:

> Shops with bloody meat, stuck on prongs – 'cats meat'; at every street corner a 'wine and spirits' house; torn posters on the walls, still in loud colours; a crowd of young men passes by – they shout and sing; down the side street a drunken form is feeling its way along the wall, muttering to itself and gesticulating . . .[34]

This is Bury, the country boy cast into the unending slum, nursing his fantasies at the bottom of a glass and trying to escape from the futility of the cat-meat shop. Tomorrow, when he is sober, his demons will be back clawing at his throat again, growing stronger all the time.

NOTES

1. Jack London, *The People of the Abyss*, 1977, pp. 29–32.
2. Ibid., p. 41.
3. Ibid., pp. 36–7.
4. Ibid., p. 62.
5. Ibid., p. 25.
6. William Fishman, *East End 1888* (hbk), p. 49.
7. Ibid., p. 50.
8. Harkness wrote under the pseudonym 'John Law'. This prophecy appears in her 'factional' work *In Darkest London*; those of Kendall and Newlands in the *East End News*, of 21 September and 19 October 1888. They are recounted by Fishman, op. cit., pp. 52–3.
9. Fishman, op. cit., p. 4.
10. Ibid., p. 44.
11. John Carey (ed.), *The Faber Book of Reportage*, pp. 312–13.
12. Fishman, op. cit., p. 28.
13. *Justice*, 28 January 1888; Fishman, op. cit., p. 123.
14. *Timewatch*: 'Shadow of the Ripper', BBC documentary, July 1988.
15. Fishman, op. cit., pp. 7 and 306.
16. *East London Observer*, 27 April and 4 May 1889.
17. Fishman, op. cit., p. 198.
18. *East End News*, 5 October 1888; Fishman, op. cit., p. 28.

19. Fishman, op. cit., p. 11.

20. *Justice*, 3 March, 1888; Fishman, op. cit., p. 40.

21. Joseph Blank, secretary to the Jews' temporary shelter in Leman Street, gives a figure of 33,218 (July 1888), while the philanthropist Charles Booth had estimated 45,000 the previous year.

22. *Times*, 13 July 1887.

23. Fishman, op. cit., p. 158.

24. Ibid., pp. 131–4.

25. *East End News*, 14 September 1888; Fishman, op. cit., p. 155.

26. See Martin L Friedland, *The Trials of Israel Lipski*.

27. Fishman, op. cit., p. 208.

28. *The Bitter Cry of Outcast London*, p 7; Fishman, op. cit., p. 304.

29. *East London Observer*, 7 April 1888; Fishman, op. cit., p. 39.

30. Brian Harrison, *The Victorian City, Images and Realities* (eds H J Dyos and Michael Wolff), Vol. 1, pp. 161–70; Fishman, op. cit., p. 303.

31. J H McKay, *The Anarchists*, p. 170; Fishman, op. cit., pp. 23–4.

32. *Nineteenth Century*, Vol. 24 (1888), p. 260; Fishman, op. cit., p. 2.

33. *East London Observer*, 10 and 31 March 1888; Fishman, op. cit., p. 36.

34. McKay, op. cit., p. 170; Fishman, op. cit., p. 24.

CHAPTER FIVE

THE BRIDEGROOM
FROM HELL

There are no extant photographs of Ellen Elliott and only the scantiest of descriptions. She was 32 at the time of her death and her corpse was measured at 5ft 1½in. She is said to have been slim and fair-haired, so perhaps her figure conveyed a misleading impression of her height because, according to one newspaper, Ellen was 'tall and attractive'.[1]

We know that she was not very well educated, although she could read and write.[2] Perhaps because of this she comes down to us as something of a cipher, a woman eclipsed both by her husband and her environment. Perhaps, too, this is why nobody took any notice of her when, at the end of a wretched life and a marriage made in hell, she told the world just who the appalling creature she had wed really was.

Ellen's story originates in the Northwest of England. George Elliott was a Derbyshire man who moved south to meet and marry Harriet Barron, a young woman 20 years his junior from Walworth in South London. Their first child, Mary Ann, was born in 1848, after which they tried their luck in the North, settling for a time in Mansfield, where George worked as a grocer and Harriet gave birth to two more children, Margaret in July 1852[3] and George Jr two years later. After his birth, they returned to South London, where George took over a pub, the Bricklayers Arms in Queens Row, Walworth.[4]

He was 'guvnor' there when their fourth child, Ellen, was born on 24 October 1856. She was christened a month later, 23 November, at St Peter's Church, Liverpool Grove, Walworth,[5] and this is the only listing we have of her birth, because it is not on file at the Family Record Centre.[6]

Probably due to lack of educational attainment, Margaret and Ellen tended to be hazy about their ages. Margaret repeated the common error of going by the current year instead of the month and day, even though she remembered the dates clearly enough.[7] Ellen had only the vaguest idea of the year of her birth. She was to get her age wrong on her marriage certificate, and before that gave different years of birth to the Poplar Workhouse authorities twice within the space of a few weeks.[8] Neither was correct.

The Elliott family were completed by three more daughters, Harriet (1858), Emily (1863) and Charlotte (1868), the last when their father had turned 60.[9] As a pub landlord in the strictly working-class district of Walworth, George would have been regarded as a cut above his customers and he himself gave his occupation not as 'publican' but 'beer retailer'. Later, his posthumous son-in-law was to outdo this by pompously describing George as a 'licensed victualler' on his and Ellen's marriage certificate.

We know next to nothing abut Ellen's upbringing. We can picture her on family outings at around the age of six being shepherded by her elder sisters while she in turn clasps little Harriet firmly by the hand, all ribbons and bows and no hint of a sordid future. Some vignettes of their family life survived, a litany given to Ellen in 1868 by her brother and a book about travel inscribed 'Harriet Elliott – a gift by Mrs Clarke, August 11th 1867'.[10]

The family lived above the pub but the environment does not seem to have adversely influenced Ellen because by all accounts she drank only sparingly. She did have a penchant for comparatively expensive jewellery and by the time she died had accumulated an assortment of rings, bracelets and earrings of better quality than those normally owned by women from the East End of London. Some of the pieces were purchased in Birmingham in August 1888 and she is recalled as proudly sporting one of them, a brooch in the form of a jubilee £5 piece, on holiday in Wolverhampton.

Margaret tells us that when Ellen grew up she went to work as a needlewoman, making waterproof cloaks. She was also employed for a time in a jute factory, an occupation that was to have a bearing on the events leading up to her death.

Sometime between Charlotte's birth and the spring of 1871, George Elliott moved his family 'across the water', as Londoners term crossing the Thames, to Bromley By Bow in East London where he took over another pub, the Prince of Wales in Upper Mary Street.[11] He died there on 20 November 1873, leaving an estate valued at under £50.[12] The family were left very much to fend for themselves. Margaret married a miller named Charles Corney on 16 January 1876 at St Stephen's Parish Church in Bow, and later set up home with him at 3 Stanley Road, just off Stratford High Street in East London.[13] Where Ellen was residing between 1873 and 1883 is unknown. Possibly she was living with an aunt, Margaret Barron, along with Emily and Charlotte, because when Miss Barron died (*circa* 1881) she left Ellen the not insignificant legacy of six £100 railway shares, nominally £40,000 on today's values.[14] Emily and Charlotte had similar inheritances.

It is often said that money cannot buy health, happiness or love. This was never more true than in Ellen Elliott's case. The windfall was followed by less welcome news: she was pregnant. In 1889, her last 'employer', James Martin, told the police, 'Elliott told me on one occasion that she had given birth to a child in some workhouse.'[15]

In fact, Martin got it the wrong way round. The child, a girl named

Ellen, after her mother, was born at 11 Kenilworth Road, Bethnal Green. The father's name – if indeed Ellen knew it – was a secret she took to her grave. Number 11 Kenilworth Road was not a workhouse but an apparently respectable dwelling place. The 1881 Census shows two families sharing the premises, one named Reynolds, the other headed by a dyer named Susannah Ward and consisting of her uncle, his common-law wife Mary Sykes and Sykes's two children. But the interesting point about Mary Sykes is her occupation – needlewoman, the same as Ellen Elliott, who described herself as a seamstress on the birth certificate (although this was also a euphemism for prostitution). Possibly Elliott and Sykes were workmates and Ellen was lodging with her at the time of the birth, 5 August 1883.

The little girl was not destined to have a long life. On 13 October 1885, mother and daughter were admitted to Poplar Workhouse, and on 27 November the child was remanded to the infirmary. On 6 December, her mother was discharged from the workhouse. Although it is not stated in the institution's records, there is evidence that she went as a domestic servant to 374 Old Ford Road.[16] Nine days later, little Ellen died, her mother apparently being present at the bedside. Poverty was a prime factor in 55 per cent of East End children's deaths before their sixth birthdays, but Ellen Elliott was not destitute: she had her inheritance and it is difficult to fathom why she chose to inflict a pauper's existence on her daughter and herself. Perhaps, like Victorian society as a whole, she opted for mammon instead of humanity. Yet she kept the little girl's clothes, so she obviously cared about her.

Dickens again, that whiplash scourge of the blighted times in which he lived, might have written the part that Ellen Elliott played in her own life. She was a combination of Clara Copperfield's timid little mouse and Molly Provis's masochistic self-image, neither a heroine nor a villain, instead, like them, a feeder character for its main players.

Ellen was back at the workhouses on 21 December. She spent a cold, cheerless Christmas there before going into service again. This time Poplar's register does confirm her leaving: on the 29th to work for a Mrs Davies of 69 Stafford Street, Old Ford. William Fishman notes that workhouses commonly supplied girls to the domestic-service market, but that the backbreaking workload made a life of prostitution more attractive by comparison.[17] Certainly this was the case with Ellen. She left Mrs Davies after only a few months and by spring 1886 was working in a brothel.

Her new employers were James Martin and Kate Spooner at 80 Quickett Street,[18] off Arnold Road in Bow. Then aged 36, Martin is described as a 'tall, acute looking cockney' with dark hair and a heavy brown moustache.[19] Like so many other characters in this story, he originated from the south side of the Thames, Lambeth, and he had then lived in the East End for at least five years. The 1881 Census finds him lodging at the Quickett Street address with two sisters, Rosina and Sarah Styles, and a 'visitor', Maria Walker. All three girls were in their twenties and it is a reasonable assumption that Martin was their pimp. Little is known of Spooner, who died around 1887 or 1888. Martin claimed she was a hawker,[20] but other evidence portrays her as living with Martin and helping him run the brothel.[21] By 1891, he was married to a woman named Eliza.[22]

Early in 1887, Ellen rented and furnished a room at 3 Swaton Road, Bow, owned by Thomas and Elizabeth Haynes. In her early fifties, Elizabeth came from Stourport of all places![23] According to both Martin and Mrs Haynes, Ellen continued to spend most of her time at Quickett Street, sleeping at Swaton Road only infrequently. She explained this to Haynes by saying that she was caring for an invalid woman. Not till spring 1888 did Ellen's landlady learn the truth:

It was then that I heard that Mrs Bury [Ellen] had been a servant in the employ of Martin who kept a brothel in

73

Arnold Road, Bow. She told me that she had been there the whole of the time that she rented a room off me before she was married and that it was not true that she had been attending an invalid lady.[24]

Martin confirmed that 'service' had a different meaning in his household: 'I know that she [Ellen] was no better than a prostitute and she occasionally fetched men home and they slept with her at my house.'[25]

The autumn mists of 1887 brought a newcomer to 80 Quickett Street. The following autumn he would hue them deepest red throughout the poorest quarter of East London, but at the moment William Bury was more interested in avarice than mutilation. How he met Martin is anybody's guess, but they were birds of the same feather and Martin was happy to rent a horse and cart out to Bury and supply him with sawdust and silversand, which he hawked around the pubs and restaurants of the City and of the East End. Bury was supposed to pay Martin 16 shillings a week rent plus the cost of the sawdust and sand, keeping the profit for himself.

Bury initially slept mainly in the stable with the horse, but was subsequently allowed to move into the house. His and Ellen's opening responses to each other were hardly love at first sight. Martin recalled, 'They were always bitter with one another. Before me they seemed so.'[26]

But it was common knowledge in the house that Ellen had money. Martin was under the misapprehension that her shares were worth their face value of £600. In reality, the recession meant that their actual value was nowhere near that amount, less than half in fact, though it is unlikely that anybody at Quickett Street appreciated this.

Outwardly, Bury's feelings appeared to change. Inwardly, his hatred of women made it impossible for him to feel anything for Ellen beyond the mercenary instincts of a predator. Whether Ellen deliberately chose to ignore the pound-note signs dancing in his eyes nobody can say, but before spring arrived in 1888 she was engaged to this mean, grasping little weasel of a man. To complete the Dickens analogy, the villain of his life would take as a wife the bit player in hers.

She was already aware of his violence: he beat her up at least once during their courtship. He, on the other hand, was also well aware of how Ellen made her living, an important point in view of the lies he later told on the subject.[27] Spitalfields is approximately 40 minutes' walking distance from Bow, but much quicker if you have a horse and cart, as Bury did. At around 5pm on Saturday, 25 February 1888, Annie Millwood, a 38-year-old army widow living in a common lodging house in Whites Row, was attacked by a man who stabbed her several times in the legs and lower body with a clasp knife. Millwood's wounds were not life-threatening and she was discharged after treatment at the Whitechapel Workhouse infirmary. Five weeks later, however, she died of heart failure. Only one newspaper, the *Eastern Post* of 7 April, reported the incident and not in very great detail, so we have no precise knowledge of where the attack took place, how many times she was stabbed or a description of her assailant. Probably she was prostituting herself and he was a client, but it is not certain.

Was this attack a forerunner of the Ripper murders? It sounds like it. Experience with similar killers, Peter Sutcliffe for example, shows that they often begin with non-fatal assaults and work their way up to murder. In this instance, we have one of Bury's trigger words, the middle name of his dead sister, Ann. We also have the fact that Bury was approaching a highly charged emotional situation in his life. Marriage, especially to a prostitute, was the last thing he wanted, but something that he had to do to get his hands on Ellen's money. Nothing was more calculated to fuel his hatred of women and his self-loathing. Couple these with the increased fear and anxiety that the situation generated, add alcohol, and you have a man suffering the torments of the damned. There can have been few men in London, if any, whose inner turmoil was as great as William Bury's was that last week in February, and of course he was verging on one of his psycho-menopausal periods. The logical conclusion is that poor Annie Millwood became the epicentre of all this tumult and that Bury abandoned his attack because he lost control of her.

Early in March, Ellen ceased working in the brothel and she and Bury moved in together at Swaton Road. Towards the end of the month, Martin sacked Bury for what he termed 'appropriating some of my money'.[28] This he later clarified in court. He had terminated their contract 'the first time about the beginning of March [because] he would never "fetch" any money home.'[29]

The reference to 'the first time' is a little misleading in that it implies that he dismissed Bury, reinstated him and then fired him again within the space of a few weeks. In fact, this was almost certainly an oblique reference (and not the only one in Martin's testimony) to a subsequent business arrangement that commenced early in May. What is not in dispute is the fact that, by the latter part of March, Bury was out of work owing Martin the comparatively large sum of £17.65, and that he was drinking heavily, likewise a point confirmed by Martin.[30]

The events of Wednesday, 28 March 1888 need to be seen against the background of these circumstances. Shortly after midnight on that date, Rose Bierman, a young woman living with her mother at 9 Maidmans Street, a tenement block situated just behind what is now Mile End Tube Station, heard screaming coming from the apartment under hers.[31] Bierman raced down the stairs to find the tenant, Ada Wilson, standing in the hallway partially dressed, shouting, 'Stop that man for cutting my throat. He has stabbed me.'

Wilson then collapsed with blood billowing from a double wound in her throat. Bierman's attention was diverted to a 'fair young man' who rushed to the front door of the apartment block and let himself out. She later told a reporter, 'He did not seem somehow to unfasten the catch as if he had been accustomed to do so before.'

Wilson was removed to the London Hospital, where it took her a month to recover. She gave her age as 39 and said she worked as a dressmaker. Wilson told the police that she had been about to go to bed when there was a knock on the door. She opened it to find a stranger of about 30 with a sunburned face and a fair moustache on her doorstep. He was wearing a dark coat, light trousers and a wide-awake hat. The man demanded money and, when she refused, he stabbed her twice with a clasp knife.

But, according to Rose Bierman, Wilson had brought a man home with her earlier that night. 'Dressmaker', like 'seamstress', was then a euphemism for prostitution, and Bierman leaves us in no doubt that the latter was Wilson's calling:

> I know Mrs Wilson as a married woman although I had never seen her husband . . . she has often had visitors to see her, but I have rarely seen them myself . . . she was under notice to quit.[32]

There is a fascinating little postscript to the attack on Ada Wilson. Five hours later, as doctors stitched her throat back together and hoped for the best, a major fire broke out at a feather mill in Colchester Street, Whitechapel.[33] Five months later, Jack the Ripper's first canonical murder would be set against the backdrop of a massive fire in the East End docks. The Ripper crimes are replete with tiny, garish coincidences.

So was Wilson one of his victims? It is more likely that she was than she wasn't. Almost certainly she was attacked by a man posing as a client who was desperate for money. She was lucky to survive. As with Millwood, the man lost control of the situation, but he clearly intended both to rob and to kill her. His description broadly fits William Bury. The 'sunburned' face is intriguing. Possibly it belonged to a seaman just back from foreign parts, but any tan would have faded by the time he docked. There are other interesting possibilities to account for it: a dark complexion or a face flushed by alcohol. Both would tie in with Bury.

There is one obvious departure from Bury's methodology: the name, Ada. But there are no absolutes with serial killers. On 28 March 1888, Bury was a desperate man, desperate for money and desperate emotionally, for the wedding he dreaded was now only five days hence, causing all his cacodemons to come bubbling up to the surface. Burgess, Douglas and Ressler note,

> In 48 per cent of 86 murder cases, the murderers stated that financial difficulties were present at the time of their crimes. Again, this stress factor may be closely related to another . . . the man's high level of aggression was linked with financial, alcohol and family member problems.

This passage might have been written for William Bury, particularly as the authors then go on to state,

> Difficulties with employment were given as precipitating stress factors in 39 per cent of 90 murders . . . Employment problems involved situations in which the murderer was unemployed or was having difficulty at work.[34]

A final factor is the proximity of Maidmans Street to Swaton Road, about 10 minutes' walk. Professor Canter believes that the Ripper would have established a 'safety zone' of about half a mile between his abode and his crime scenes. This is based on his being on foot. I think it fair to lengthen this for somebody using a horse-drawn conveyance. When Annie Millwood was stabbed, Bury had access to a horse and cart, and we will see that this was also the case at the time of the established Ripper murders. The one time in which he was on foot was at the end of March after Martin had fired him. Here we find that the attempted murder of Ada Wilson adheres very closely to Canter's safety zone.

On Easter Monday, 2 April, William Bury and Ellen Elliott were married at Bromley Parish Church. One is tempted to think of two death's heads going down the aisle together, because in just over a year's time both partners in this blissless union would have perished violently, each at the hands of the other.

Ellen's witness was Elizabeth Haynes. The signature of Bury's is difficult to decipher but the gentleman's name would appear to have been 'L Tollfree'. He plays no further part in this story and his relationship to Bury is unknown. Bury gave his age a little prematurely as 29, perhaps to minimise the gap with Ellen's, for she mistakenly recorded hers as 32 instead of 31. Apparently, no family members were present, not even Margaret.[35]

A covenant had been made but with death, not life. For those who believe in portents, the East End of London was replete with them on that Easter Monday, all presaging a bloody end to this union of the damned and the desperate.

The sudden squalls of violence blew first in Bow, where James Brown, a private in the Dragoon Guards, attempted that morning to cut the throat of the woman he was living with. The victim, Eliza Lowe, disappeared after she was discharged from hospital.[36]

The sense of foreboding is added to by the surname of the next victim. In the evening a policeman found Malvina Haynes lying unconscious with severe head injuries near Leman Street railway station, on the border of Whitechapel and St George in the East. Ostensibly a respectable married woman, Haynes lay in a coma for a week. On recovering, she was able to recount how she had been attacked, but when asked to describe her assailant she claimed her mind had gone blank. Meanwhile, a man was seen 'near' her at the time fled the district, which leads to the suspicion that Malvina was not quite the paragon of virtue that she pretended to be.[37]

The London Hospital had a busy 24 hours. While Lowe and Haynes were joining Ada Wilson in the recovery wards, a sad middle-aged prostitute's luck was about to run out. Not that Emma Elizabeth Smith had ever had much of it in the first place. Aged 45, she is alleged to have seen better days, but by Easter 1888 she was living in a common lodging house at 18 George Street, Spitalfields, and soliciting in Bow. She may well have travelled so far afield because of past encounters with the Old Nichol gang. A woman saw her just after midnight on the 3rd talking to a man in Burdett Road, a main thoroughfare running between Mile End and Poplar. Remarkably, Emma's spotter had herself just been punched in the mouth by two men; even more remarkably she was still recovering from an attack prior to that and had spent a fortnight in hospital. It is hardly surprising that the *Morning Advertiser* summed this bloody little montage up as 'rough work'.

Emma Smith was unharmed when she parted from her erstwhile beau. She then walked into history with an undeserved reputation as the first victim of Jack the Ripper. Three men, probably thugs from the Old Nichol, picked up her trail at Whitechapel Church. They shadowed her back to Spitalfields, and, on the corner of Wentworth Street and Brick Lane, they jumped her. One of them rammed an object of some kind, most likely a wooden stick, into her vagina and she was left to stumble home trying to staunch the blood the best she could. At her lodgings, Emma was persuaded to go to the London Hospital, where it was found that her peritoneum had been ruptured. She died there at 9am on the 4th. Her murderers were never caught and the ongoing investigation was later lumped in with the Ripper's. Whatever faults she may have had, Emma Smith did not deserve to die in such a way.[38]

Meanwhile, back at Swaton Road, Ellen was proving intransigent about yielding up her shares to her new husband. Bury had his own way of dealing with stubborn females. Elizabeth Haynes takes up the story:

> He was drunk and wanted her to give him some money, she refused and he assaulted [her] she screamed for help and I went into their room. I found him kneeling on her in bed. He had a [large] table knife in his right hand and was apparently about to cut her throat . . . Mrs Bury asked me on this occasion to take the key of the door and keep it to prevent him locking her in for she was afraid he would kill her.[39]

Haynes threatened to call the police but relented when Bury promised it would not happen again. In fact, this incident, which took place on Saturday, 7 April, was the third in the five days since the wedding!

The first occurred on Wednesday, 4 April. The newlyweds had bought a rug and Bury was, as usual, pining for a drink. He asked Ellen for money and, when she refused, floored her with a punch in the mouth. James Martin, who was passing at the time, intervened and struck Bury to prevent him from hitting Ellen again.

This rather unlikely Sir Galahad was unwittingly the instigator of the Burys' next quarrel. The couple were drinking in a pub in Whitechapel when Martin loomed up at them demanding some of the money Bury owed him. Ellen was apparently about to pay him when Bury intervened and stopped her by striking her in the face. On this occasion, Martin contented himself with telling Bury that he would not work again till the debt was settled. He later said in court that Bury had been drunk on both occasions.[40]

The vexed issue of Martin's money was finally resolved the

following week when he called at Swaton Road and Ellen gave him what he was due.[41]

Bury's response to this is unknown, but Haynes says that he chivvied away at Ellen with threats and blows throughout their stay at Swaton Road, adding that she 'never saw him sober when he could get drink'.[42] Finally, on 28 April, Ellen gave in and sold one of her shares, realising £39.37 on it, less than 40 per cent of its face value.[43]

The amount must have come as a bitter disappointment to the Burys. Another, following hot on its heels, was that Mrs Haynes evicted them. It seems clear that only her liking for Ellen prevented her from telling them to go earlier.

The couple did not travel far. They rented rooms at 11 Blackthorn Street, just a stone's throw from Swaton Road.[44] Here Ellen gave Bury the money to buy a pony and cart and he set himself up as a sawdust and silversand salesman, apparently purchasing his supplies from Martin. How seriously Bury took the business can only be guessed at. He had cards printed:

W H Bury
Sawdust and Silversand Merchant
5 Spanby Road Bow E
Private Residence 11 Blackthorn Street Devons Road
Bromley E[45]

But William Henry Bury was not the sort of man to let work interfere with drinking. Certainly, as the Ripper's atrocities mounted and Bury gave way more and more to a virtual state of siege by alcohol, so he was less and less inclined to make his rounds. As we shall see, he eventually became increasingly fearful of travelling beyond Bow lest he be recognised.

In May, Ellen found she had something else to worry about. Martin picks up the story again: 'Bury told me he had the venereal disease very bad in May and that he had given it to his wife. She also told my wife in my presence about this time that she had the bad disorder.'[46]

This suggests that it was syphilis. What a blow this must have been to Ellen, who seems to have avoided it at the hands of her clients only to become infected by the man she should have been able to rely on! Clearly, Bury was sleeping with prostitutes after his marriage. Given the man he was, it is unlikely that he was able to maintain a normal sexual relationship with Ellen. His yet-to-be-discovered habit of sleeping with a knife under his pillow is indicative not only of paranoia but also of sexual fantasies involving the weapon being used as a penile surrogate – exactly as one would expect from Jack the Ripper.

Ellen's beatings went on repetitively. There is no statement from the Blackthorn Street landlord because the London Police, due to a subsequent communication failure, never found out where the Burys were between the end of April and the middle of August. The owner does not appear to have lived on the premises, anyway. The 1881 Census lists two families, the Skiptons and the Pughs, living there, while in 1891 it was occupied by a single family called Honney, who divided it up into two apartments. But the ever-present James Martin records seeing Ellen in the street sporting a badly bruised face, and in June he witnessed a particularly nasty little assault on her. Bury had not been home for two nights and Ellen, frantic with worry, was combing the area looking for him. Just after 6am, she spotted Martin in a pub in Campbell Road, Bow, and was asking him for news of her husband when Bury turned up and, seeing her, went into a rage, which culminated in his hitting her several times and knocking her down in the doorway. He was, said Martin, 'getting better of the drink', an unintentionally comic remark that drew laughter in a Dundee courtroom the following year.[47]

This assault may finally have done the trick for Bury, because, on

7 June, Ellen sold the rest of her shares for £194.35, around £12,500 on today's values.[48]

At some point between his arrival in London and the summer of 1888, Bury made the acquaintance of a man named Dodd, who managed a wine vault in Shoreditch, East London. Dodd was a native of Wolverhampton and the two men appear to have had a drink together when Bury said that he too had grown up there. During the conversation, Dodd revealed that his father, James, was the licensee of the White Rose Inn in Powlett Street, Wolverhampton, and invited Bury to stay there if he visited his old haunts. Dodd's invitation was to benefit Bury at a time when he needed a bolthole.

By the beginning of August, another unhappy relationship was fast approaching its end. William Turner, a carpenter turned hawker, and his consort, a married prostitute named Martha Tabram, were about to split up for the umpteenth time over the past nine years. But on this occasion a murderer's knife would put paid to any reconciliation.

NOTES

1. *Midland Wednesday News*, 13 February 1889.
2. Margaret Corney, evidence at the trial of William Bury, 28 March 1889.
3. Birth certificate.
4. 1861 Census.
5. Baptismal record.
6. She is also missing from the 1881 Census, as is Margaret. Two Ellen Elliotts, aged 25 and 27, are listed in London, one the daughter of a gardener from the Isle of Wight, the other a machinist from South London. Both had fathers named George, but neither is the correct Ellen. There is a Margaret Corney of the right age, but her husband was Henry Corney and her maiden name was Storey.
7. At Bury's trial on 28 March 1889, Margaret gave her age as 37 and her sister's as 33; she was in fact only 36 and, had Ellen still been alive, she would have been 32.
8. 1857 and 1858.
9. 1861 and 1871 Censuses.
10. Dundee Police files.
11. 1871 Census.
12. Probate records.

13. They were not living there at the time of the 1881 Census.

14. Union Bank of London.

15. Statement to the London Metropolitan Police, 14 February 1889.

16. Daughter's death certificate.

17. William Fishman, *East End 1888* (hbk), p. 97.

18. Now Dimsun Crescent.

19. *People's Journal for Dundee*, 30 March 1889.

20. Evidence at the trial of William Bury, 28 March 1889.

21. Margaret Corney, evidence at the trial of William Bury, 28 March 1889.

22. 1891 Census.

23. Ibid.

24. Elizabeth Haynes, statement to the London Metropolitan Police, 14 February 1889.

25. James Martin, statement, 14 February 1889.

26. Trial evidence, 28 March 1889.

27. James Martin, statement, 14 February 1889.

28. Ibid.

29. Trial evidence, 28 March 1889.

30. Trial evidence, 28 March, and statement, 14 February 1889.

31. Now Wentworth Mews.

32. *Eastern Post*, 31 March 1888; *East London Observer*, 31 March 1888.

33. *Eastern Post*, 31 March 1888.

34. Ann Burgess, John Douglas and Robert Ressler, *Sexual Homicide: Patterns and Motives* (pbk), pp. 46–7.

35. Trial evidence, 28 March 1889.

36. *Eastern Post*, 7 and 14 April 1888.

37. Ibid., 14 April.

38. Most of the police files on Emma Smith's murder are now missing. This account is culled from the two surviving police reports: Inspector Edmund Reid, head of 'H' division (Whitechapel), CID, and Chief Inspector John West, of 'H' division, plus the *Morning Advertiser*, 9 April 1888, and *Lloyds Weekly News*, 8 April.

39. Elizabeth Haynes, police statement, 14 February 1889, and evidence at the trial of William Bury, 28 March 1889.

40. Trial evidence, 29 March 1889.

41. Police statement, 14 February 1889.

42. Trial evidence, 28 March 1889.

43. C H R Wollaston of the Union Bank, London, statement to the Procurator-Fiscal of Forfar, 15 February 1889.

44. No. 11 is now a parking bay; 3 Swaton Road has also gone. The first few houses on that side of the road are now a green patch.

45. *Express & Star*, Wolverhampton, 13 February 1889.

46. Police statement, 14 February 1889.

47. Trial evidence, 28 March 1889.
48. C H R Wollaston, Secretary of the Union Bank, London, statement to the Procurator Fiscal, 15 February 1889

CHAPTER SIX

THE LATE-SUMMER MURDERS

T he serial killer does not necessarily mean to begin where he does, but sooner or later the final barrier is crossed. In the early hours of Tuesday, 7 August 1888, William Bury crossed his Rubicon into murder.

Martha Tabram was 39. Born Martha White in Southwark, South London, on 10 May 1849, she was the estranged wife of Henry Tabram, a foreman packer who married her on Christmas Day 1869. They had two sons but parted around 1875. A few years later, she embarked on her up-and-down relationship with Henry Turner, who may have been somewhat younger than she was. Both Henrys claimed that Martha's drinking made her difficult to live with. Maybe, but Turner is described as dirty and slovenly and by 1888 had long since abandoned his trade to earn a precarious living on the streets, so perhaps he wasn't the perfect partner either.

Turner's evidence at Martha's subsequent inquest is traditionally skipped through, but one thing he said may provide us with an important clue about her death:

At times the deceased had stopped out all night. After these occasions she told him she had been taken in a fit

and was removed to the police station or somewhere else
. . . He knew she suffered from fits, but they were brought
on by drink.[1]

The condition that Turner describes is a form of epilepsy commonly
referred to as 'rum fits'. The seizure occurs when the level of alcohol
in the body begins to fall and it can be an isolated phenomenon of
epilepsy, i.e. the victim may not otherwise suffer from that illness.[2]

Martha was then living in a lodging house at 19 George Street,
opposite what had been Emma Smith's lodgings, and she was herself
using the name 'Emma'.[3] She had been parted from Turner for three
weeks and was supporting herself by prostitution.

The autumn bank holiday that year fell on Monday, 6 August. It
was a day to spend with the family or paint the town red. For William
Bury, married in name only, it was merely an official drinking day.
Oblivious as usual to Ellen's needs, he unstabled his horse and cart
and headed for the stewpots of Whitechapel. He did not realise it but
he was on a collision course with an evil destiny.

Monday evening found Martha and another prostitute, Mary Ann
Connolly, working the pubs around Whitechapel and Spitalfields.
About 10 o'clock they picked up two Coldstream Guardsmen. The
quartet toured the hostelries till 11.45, when they split into
twosomes and went off separately to round things off with a spot of
illicit sex. Connolly saw Tabram and her soldier make their way into
George Yard, a bleakly narrow thoroughfare running between
Whitechapel High Street and Wentworth Street. It was the last time
she saw Martha alive.[4]

Two hours later, the beat constable, PC Thomas Barrett, came
across a Grenadier Guardsman on the corner of Wentworth Street
and George Yard, who said that he was waiting for his mate, who had
'gone away' with a girl.[5] Given the circumstances, it was probably
Tabram but, as the Grenadier was never traced, there is no way of

verifying this. What we do know is that sometime within the next 30 minutes or so she met her murderer.

The following three hours of Barrett's patrol passed uneventfully. All this changed at 4.50,[6] when a man came running up to him. John Reeves had just had the fright of his life. A resident of George Yard buildings, a tenement block at the Wentworth Street end of the yard, Reeves had been on his way to work when he discovered the body of a woman lying in a pool of blood on the first-floor landing.[7]

Barrett immediately sent for a doctor. The nearest was Dr Timothy Killeen, who had a surgery at 68 Brick Lane, just a couple of minutes round the corner from Wentworth Street. Killeen would have reached George Yard at approximately 5.15. He pronounced life extinct and estimated that Martha had been dead for about three hours. Other testimony supported this. Joseph and Elizabeth Mahony had returned home to George Yard buildings at 1.40. Later, Elizabeth went out again to buy supper for them. There was nothing on the landing at this time. However, when cab driver Alfred Crow came home at 3.30, he saw what he assumed in the darkness to be a down-and-out lying there. It was a frequent occurrence, and Crow took no notice.[8]

The mortuary photograph of Martha Tabram is as far removed from the film industry's image of a Ripper victim as it is possible to be. The impression is of a chubby, middle-aged housewife dozing in an armchair while she waits for her husband to come in for his tea. But the blanket covering her body concealed from view no fewer than 39 knife wounds, one for each year of her sad life. These included seven to the lungs, seven in the liver and spleen, six to the stomach and one that penetrated her heart – 'sufficient', said Killeen, 'to have caused death', although all the injuries had, in his opinion, been inflicted during life.[9]

Elsewhere, there were clusters of wounds to the throat, breasts and genitals.[10] A great gout of blood between her legs bore mute testimony to the assault on Martha's private parts. Her clothes, said PC Barrett, had been pulled up to the middle of her body, 'leaving the lower part exposed; the legs were open and altogether her position was such as to suggest in my mind that recent intimacy had taken place'.[11]

In a manner of speaking, it had.

Killeen decided that all but one of the injuries had been made with a weapon like a penknife, but the other, a deep wound in the breast that had penetrated through to the bone, had been caused by a long, strong-bladed instrument such as a dagger or bayonet. This suggests a link with the Guardsmen but in fact bayonets were so commonly on sale in London's East End that children played with them in the street. Martha's and Mary Ann's various soldier clients were never traced but there can be little doubt that clients were all they were.

I have no real hesitation in saying that Martha Tabram was the first fatal victim of Jack the Ripper. This view does not find favour everywhere, which is why she is not listed among his so-called 'canonical' victims. The main reason given by the doubters is that her murder differs in mode from those that followed. The wounds were punctures, not incisions; her throat was not cut according to his modus operandi (MO); and there were not the deliberate mutilations we usually associate with the Ripper. A second, though far less serious, objection is the use of two weapons.

Knowledge, however, marches on, and those who do not move with it are left at the side of the road. Robert D Keppel, a leading homicide investigator and consultant on multicides and their crimes, writes in his book, *The Riverman*:

> Because it can change, simply saying that the homicides can't be related because there are different modi operandi in a number of cases otherwise related by time, place or

90

area is foolishness ...A killer might use strangulation in the first case, and in a subsequent case, to accommodate resistance by the victim, use a firearm because the strangling method was unsuccessful. Therefore, the killer's modus operandi can change over time as the killer discovers that some things he/she does are more effective than others.[12]

Today, investigators like Keppel and the FBI's behavioural scientists look at a variety of contributing factors when determining whether a victim can be attributed to a particular killer: victimology, locale, forensics, MO and what they term *signature*. Signature is what satisfies the murderer's emotional needs, how he derives his satisfaction from his crimes. John Douglas, who is neutral on whether Martha Tabram was or was not a Ripper victim, gives another uncaught multicide, the infamous 'Zodiac' murderer in California in the 1960s, as a case in point: Zodiac's signature was his persistent taunting of the police.13 Keppel recounts the case of George Russell, who murdered three young women in the state of Washington between June and September 1990. Modi operandi differed in each case, but what linked them together were objects inserted into orifices in the victims' bodies and arranged in sexually degrading poses. This was how he attained his pleasure; this was his signature.[14]

Failure to take all the relevant data into account, and adhering slavishly to modi operandi to the exclusion of all other factors, may result in what is described as 'linkage blindness', the refusal to believe that a crime is one of a series.

With these strictures in mind, let us return to Martha Tabram. She was found lying in a pool of blood and Killeen attributed her death to 'haemorrhage and loss of blood', although much of it may have come from bleeding after death.[15] Normally, stab wounds bleed little externally – the victim tends to haemorrhage internally[16] – but

Killeen was in fact wrong in stating that all the injuries were puncture wounds: at least one, found in the 'lower portion' of the body, 3 inches (7.6cm) in length and an inch (2.5cm) deep, was by definition an incised wound. Incised wounds do bleed a lot externally and, while life persists, they will spurt as well as ooze blood if a main artery is severed. Given the quantity of blood between Tabram's legs and the fact that they were open and her clothes pulled up to her waist, this is the injury that probably accounted for most of the blood she lay in. We can also be pretty sure that it spurted or flowed, or both, on to her killer, enough, certainly, for some to have got on to his clothes, creating a risk to him. But equally important, as John Douglas and Roy Hazelwood point out, would have been the psychological effect of being made to feel unclean by coming into contact with a prostitute's blood, especially on his clothes.

Contamination by a victim's blood can cause a multicide to alter his MO completely. David Berkowitz, New York's 'Son of Sam' killer, wounded his first victim with a knife but got blood on himself and changed to blasting his victims with a .44-calibre revolver instead.[18] Bury's change of MO was not quite so drastic, nor could it be, for his signature, the motivating force behind his murders, was his need to mutilate.[19] This meant using the knife and having contact with his victim, which in turn meant that, like it or not, he could not altogether eliminate the likelihood of getting some blood on himself, particularly when, in the later murders, his needs drove him to remove body parts. But he could minimise it, especially on his clothes where there were two attendant risk factors. One was that somebody might notice the stains as he was walking back to his horse and cart; the other, obviously, was Ellen's seeing them. The upshot was that Bury refined his technique to ensure that the victim was dead before he cut into her.

This was accomplished by strangulation. Although not readily apparent in 1888, two of Britain's post-war giants of forensic pathology, Professors Francis Camps and James Cameron, concluded that the Ripper first throttled his prey. Paul Begg, Martin Fido and Keith Skinner's *The Jack the Ripper A to Z* notes that swollen and protruding tongues (Annie Chapman) and clenched fists (Stride and Eddowes) are signs of strangulation. To this we can add congested features (Chapman again), which is one of the classic indications of asphyxia.

The method used remains a matter of debate. Ellen was to be strangled with a piece of rope, as was Catherine Mylett, although there is a large question mark over whether Mylett was in fact one of Bury's victims. Elizabeth Stride's death was probably caused by her being partially garrotted with her own scarf. Thereafter, the picture grows misty. Professor Cameron believes that all the victims were strangled from behind.[20] A ligature would accomplish that more efficiently than finger pressure. Cameron, however, is also of the opinion that the victims had their throats cut from the rear, and this is unconvincing.

Dr George Bagster Phillips, whom we shall soon meet at the postmortem on Annie Chapman, Liz Stride and Mary Kelly, was the only contemporary doctor to mention strangulation, albeit fleetingly. Phillips subsequently opted for a ligature, if the *Star* newspaper can be believed, but the journalist's information was second-hand (Phillips declined to comment directly) and Chapman's death is more indicative of manual strangulation. On the other hand, for reasons that will become clear in the next chapter, it may have been easier for him to use a piece of rope to strangle Catharine Eddowes.

Overall, the evidence suggests that Bury could well have used both methods, as did Frederick Cummins, the London so-called Blackout Ripper of the early 1940s.

After choking his victims, Bury then cut their throats to make doubly sure they were dead. He needed to: there is speculative evidence that Annie Chapman was strangled only into unconsciousness, while Mary Kelly appears to have warded off attempts to throttle her. Nichols's, Chapman's and Eddowes's throats were cut left to right, twice, Stride's in the same direction but only once, while Kelly had hers cut right to left; exactly how many times is unclear from the rather perfunctory autopsy report.

The purpose of ensuring that the victims were dead was to avoid spurting blood, as had apparently happened with Tabram, although strangulation by itself is a homicidal form of foreplay in serial murder. The wounds would still have haemorrhaged, but the blood would then have only oozed out, and on the available evidence there was not a great amount of bleeding. To avoid contact with it, Bury knelt, generally on the victim's right, except in Kelly's case, where he stood both facing her and to her left at different times. He likewise cut their throats from these positions, the blood running off to the side from which the incisions to the neck had first been made.[21]

The outcome was that, whereas he almost certainly got blood on himself in the Tabram murder, Bury would have got very little, if any, on himself in the next four, aside from handling the organs. What happened with Mary Kelly is strictly conjecture, but there is a belief that he was naked when he mutilated her. We can see here how Bury is learning from initial mistakes as the murders progress, 'getting tighter and tighter', to echo Burgess, Douglas and Ressler's anonymous multicide.

The main area of contention as to whether Martha Tabram was a Ripper victim is summed up by his *nom de guerre*: the wounds were not rips but punctures. As we have seen from the above, this was a learning-curve murder, a first-time effort by a man primed to kill but who would not necessarily have done so that night, except that something ignited the powder in the tinderbox. Basically, he began by hacking away, but we can see that he was not deriving a great deal of satisfaction from this, and not realising his fantasies, because, when he reaches her private parts, he also starts to rip her (the incised wound we noted earlier). Additionally, the deep wound with the separate weapon implies an early attempt to cut off a breast, hence the change to a longer knife. Here he was thwarted by coming up against the breast bone. Three months later, he removed both Mary Kelly's breasts with what the medical examiner described as 'circular incisions'. Once again, he has learned from experience and when an opportunity allowing more time presents itself he takes full advantage of it.

Which brings us to signature. The punctures becoming evisceration to Martha's genital area is only too symbolic of the Ripper's sexual lusts. The same fantasies are on display, the same centrifugal force that links the murders of Nichols, Chapman, Eddowes, Kelly and the final victim with each other. Moreover, these crimes were progressive. In his next outing (Nichols), Bury again *stabbed* the genital organs, but this time through the incisions he had already made.[22] This indeed was the precise purpose of the evisceration, to satisfy himself by getting at the reproductive organs and either stabbing or, later on, removing them. Martha Tabram's murder had shown him that he could not do this by simply stabbing externally; hence he began to incise the victims, even in that first killing. He began the process of cutting out organs a week after Nichols with Annie Chapman, and three weeks later we find him both taking away one of Eddowes's reproductive organs (the uterus) and simultaneously stabbing and incising what he clearly took to be another (the liver).[23] The ghastly parade of butchery reached its zenith with the annihilation of Mary Kelly in November. That was, in effect, the climax. He could do more than what he did to Kelly and, as we shall discover, afterwards started to weary of his killing spree.

To believe that Martha Tabram was not slain by the same man means that you have to believe that two separate woman-hating psychopaths – one who appears, kills once and then disappears as suddenly as he came and a second who takes up where he left off, learning from his unknown mentor's errors, sharing his fantasies and duplicating his signature – were both at large in the same grimy collection of mean little streets at the same time. Now how likely is *that*?

We turn now to the use of the two separate weapons. This is entirely consistent with Jack the Ripper's profile. John Douglas writes that he would have been 'paranoid and carried one or more knives around with him'. Bury, in fact, confirms this. Even when he went to the police station where he was subsequently arrested, he was carrying a knife, and a subsequent search of his apartment revealed two more, one a murder weapon still bearing the residue of the crime.

That he carried two knives with him is evidenced by the fact that his double murder on the night of 30 September 1888 was accomplished with two separate weapons. He also slaughtered Mary Kelly with both a knife and a hatchet, the latter probably a household implement present at the scene. It would not have been out of character for Bury to have used such an easily attainable weapon, such as a dagger, on Tabram, but his second weapon may well have been the knife that he most favoured in his later crimes. Killeen did not elucidate on why he thought a dagger was used but the inference would be that he thought the injury was caused by a double-edged instrument. However, Professor Bernard Knight, one of our most prominent forensic pathologists, has this salutary warning for the inexperienced examiner: 'the skin may split at the blunt end [of the blade] and produce two sharp points, which may mislead the examiner into thinking that a double edged dagger was used.'[24] Killeen had been qualified for only three years and was not a police surgeon.[25]

At first sight there is one flaw in the scenario of Martha Tabram as one of Bury's victims: her name. Neither 'Martha' nor 'Emma', as she was then calling herself, conformed to either his mother or sister. But, as we have already seen, it is unwise to apply precepts too rigidly when dealing with a serial killer, another cause of linkage blindness. Victimology is flexible depending on need. Peter Sutcliffe and Arthur

Shawcross hated prostitutes but Sutcliffe also murdered a student and a librarian and tried to kill a doctor, while Shawcross initially murdered children and, in the midst of his later crimes, an elderly down-and-out. Zodiac departed from targeting courting couples to gun down a taxi driver. We have to remember that we are dealing with people whose stability is best summed up as volatile, none more so than that of William Bury, who had recently been treated for venereal disease. Plausibly, Tabram reminded him of a prostitute who might have infected him.

And there is a second, perhaps likelier, possibility. Anything that reminds a multicide of an object of hatred can unleash the venom that he carries around inside him. Peter Kurten, Germany's most infamous serial killer, butchered young women and little girls but on one occasion stabbed to death a middle-aged man who made the mistake of drunkenly lurching into him. The victim, Rudolph Scheer, undoubtedly brought to mind Kurten's brutal, alcoholic father. This twins with what I am about to suggest.

Martha Tabram, as we know, was prone to 'rum fits'. The pubs stayed open till the early hours that night. The blood-alcohol level peaks 30–60 minutes after the last drink and then begins to fall. It is at this point that the sufferer is most vulnerable to such a fit.[26] If, having solicited Bury as a client, Martha then went into such a seizure on the landing, its effect on him would have been traumatic. The convulsions are the same as in epilepsy. Here was the illness he most dreaded and it was the 7th, the same day of the month his hated sister had succumbed to it, again reminding him of her. So he murdered this dread apparition in front of him to remove the torment and of course this released his pent-up sexual frustrations.

It would be difficult to imagine a more potent trigger and would explain several facets of Martha's death that have never been explained.

Killeen said her injuries were inflicted during life but nobody heard anything, nor did Martha exhibit any signs of a struggle. One newspaper described her head as swollen and distorted and suggested she had been throttled.[27] However, it is clear that their informant was Tabram's landlady, who identified the body several days after death, and what she saw were symptoms of the bloating, which takes place after decomposition has set in. Killeen makes no mention of bruising to the throat (unlike incisions, puncture wounds would not have obscured it), and, although PC Barrett mentions that her hands were clenched, this may have been due to the muscular contractions during a rum fit.[28]

If Martha was upright and alert when Bury launched his assault, one would have expected her to struggle till shock and loss of blood set in – scream too, but there was nothing: no bruising, no cries. There had been a shout of 'murder' but it was early the previous evening, came from outside the building and was often heard in the vicinity.[29] Forensic investigation showed that the attack had been confined to the first-floor landing.[30] The whole scene conveys the impression that Martha was already helpless and that she was attacked by a client who had suddenly taken leave of his senses.

We can imagine Bury's state of mind as he made his nightmare journey home. If the profile is accurate, he would have felt horrified as a result of coming into contact with Tabram's blood and there would have been stains of some description to rid himself of without Ellen's being aware of it. Doubtless he slept restlessly and once he awoke he faced the awful reality that he had now irrevocably sundered his bonds with society. If caught, he would hang.

Several killers live with fear and it is at its worst after they kill for the first time. The next four days saw Bury in a panic. Blackthorn Street now held horrible memories for him. Here his life had suddenly, cataclysmically, gone bad, and number 11 constantly reminded him of how he had returned home that terrible morning, reeking of his victim's blood. On 11 August, he and Ellen moved into 3 Spanby Road, next door to where he stabled his horse.[31] His new home was two minutes' walk from Blackthorn Street, and Spanby Road connects with Swaton Road.

The proximity of his new home to his transport is revealing. In future there would be no journey on foot between the stable and his lodgings, nobody to observe him making it. But even more interesting is how it illustrates Bury's fear and paranoia. It is possible to walk in a circle from Swaton Road to Blackthorn Street and then Spanby Road in only a few minutes, and Quickett Street is again only a few minutes' walk away, in a northerly direction. What we see here is a cramped, inward-looking mentality at work, exhibiting a desperate need to be in control of his environment lest he wander out of its circle and back into the world of the down-and-outs he had inhabited in Dewsbury and Birmingham.

The crime locale displays a similar constricted vision at work. All the murder sites were within a few minutes' walk of each other, save Bucks Row, which was on his way home. All thronged and throbbed with the homeless prostitutes who exercised such a lure. The consanguinity of Bury's residences to his crime scenes is part of his psychological signature to these atrocities.

Once inside Spanby Road, the Burys barely had time to unpack before they were off again, this time to Wolverhampton for a week. Bury was desperate for a break, to get out of London till his fear subsided and the hue and cry died down. The holiday has all the hallmarks of being hastily arranged. The Corneys were unaware of it till they were back;[32] they had no place to stay beyond a vague invitation from a man in his cups; and they had just moved into a new apartment.

In the event, James Dodd was happy to accommodate them. The exact day they travelled is not recorded, but on either Monday, 13 August or the Tuesday they attended a race meeting at Dunstall Park, a new venue for horseracing after the sport had been absent from Wolverhampton for some time, and this was the inaugural meeting there. It was not used again that month.[33]

To his former workmates at the warehouse and the lockmaker's, Bury posed as a man who had gone up in the world, passing out business cards and portraits of Ellen and himself that were done during the visit. According to one source, probably Richard Swatman (see Chapter 3), Bury dressed in a 'very flash style' and on one occasion changed a £50 note. The portrait was reproduced in the *Midlands Weekly News* on 16 February 1889 and shows the Burys in typical Victorian style, he on a chair holding his hat, Ellen standing beside him on his right, her left hand resting on his shoulder. She appears overdressed and stares ruefully into space as though wishing she were somewhere else, an impression heightened by comments she made during the week.

Perhaps the main interest of the portrait is that it shows Bury clean-shaven aside from his moustache. Five months later, he turned up in Dundee with a full beard and whiskers.

Bury depicted Ellen as the daughter of a wealthy London publican and boasted that he was assured of an income for life (actually correct!). In fact, George Elliott's estate was valued at under £50 on his death. In James Dodd's eyes, Ellen cut a rather forlorn figure: 'a quiet submissive sort of woman who was too prone to give way to her husband's wishes'.

With one exception. Try as he might, Bury could not induce her to join him in his drinking sprees – very much in evidence during the holiday – although one unnamed source (possibly Wakeman, licensee of the Summer House Inn; see Chapter 3) does claim to have seen both drinking heavily on one occasion. Dodd, however, only ever observed her to drink the odd glass of wine. To Dodd, she complained about her husband's drinking and said that she had made a mistake in marrying him. These quiet words destroyed the façade he was trying to erect.

As the week wore on, Ellen began to sport a brooch inlaid with a jubilee £5 piece, one of several pieces of jewellery she bought when

Portrait of William and Ellen Bury during their visit to Wolverhampton in August 1888. Note Bury is then sporting only a moustache. (*Midland Weekly News*)

Bury took her to Birmingham for the day. This is almost as significant as the hasty way in which the holiday was arranged. Although it was Ellen's money and Bury was anxious to create an impression of wealth, he was certainly not the sort of man to countenance his wife's spending money he regarded as his. Yet he did. Suddenly, the beast of Blackthorn Street had become a kind and benevolent husband. This behaviour is typical of men with something to hide from their wives. Sadly for Ellen, it was not to last. As he waded deeper and deeper in blood, Bury became inured to his crimes.

There is a saying: when they're ringing down your curtain, make it look as though you're taking an encore. For William Bury, the curtain was gathering momentum on its descent. He was not to know that, far from impressing those he encountered that week in Wolverhampton, the image he left behind was that of a madman.[34]

The term 'canonical victim' was coined to describe the five women who, everybody is supposed to agree, were killed by Jack the Ripper. Far from it. Even in 1888, there was no unanimity on the subject, and today it has ceased to have much meaning. Who was and who was not a victim is very much a matter of individual interpretation.

However, nobody has ever questioned the credentials of Mary Ann Nichols to be included in the list. Born on 26 August 1845, she was the daughter of Edward and Caroline Walker of Dean Street, just off Fetter Lane in central London. The area is not far from the East End, so, technically, Mary Ann's ship of life had the shortest distance to navigate between birth and death, although she came to the latter via a rather large diversion to South London. Here, in Walworth, she spent most of her married life with her husband, William Nichols, and their five children. The couple parted amid the thrust and parry of family break-up in 1880.

Between 1880 and 1887, 'Polly', as her friends knew her, flitted between workhouses, dalliances with other men and her father's home before finally and irredeemably ending up as a vagrant. She did try working for a brief period, as a housemaid to a family in Wandsworth, but absconded with items worth about £3. From here it was just steps going down to the grave. August 1888 finds her working as a prostitute out of lodging houses in Thrawl and Flower and Dean Streets. Born in one Dean Street and residing in another, she had, in a sense, come full circle at her end.

Mary Ann Nichols spent the last complete day of her life, Thursday, 30 August 1888, selling herself to buy drink and a new hat. That night, the East End seemed to burst into flames. Down by the Thames, first South Dock and then Shadwell Dock caught fire. The night sky blazed as incendiaries leaped a hundred feet into the air.

At 1.40am on the 31st, she was turned out of the Thrawl Street lodging house because she was penniless.[35] 'Look,' she said, 'what a jolly bonnet I've got!' and went off to find a client who would pay her bed for the night – in eternity, as it worked out.

Fifty minutes later, her friend Ellen Holland encountered her on the corner of Whitechapel Road and Osborn Street. Holland noted that 'Polly' was much the worse for drink.[36]

So, as usual, was William Bury. He may have gone down to the Thames to see the conflagration. Fire has a peculiar sexual fascination for serial killers; many commit arson during their adolescent years. Whether Bury did we will never know.

He was driving his pony and cart back along the Whitechapel Road on his way home when he espied Nichols's tipsy figure as she was passing what is now Whitechapel Tube station. It was just before 3.30. In the eerie glow cast by the firelight he saw a woman who appeared to be around his mother's age when she died; although just turned 43, some thought Mary Ann looked 10 years younger.[37] Hatred mingled with the sexual arousal caused by the fires. When the woman came up to him he saw that she was wearing a jacket embroidered with a man standing next to a woman sitting on a horse.[38] Visions of his father's death flooded into his mind, another demon adding its voice to the mental cacophony raging inside his head. Mary Ann's name sealed her fate.

Just past Whitechapel station on the left is Brady Street, and a little way down there, past Winthrop Street, is Bucks Row, as it was then called.[39] Bucks Row runs east–west from Brady Street to Bakers Row, behind the railway station. The first half of the row commencing at Brady Street is comparatively narrow. Today the south side accommodates a block of security-conscious luxury flats, but in 1888 they were a line of terraced houses ending at a stable yard. There was then a boarding school (now derelict) after which Bucks Row converges with the western end of Winthrop Street and broadens out before running into Bakers Row.

On 31 August 1888, Baker's Row was part of the beat of PC John Neil. At 3.45, he turned its corner into Bucks Row and proceeded towards Brady Street. He just missed two workmen, Charles Cross and Robert Paul, who had gone in search of a policeman to report a woman they had found lying in the entrance to the stable yard. Now Neil saw her too. Bending down, he shone his lantern on to her features and discovered that her throat had been cut from ear to ear.[40] With the fires still dancing away in the distance the setting was distinctly Wagnerian.

Neil summoned a second constable, John Thain, and sent him for the police surgeon, Dr Rees Llewellyn, of 152 Whitechapel Road, 300 yards away. Llewellyn inspected the corpse and then directed it to be removed to the mortuary. He noted that there was not a lot of blood on the ground, about the equivalent of a wineglass and a half, but further investigation was to show that most of the bleeding had been absorbed into Nichols's clothes and her abdominal cavity.

While Llewellyn was making his examination, three onlookers turned up in the shape of Henry Tomkins, Charles Brittain and James Mumford, all horse slaughterers working for Harrison & Barber, a slaughterhouse in adjacent Winthrop Street. Even today Winthrop Street has the capacity to chill blood and bone, a desolate windswept and now derelict thoroughfare which makes you quail at the thought of traversing it after dark. In 1888, it was an even more forbidding place, resounding with the shrieks of animals about to be butchered. Whether Bury obtained the horsemeat he had once cut up for cats from Harrison & Barber is anybody's guess.

Adding to this wonderfully gay ambience was a sewage works, 70 yards along from the abattoir, which was watched over at night by Patrick Mulshaw, a council employee. Mulshaw had come on duty at 4.45 the previous afternoon and admitted to dozing off at times, although he claimed, in best jobsworth traditions, to have been awake between 3 and 4am This may be doubted, but he was not asleep at 4.30, when a man passed him saying, 'Watchman, old man, I believe somebody's murdered down the street.' Mulshaw went to have a look and found a number of policeman and several 'working men' clustered around a body[41] on the ground. Up to then, he had apparently seen and heard nothing. Later, the police announced they had been 'unable to find the man who passed down Bucks Row while the doctor was examining the body'. These enquiries could have originated directly from Mulshaw's encounter, but the latter part of the statement suggests a separate sighting, in all probability of the same man.

Was this William Bury, and, if so, what was he still doing in the area 45 minutes later? The term 'old man' was certainly used by him to a fruiterer at the end of September. More importantly, if the man who spoke to Mulshaw was not the killer, then how did he know the woman was even dead, let alone murdered? The parish of Whitechapel had actually been a murder-free zone during 1886 and 1887 and was to record only a solitary homicide in each of the two years following 1888. By contrast, in 1887, 69 people had perished in accidents and two had committed suicide.[42] But, if it *was* Bury, why was he walking past the murder scene at 4.30? We shall return to this a little later.

Police enquiries in Bucks Row established that nobody had heard a thing, but round the corner in Brady Street a Mrs Sarah Colwell had been awakened by her children telling her that somebody appeared to be trying to get into the house. Listening, she heard a woman scream, 'Murder! Police!' followed by a person's receding footsteps. That morning spots of what looked like human blood were found near the intersection of Brady Street and Bucks Row.[43] The *Evening News* of 31 August mentions an affray in the neighbourhood shortly after midnight and it is likely that the blood and the sounds Colwell heard were connected with it. Certainly, the police thought her evidence to be of no significance.

PC Neil made a thorough search of the surrounding area in daylight and discovered nothing that might be of assistance. He found no trace of wheel marks, which means that Bury and Mary Ann entered Bucks Row on foot.[44]

Nichols's only apparent injury as she lay on the ground was the huge rent in her throat. But after her corpse was taken to the mortuary the police discovered that she had been disembowelled. Dr Llewellyn performed an autopsy later that day. His findings, given at the inquest, make gruesome reading:

> There was a bruise running along the lower part of the jaw on the right side of the face. That might have been caused by a blow or pressure from a thumb. There was a circular bruise on the left side of the face, which might also have been inflicted by the pressure of the fingers. On the left side of the neck, about 1 inch [1.5cm] below the jaw, there was an incision about 4 inches [10cm] in length, [which] ran from a point immediately below the ear. On the same side, but an inch below and commencing about 1 inch in

front of it, was a circular incision, which terminated at a point 3 inches [7.5cm] below the right jaw. That incision completely severed all the tissues down to the vertebrae. The large vessels of the neck on both sides were severed. The incision was about 8 inches [20cm] in length; the cuts must have been caused by a strong[45] bladed knife, moderately sharp, and used with great violence. No blood was found on the breast either of the body or clothes. There were no injuries about the body till just about the lower part of the abdomen. Two or three inches [5–7.5cm] from the left side was a wound running in a jagged manner. The wound was a very deep one, and the tissues were cut through. There were several incisions running across the abdomen. There were also three or four similar cuts, running downwards on the right side, all of which had been caused by a knife which had been used violently and downwards. The injuries were from left to right and might have been done by a left handed person. All the injuries had been caused by the same instrument.[46]

Questioned, Llewellyn attributed 'some rough anatomical knowledge' to the perpetrator. This view would be endorsed in the coming weeks by other doctors who examined the Ripper's victims. It was the sort of knowledge that a man accustomed to cutting up horsemeat might acquire; equally, it has to be said that similar mutilations have been performed many times since by killers with no known knowledge of anatomy.

Less enduring was Llewellyn's theory that the murderer was left-handed. Llewellyn himself came to doubt this.[47] No subsequent doctor or expert has endorsed it; quite the contrary. Expert opinion now propounds the Ripper as right-handed, as indeed was William Bury.

The original autopsy report is missing, as indeed are many other statements and documents pertaining to the murder. This is one of the more galling aspects of the Ripper murders. Most of the available documentation is in the shape of *Times* reports preserved in the police files because of their accuracy. Indeed, *The Times* was Scotland Yard's 'house' newspaper and was used by them to release information to the public, including, in one instance, details deliberately calculated to weed out bogus confessions. Aside from *Times* extracts, the most important material available from the police files consists of a series of overviews written by the man in day-to-day control of the Ripper investigation, Chief Inspector (later Superintendent) Donald Sutherland Swanson. Swanson's review of Mary Ann's case summarises the main points of Llewellyn's examination:

> ... throat cut nearly severing head from body, abdomen cut often from the centre of bottom of ribs along right side, under pelvis to left of stomach, there the wound was jagged; the coating of the stomach was cut in several places and two small stabs on private parts.

However, one essential detail is missing. Despite a lacerated tongue, nobody realised Nichols had been throttled. In general, the incised throat wounds obliterated the asphyxiation marks. The only exception, aside from Ellen Bury, were scratches on the left side of Annie Chapman's neck.[48]

Without building a time machine and travelling back to the early hours of 31 August 1888, we have no way of knowing precisely what took place that morning. Bury must have posed as a client and left his horse and cart nearby to walk round to Bucks Row with Nichols. Robert Keppel notes that a serial killer travelling by vehicle will generally walk the last couple of hundred yards to the murder scene with his victim as each step builds up the combination of hate and lust surging inside him.[49]

The quiet backstreet in the deadfall hours was most convenient for Nichols to do what she imagined they were going to do. His fingers tightening around her throat prevented her from crying out. The rest of it would have taken no more than two to three minutes to accomplish.[50] And then he was gone.

But did he return? Many serial killers have mingled with the crowds gawping at the murder scene. Wayne Williams, convicted of the Atlanta child murders, offered to take the scene-of-crime photos for the police after the discovery of one of his victims. And a Michigan multicide, sadly never caught, stood chatting with onlookers at the site of a murder he had committed.[51] Bury would have been on a high immediately following the Nichols murder. He had corrected the mistakes he had made with Tabram, and had avoided getting blood on him. Fear would hit him again later, as a hangover hits a man waking to what he has done the previous night, but for now there was a feeling of elation, and the confidence to go and view his handiwork. He may well have been the man who walked past the murder site and the man Mulshaw spoke to. If not, then how did he know Nichols had been murdered – and was it coincidence that he used the same words to the night workman as the killer did to someone else on another occasion?[52]

The killing of Mary Ann Nichols marked the beginning of Jack the Ripper's reign of terror. It was also the herald of a grand illusion, a master murderer who could walk between the raindrops and 'beat every policeman in London' as one disgruntled commissioner put it.[53] The reality was very different. Jack was an impulse murderer, responding to triggers in a diseased mind befuddled by alcohol, and his ability to avoid capture for a brief few months was based on the shifting sands of fortune.

Meanwhile, remember what Dr Llewellyn said about the pattern of Nichols's abdominal injuries: downwards and oblique. Keep this in mind, for we shall see the pattern again when William Bury's luck runs out in a Dundee hovel.

NOTES

1. *Times*, 24 August 1888.
2. Dr Richard Lechtenberg, *Epilepsy and the Family*, 2nd edn, pp. 205–6.
3. Police report, 16 August, and *Times*, 24 August.
4. Police report, 16 August. George Yard is now called Gunthorpe Street.
5. Police report, 16 August.
6. Police report, September 1888.
7. *Times*, 10 August.
8. Ibid. and Police report, September, 1888
9. *Times*, 10 August.
10. Police report, September 1888.
11. *East London Observer*, 11 August.
12. Robert Keppel, *The Riverman* (hbk), pp. 340–1.
13. John Douglas and Mark Olshaker, *The Cases that Haunt Us* (hbk), p. 233.
14. Keppel, op. cit., pp. 333–9.
15. Professor Bernard Knight (ed.), *Simpson's Forensic Medicine*, 11th edn, p. 100.
16. Brian Lane, *The Encyclopaedia of Forensic Science* (pbk), p. 410; Knight, op. cit., p. 63.
17. Knight, op. cit., p. 100.
18. Robert Ressler (with Tom Shachtman), *Whoever Fights Monsters* (pbk), pp. 108–9.
19. Douglas and Olshaker, op. cit., p. 47.
20. Paul Begg, Martin Fido and Keith Skinner, *The Jack the Ripper A to Z*, 1st edn (pbk), p. 297.
21. Except in Mary Ann Nichols's case, where it ran down the back and into her clothing. Chapman's ran towards a fence and Stride's into a gutter, both on their left. Eddowes's, likewise, seeped to the left but also flowed under her head as far as her right shoulder and Mary Kelly's blood saturated the right-hand corner of her pillow.
22. Police report, 19 October 1888.
23. Autopsy report, 30 September 1888. There was also a stab wound on the left groin.
24. Knight, op. cit., p. 52.
25. Begg, Fido and Skinner, op. cit., p. 229.
26. Guy Norfolk and Margaret Stark, in W D S McKay (ed.), *Clinical Forensic Medicine*, 2nd edn, p. 174.
27. *Illustrated Police News*, 18 August.
28. *East London Observer*, 11 August.

29. Ibid., 18 August.

30. Police report, 10 August.

31. William Smith (landlord), statement to the London Police, 14 February 1889.

32. Margaret Corney, William Bury trial evidence, 28 March 1889.

33. *Midland Evening News*, 13 August 1888.

34. *Midland Wednesday News*, 13 February 1889, and other Midlands newspapers.

35. Police report, 19 October 1888.

36. Ibid. Holland also seems to have gone by the name 'Jane Oram'.

37. Nichols's father thought so, as did a journalist who viewed the body. The mortuary photograph is a tad too faded either to confirm or deny this.

38. Police report, 13 August 1888.

39. Because of the murder, the residents successfully petitioned for Bucks Row to be renamed. It is now Durward Street.

40. *Times*, 3 September 1888.

41. *Times*, 18 September 1888.

42. Annual report on the sanitary conditions of Whitechapel 1887–88; John C Smithkey III, *Jack the Ripper: The Inquest of the Final Victim Mary Kelly* (pbk), p. 18.

43. *Evening News*, 1 September.

44. *Times*, 3 September.

45. Ibid. Llewellyn was actually reported as saying 'long-bladed', but seems to have been misheard by the reporter, as two police reports, 31 August and 19 October, refer to the weapon as 'strong-bladed'.

46. Ibid.

47. Police report, 19 October.

48. *Times*, 20 September.

49. Robert D Keppel, *Signature Killers*, p. 98.

50. A view expressed by another eminent modern-day pathologist, the late Dr Iain West, in the Channel 4 documentary *Secret History*: 'The Whitechapel Murders', November 1996.

51. Keppel, op. cit., pp. 117 and 134. The Michigan crime was never officially listed as one of this particular killer's murders, but Keppel believes it was.

52. Paul Begg, *Jack the Ripper: The Uncensored Facts* (pbk), pp. 44–5, deserves the credit for drawing our attention to this point.

53. Sir Henry Smith, head of the City of London Police, in his autobiography, *From Constable to Commissioner*.

CHAPTER SEVEN
SEPTEMBER MO(U)RNS

In August 1888, the Metropolitan Police force was in a state of flux. James Monro, the assistant commissioner for the detective branch, had just been transferred to the Home Office after losing a bout of political infighting with the commissioner, Sir Charles Warren.

His logical successor was Frederick Adolphus Williamson, the first head of the CID and eventual chief constable. But Williamson had reached the ceiling to which an officer who had risen from the ranks could then aspire. He was also suffering from a debilitating heart condition, which killed him 15 months later. So, instead, the choice fell on Robert Anderson, a Home Office spymaster, although at this stage in the game he had been shunted off to the prisons department. Anderson was a doctor of law who maintained a ferocious output of literature on Christian theology, and his appointment to Scotland Yard was probably the result of some subtle scene shifting by the permanent undersecretary, Godfrey Lushington, with whom he had a somewhat ambivalent relationship.

If this all sounds like an exercise in office politics, it is because that is what it was. In time, Robert Anderson would become one of the most statistically impressive crime fighters in the Yard's history, presiding over a steep decline in the crime figures, but in 1888 he allowed himself to be guided by the person he wanted the killer to be rather than who he actually was.

Anderson's subsequent success was perhaps inevitable given the quality of the man who did his fieldwork for him. Donald Sutherland Swanson was a Scot by birth, who had joined the police service after a brief spell in teaching. Fluency in Latin and Greek and a keen interest in philosophy marked the breadth of his mind. Only 40 years of age, he was by 1888 a chief inspector. A very long track record of success marked his progress to being one of the Yard's top men.

Anderson took over on 1 September 1888 on the understanding that, having introduced himself to his men, he would then embark on a lengthy holiday in Switzerland before taking up his duties in earnest. There is a letter to him from Commissioner Warren in the files confirming an indeterminate period of leave, although Warren makes it clear that he wants him 'back by October'.[1]

The murder of Mary Ann Nichols thus found the Met's detective branch effectively leaderless. Worse, the investigation into what the police now saw as a series of murders by one man was being handled by two different units. In Whitechapel, 'H' division CID under its local inspector, Edmund Reid, was probing Emma Smith's and Martha Tabram's deaths, while, 'J' division CID's[2] local inspector, Joseph Helson, was heading the enquiry into Nichols. By a quirk of the divisional boundary lines, Buck's Row fell into his jurisdiction. Early in September the decision was taken to appoint a Yard man to coordinate their efforts locally. The obvious choice was Inspector Frederick George Abberline, a very able and charismatic officer who had been Reid's predecessor before being elevated to Scotland Yard the previous year.

Anderson departed on his holiday on 8 September, leaving nobody in overall command of the murder hunt at the Yard. There appears to have been a rather ad hoc committee consisting of Williamson, Swanson, Superintendent John Shore and the senior assistant commissioner, Alexander Carmichael Bruce, who was looking after Anderson's department during his absence. All this changed on the 15th. The previous day a communication had been sent out without Swanson's knowledge.[3] Warren, who was already under pressure to sanction a reward for the killer's capture – a subject that would occupy a great deal of his time over the coming weeks – responded sharply with a memo to Bruce directing that Swanson should be put in sole day-to-day running of the case with no other duties to distract him, although he was careful to add that the chief inspector should clear any important decisions with Bruce, Williamson or himself.[4]

A similar command-and-control system, with all information flowing through one person not employed on field duties, is now regarded by some experts as being the most effective way of running a serial-killer investigation.[5]

Given the undoubted talents of Swanson and Abberline, the efficacy of their operating module and the prodigious amount of work that was to be put into the case by Reid and Helson and their teams, why did this investigation fail?

Perhaps the question we should really ask is: *did* it fail?

The impression that has lingered through the years is of a group of bumbling incompetents plodding around Whitechapel in hopeless disarray. 'The Queen fears that the detective department is not so efficient as it might be,' shrilled Victoria's private secretary, Sir Henry Ponsonby, on 13 November 1888.[6] Fifteen years on, Abberline indirectly rebutted his late sovereign's view:

Many a time . . . instead of going home when I was off duty, I used to patrol the district till four or five o'clock in the morning, and while keeping my eyes wide open for clues of any kind, have many and many a time given those wretched and homeless women, who were Jack the

Ripper's special prey, fourpence or sixpence for a shelter to get them away from the streets and out of harm's way.[7]

There is something deeply touching about this lonely odyssey to catch a killer. Abberline was an intensely private man who left not even a photograph of himself, let alone any memoirs. This is the one glimpse of him as a human being that has come down to us and it suggests a man as compassionate as he was conscientious.

It is an image far more in keeping with the way the Ripper hunt was actually conducted than has previously been supposed. Certainly, the police did make errors and there were moments of disarray, but overall, with no previous experience to guide them, they did remarkably well. Anderson himself began the process of bringing in outside consultants, which is standard today. 'Your eminence as an expert in such cases,' he wrote to Dr Thomas Bond on 25 October 1888, 'will make your opinion specially valuable.' Bond went beyond his original brief, assessing the killer's medical knowledge, and prepared criminal history's first offender profile, anticipating modern-day practice by almost a century.

Indeed, many of the intuitive observations that he made about the Ripper have been echoed by the experts who came after him, and can be found in the profile we examined in Chapter 2.

The Ripper investigation also saw the first recorded use of what have become known as *proactive* techniques, i.e. initiatives undertaken to identify a criminal. When the police received the now legendary 'Dear Boss' letter – which we will catch up with in a later chapter – they distributed posters around the East End bearing facsimiles of it in the hope that somebody would recognise the handwriting. John Douglas remarks that, if the letter had been genuine, this might have worked.[8]

Another example was the use of misleading information to test the value of confessions. Here the police encouraged the belief that the murderer had taken away Mary Kelly's uterus and left her breasts on the bedside table. In a variation on this – what might be called a proactive technique in reverse – they persuaded the coroner to withhold selected information at Kelly's inquest. Arguably, this was first attempted at Annie Chapman's inquest.

So, in terms of efficiency and farsightedness, this investigation was not a failure. But – and for a very obvious reason there has to be a 'but' – it did have one major Achilles heel. The first hint of it came on 7 September in a report to Scotland Yard by Inspector Helson:

> The Inquiry has revealed that a man named Jack Pizer, alias Leather Apron, has for some considerable period been in the habit of ill-using prostitutes in this and other parts of the Metropolis ... although at present there is no evidence whatsoever against him.

Nor would there ever be. Pizer had a cast-iron alibi for the Nichols murder. But in one form or another this Polish Jewish boot finisher would haunt the inquiry from beginning to end, leaving Scotland Yard with nothing to show for all their good work.

Colloquially known as 'Leather Apron', Pizer hove into view during the days following the Nichols murder. Prior to her death, the police believed that Smith and Tabram had been murdered by a gang, correct in the former instance. Now they switched focus, attributing all three crimes to one person. This change was reflected in the mood on the streets, where fear of what people termed as a 'high-rip' gang was replaced by fear of an individual. John Pizer was ready made for the role: he had served a prison sentence for stabbing a man and had recently been acquitted of indecent assault. Chinese whispers caused a chain reaction in the press, resulting in mass hysteria. Suddenly, Pizer became the embodiment of all those villainous Jews who had skulked through the pages of Dickens.

The Leather Apron scare died down by mid-September (Pizer

sued several newspapers), but the image remained fixed in the minds of the men who had charge of the case. Anderson later wrote in his memoirs, 'The conclusion we came to was that [the Ripper] and his people were certain low class Polish Jews.'[9]

This belief was not fashioned from any conscious racism; there is no evidence that Anderson, Swanson and Abberline were anti-Semitic, but were simply reflecting the attitudes of the day. Here, even the *Jewish Chronicle* was unhappy about the failure of immigrant Jews from East Europe to integrate into the community.[10] Mix this up with the quaint notion that no Englishman would commit such crimes and you have a main course of suspect garnished with Hebrew and marinated in Poland.

When Pizer proved a non-runner, Anderson quite literally looked just along the street, because his belief that the murderer was a Polish Jew found its apotheosis in Aaron Kosminski, who lived in Sion Square at the top of Mulberry Street, where Pizer lived! Kosminski was a paranoid schizophrenic who was incarcerated in lunatic asylums from February 1891 till his death in March 1919. Anderson never named him directly, but Donald Swanson confirmed, and tacitly endorsed, Kosminski as the man concerned in some notes he made in his copy of Anderson's memoirs.[11]

Abberline was not nearly as impressed by Kosminski. He is believed to be the suspect the inspector was referring to when he wrote that there was 'nothing of a tangible nature to support such a theory'. But in 1903 Abberline came up with a Polish suspect of his own, Severin Klosowski, who sometimes posed as a Jew. Klosowski was a serial poisoner who was hanged early that year for the murder of one of his victims.[12]

The big three's obsession with Polish Jews was the fatal flaw that ran through the investigation. After October 1888, there was no going back on it, because Anderson had indoctrinated the Home Secretary with their beliefs.

However, officers of similar status who were not directly responsible for the day-to-day running of the case could afford to take a more altruistic view. In 1894, Sir Melville MacNaghten, Williamson's successor as chief constable, named three suspects: Kosminski, another Pole (or Russian) called Michael Ostrog and an Englishman, a 31-year-old barrister, Montague John Druitt, who was found drowned in the Thames on 31 December 1888. In a preliminary draft of his report MacNaghten says of Druitt, 'I have always held strong opinions regarding [him] and the more I think the matter over, the stronger do these opinions become.'

Abberline, it is fair to say, dismissed Druitt almost with contempt in 1903,[13] while another senior officer, Chief Inspector John Littlechild, wrote in 1913 that he had never heard of him as a Ripper suspect. For good measure, Littlechild also seems to take a sideswipe at Kosminski: Anderson only 'thought he knew'. In 1888, Littlechild was head of Special Branch and, in his 1913 letter to the journalist and author George Sims, he mentions Francis Tumblety, an American quack doctor, as a 'very likely' suspect whose 'feelings towards women were remarkable and bitter in the extreme'.

Perhaps the greatest irony of the 'Aaron the Ripper' debacle is that, when a credible Jewish suspect did arise, the Ripper squad failed to notice him because they were off chasing another Polish red herring. On 6 December 1888, Joseph Isaacs was hauled in for questioning on nothing more substantial than the fretting of his overanxious landlady. While Isaacs was being interrogated police were called to a fracas in an East End brothel. They arrested a man who appeared in court the following day and was later confined in the Cobney Hatch asylum, where he died in October 1889.

The mystery man's name is given as David Cohen. Beyond the fact that he was a Jew of foreign extraction, little is known of him, but, unlike Aaron Kosminski, he turned out to be a violent patient who had to be separated from the other inmates.

One name missing from all this activity is that of William Bury. When Joseph Isaacs was arrested an inspector was heard to say, 'We have got the right man at last.'[14] When Bury, neither a Pole nor a Jew but very definitely an Englishman who did commit this type of murder, was arrested, a 'prominent head' at Scotland Yard told the *New York Herald*, 'You may be quite sure this man Bury is not Jack the Ripper.'

But that would change dramatically two months later, and, although their names were not recorded for posterity, we do now know that there were less exalted members of the Ripper squad who did believe that Jack was executed in Scotland on a spring morning in 1889.

While the press were whipping Whitechapel and Spitalfields into a state of frenzy, business was going on as normal at 3 Spanby Road. Bury was pursuing his usual routine: drink, beat up Ellen, more drink. William Smith, their new landlord, later told Abberline, 'During the whole of the time he resided here with the exception of Sundays he was constantly drinking and very frequently drunk. He frequently assaulted his wife.'[15]

Almost lost amid the dull repetitiveness of Bury's behaviour is a small but crucial point. He drank heavily on every day bar Sunday.

Let's translate this to the London murders, adding in also the possible killings and attacks.

Monday evening/Tuesday morning:	Martha Tabram
Tuesday evening/Wednesday morning:	Ada Wilson
Wednesday evening/Thursday morning:	Catharine Mylett
Thursday evening/Friday morning:	Mary Ann Nichols, Mary Jane Kelly
Friday evening/Saturday morning:	Annie Chapman
Saturday evening/Sunday morning:	Annie Millwood, Elizabeth Stride, Catharine Eddowes

What is missing? Sunday evening and Monday morning, the one time during the week that Bury was sober. He had good reason – not that he needed one – to be drunk on the night of 7–8 September 1888: the 7th was the 29th anniversary of Elizabeth Ann's death. That evening he set out with his pony and cart for his favourite stamping grounds in Whitechapel and Spitalfields. He did not return till the following afternoon.

Eliza Ann Chapman, a.k.a. 'Annie Siffey', 'Annie Sievey' and 'Dark Annie', resident in the East End for the previous six years, was a fully paid-down member of the tragic underclass that constituted Spitalfields' walking wounded, in her case mortally, for Annie had a serious lung complaint that would have killed her anyway within the next year; William Bury was to deny her the possibility of dying with some degree of dignity and care. When she could, Annie earned her pittances from selling flowers and matches and crochet work, which she created herself. At other times she survived by prostitution, going as far afield as Stratford.[16]

Like the other victims, Chapman was a once a respectable married woman fallen from grace. Her maiden name was Smith and she never used her first forename. She was illegitimate at the time of her birth in Paddington, Northwest London, in September 1841. Her parents married the following year and moved to Windsor in Berkshire. In 1869, at the comparatively late (for the era) age of 27, Annie married John Chapman, over a year her junior and said in some (unverified) accounts to have been a relative of her mother's. The couple set up home in Bayswater, London, close to Annie's birthplace, and in 1881 they returned to Windsor, where John took up a post with a farm bailiff. Annie later told her friend Amelia Palmer that he was a vet;[17] actually he was a coachman. By now they had three children, although the marriage was not a success. John Chapman put the blame fairly and squarely on Annie, saying that her dishonesty had once cost him a job as a valet and accusing her of being a drunken sot who slept around. Actually, it was John who was the alcoholic, dying at only 44 from cirrhosis of the liver on Christmas Day 1886. Annie is supposed to have been arrested for drunkenness in Windsor, but this is uncorroborated.

Here we have another sad story of a failed relationship – two, in fact, because by the time of her death Annie had also quarrelled with her mother and sister, according to Amelia Palmer.[18] In view of her husband's accusations, it is worth recording Palmer's testimony at the inquest that Annie had been much affected by his death and seemed broken thereafter.[19] They actually parted in 1882 shortly before the death of one of their daughters, Emily Ruth, from meningitis. At the time of her murder, Chapman's other daughter, Annie Georgina, was abroad in France and the son, John, apparently a cripple in the care of charitable institution. After the break-up, Annie lived for a while with a sieve maker, hence 'Annie Sievey', garbled into 'Siffey'. She also had a relationship of sorts with Ted Stanley, a bricklayer's labourer.

During the last few days of Annie's life, her illness had begun to take its toll. She was tired and rundown, and feeling the effects of a fight the previous week with a woman named Eliza Cooper in a pub.

The early hours of Saturday, 8 September found her in the kitchen of a lodging house at 35 Dorset Street, literally just across the street from Miller's Court, where two months later Bury was to mangle Mary Kelly so frightfully. Chapman had been living on and off at number 35 for the last four months, but at 2am the keeper, Tim Donovan, chucked her out because she did not have the money for her bed. Annie departed, vowing to return with it. Donovan said she seemed tipsy but this was probably due to her condition, because the autopsy found no evidence of alcohol in her body.[20]

Hanbury Street is only two minutes' walk northeast from Dorset Street. It runs east from Commercial Street across Brick Lane into Bakers Row. Number 29 Hanbury Street lay halfway between Commercial Street and Brick Lane, on the northern side of the thoroughfare, i.e. on the left from Commercial Street and the right looking up from Brick Lane. Today it is part of a warehouse, which occupies about two-thirds of that side of the street. In 1888, it was a three-storey dwelling house from which two businesses were run.

Mrs Amelia Richardson, who had her living quarters on the first floor, used the cellar and the backyard to make packing cases, while on the ground floor Harriett Hardyman sold cat meat. As with the slaughterhouse in Winthrop Street, the memory of his own cat-meat shop, and of cutting up the horsemeat for it, would have helped stimulate Bury's bloodlust that morning.

Number 29 had two front doors. One opened directly into Mrs Hardyman's shop. The other was the residents' entrance. Inside, it was a passage that led to the staircase to the upper floors before continuing on to the backyard. Here, the rear door opened out to the left, on to three stone steps going down into the yard. To the right of the steps was another door leading to the cellar. Because of the number of people who either lived or worked at number 29 – 19 in all! – both the residential front door and the rear door were kept permanently unlocked. This generated some annoyance among the tenants because the backyard was frequently used for another form of business, which had nothing to do with packing cases. Prostitutes took their clients there and serviced them.[21]

For this reason, and also a recent break-in, Mrs Richardson's son John made it his practice to call in and check the cellar door on market days. He did so on the 8th between 4.40 and 4.45am. Afterwards, he sat on the steps and trimmed one of his boots with a knife. All was normal. Richardson then went on to his job as a porter at Spitalfields market.[22]

At 5.25, Albert Cadosch, a carpenter living next door at number 27, went out into his backyard, where he heard voices, one distinctly saying no. They appeared to come from the backyard of number 29. A fence 1.5–1.7 metres (5–5½ft) high separated the two properties and Cadosch did not see anyone over it. He went back into number 27 but 'three or four minutes afterwards' returned to the yard and this time heard what he described as a 'sort of fall against the fence . . . something seemed suddenly to touch the fence'. Once again he did not see anybody. Cadosch then left to go to work passing Christ Church, Spitalfields, at 5.32.[23]

Shortly before this, Elizabeth Long,[24] a park keeper's wife, passed number 29 *en route* to the market. 'Close against the shutters of number 29', she saw a man and a woman talking. They were sideways to her as she passed. Long heard the man ask, 'Will you?' and the woman reply, 'Yes.' The woman she later identified as Annie Chapman. The man had his back to her as she approached, but she made out that his features were dark. He was wearing a brown deerstalker hat and a coat that may have been dark. His age she put at over 40. In height he was 'a little taller than deceased'. Long summed up her overall impression of the man as a foreigner, of 'shabby genteel appearance'. The time she was certain of as 5.30, because she heard the brewery clock opposite strike as she passed number 29.[25]

Thirty minutes later, John Davis, a resident of number 29, went out into the backyard. There, next to the fence, her head lying between it and the back steps, was the dead and horribly mutilated body of Annie Chapman.[26]

This neatly timed sequence of events was to be bedevilled by the initial estimation of the time of death – before 4.30am, thought Dr Bagster Phillips. But this was based on his erroneous belief that rigor mortis had already commenced when he saw the body at 6.30: 'The stiffness was more marked on the left side, especially in the fingers which were partly closed.'[27]

Forensic pathology was then in its infancy and what Philips was actually seeing was an example of cadaveric rigidity, in which shock causes stiffness to set in immediately after death, particularly in the grasping mechanism.[28] Phillips himself was clearly puzzled by what he saw and hedged his bets during his inquest testimony, stating that rigor could have progressed more quickly due to the chilly morning and the great loss of blood.[29]

Donald Swanson, writing on 19 October, was apparently unaware of these equivocations because in his report he uses the doctor's original estimate to cast doubt on whether the couple seen by Elizabeth Long were Chapman and Bury: 'The evidence of Mrs Long which appeared to be so important to the Coroner must be looked upon with some degree of doubt.'

This was highly unfortunate, because, aside from his age, Long gave a very good thumbnail sketch of William Bury: dark, shabby genteel and only a little taller than Chapman, who stood an even five foot tall.

This is indirectly corroborated by Albert Cadosch. At 5.25, he heard a low hum of conversation apparently coming from the backyard of number 29 and at 5.28 the sound of something hitting the fence, yet saw nobody over the top of the wooden palings. According to Cadosch, the height of the fence was approximately 5ft 6in (about 1.7 metre). Other estimates are lower: Swanson 'about 5 feet' (1.5 metre); John Davis ditto. If the man had been significantly taller than Chapman, the top of his head should have been visible.[30]

There is a slight discrepancy in times between Long and Cadosch. She heard the brewery clock strike at 5.30, five minutes *after* he heard voices in the yard. But Cadosch was basing his timings on the church clock, which said 5.32 when he passed it en route to work and it is clear that the brewery and church clocks were not in synch with each other. Had they been, Long would have heard the church clock chime as well. John Davis subsequently heard 'the bell of Spitalfields Church strike' at 5.45.[31]

The first police officer to reach the scene was an inspector named Joseph Chandler. He sent for Phillips, who on his arrival helped him make a search of the yard. One of their discoveries, John Richardson's leather work apron soaking in a tub, added of course to the Tower of Babel being erected in the newspapers about Leather Apron.

A very significant point was that Chapman had been wearing a large pocket under her skirt, tied around the waist with string. Bury had cut it open at the front and side and laid the contents out at her feet. An envelope containing two pills was also found by her head. This tiresome *non sequitur* was to consume much police time till a man named Stevens came forward to say that he had seen Chapman pick the envelope up from the fireplace in the lodging house and wrap the pills in it.[32] What was really important was the ransacking of the body. As we have noted, theft is one of the traits of the serial killer, Bury being a prime example. Chapman, citizen of the streets, was obviously not going to possess anything of pecuniary value, so he was looking for something he could steal as a trophy. And he was successful. The pocket yielded nothing suitable, but, as Abberline reported on 19 September, 'The deceased was in the habit of wearing two brass rings (a wedding and a keeper). These were missing when the body was found and the finger bore marks of their having been removed by force.' Remember this – it will come up again.

Interestingly, there had been speculation that a ring was stolen from Nichols. The *Evening News* of 31 August reported that Nichols's hands were bruised, as though she had been engaged in a struggle, and that her finger bore the imprint of a ring, although 'there is nothing to show that it has been wrenched from her in a struggle'. However, Inspector Helson sharply contradicted the newspaper's report: 'There were no bruises on the arms to indicate that a struggle had taken place.'[33] Nor was there any confirmation of a ring impression, either from the police or Dr Llewellyn. On balance, it now seems unlikely that any ring was taken from Nichols.

Phillips performed the autopsy on Annie Chapman at 2pm on the 8th. During the inquest, he strenuously objected to making public the nature of her abdominal injuries, telling the coroner on 19

September that it would not serve the interests of justice. This implies an early attempt by the police to withhold specific details. The coroner, Wynne Baxter, was a 44-year-old solicitor who had won a bruising election campaign for the post the previous year. He was subsequently accused of electoral impropriety, and his district was split into two, the other half being given to his former opponent, Dr Roderick Macdonald, a liberal MP who will also feature in this story. Baxter dressed ostentatiously, apparently in an attempt to appear flamboyant, but comes across as a long-winded bore. He carried on the Nichols and Chapman inquests simultaneously and seems not to have been well thought of by the police. At any event, he had no sympathy with Phillips's objectives and insisted the evidence be given, although it did not appear in the press, save for a potted version in the *Lancet* of 29 September.

Because of this, we have no precise details of Phillips's findings. However, it is possible to reconstruct the jigsaw that Bury made out of Annie's body from a combination of the *Lancet*, the cause of death revealed at the inquest and Swanson's report of 19 October.

We have already noted the evidence of prior strangulation in the preceding chapter. In this instance it may only have rendered her unconscious. Phillips noted 'smears of blood . . . 14 inches [35.5cm] from the ground and immediately above the part where the blood lay that had flowed from the neck', on the palings of the fence to the body's left, while, on the wall behind it, 'about 18 inches [46cm] from the ground, were about six patches of blood, varying in size from a sixpenny piece to a small point'. The latter could have been caused by spurting blood, indicating that Chapman was still alive when the knife was plunged into her neck. But we need to exercise caution here because the spots could have been caused by blood flying off the knife.

Her throat had been cut twice from left to right, the jagged incisions reaching 'right around the neck', said Phillips, beginning on the left of the spine and made with such ferocity that he thought it an attempt at decapitation.

Below, Annie's abdomen had been entirely laid open. In the absence of the actual postmortem report, we do not know the precise number of incisions, although a later writer, Norman Hastings, who had contacts at Scotland Yard, specifically states three. Donald Swanson recorded that her intestines were removed and draped across her right shoulder along with a flap of skin from the belly wall. Two more flaps and her pubis lay in a bloody little pool above the other shoulder.

Cut out and taken away by this deformity of a man were Annie's uterus, navel, the upper part of her vagina and two-thirds of the bladder.

Phillips opined that the murder weapon was a very sharp, thin-bladed knife at least 6–8 inches (15–20cm) long, the sort of instrument common to a slaughterman, though 'well ground down'. In the coming weeks, the police would get used to the smell of the abattoir as they went about their enquiries.

The doctor's view of the killer's medical knowledge was, and is, controversial. Initially, he told the inquest that the abdominal injuries showed 'some anatomical knowledge', but, when it resumed a week later, 'some' had become inflated to 'great' and the crime was 'the work of an expert' whose surgical skills were of an order to 'secure the pelvic organs with one sweep of the knife'. He, Phillips, 'could not have performed the injuries in under a quarter of an hour. If he had done it in a deliberate way . . . it probably would have taken him the best part of an hour.'[34]

Whether this assessment greatly influenced the police at the time is a moot point. The fact that Dr Bond's original brief was to advise on the extent of the Ripper's medical knowledge (he assessed it as nil) suggests that, between mid-September and mid-November, they kept a collectively open mind on the subject. Phillips's opinion, which as far as *surgical* skill is concerned he alone held, has had much more influence in historical terms. The public consciousness, even to this day, remains very much in favour of the murderer's being a doctor, particularly as some of the more wild-eyed Ripper theories have perpetuated this myth. The truth is that the knowledge that William Bury gained from having been a horsemeat butcher may have assisted him in a small way in providing a rough diagram of whereabouts to cut, but, as we shall see from his dissection of Catharine Eddowes, he was really guessing about which organs were or were not sexual.

One thing that would have mightily interested the police had they known of it at the time was the behaviour of Bury on that Saturday afternoon. His manner was described as being that of a madman.[35]

It was possibly this that gave Ellen her first inkling that she was not the only recipient of his violence. It was something that at first she would have quickly expunged from her mind. But, as the evidence mounted piece by piece, so the doubts would have kept nagging away inside her head. Spouses are simultaneously both the most and the least likely to suspect their husbands of being a serial murderer. They are the closest observers of their behaviour, the best placed to add two and two together. But a spouse is also the person who least wants to believe that her partner can be guilty of such atrocities. Deep down, John Christie's wife, Ethel, probably knew for years but ignored the reality till it could no longer be avoided. Then, as with Ellen Bury, it was too late. Ted Bundy's partner, Cas Richter, was luckier. They had ceased living together when she telephoned the police with her suspicions. Later, after his arrest, she went back to believing that he could not possibly be such a monster. Ellen Bury never enjoyed the luxury of being able to have second thoughts.

The events of 29–30 September would have served only to fuel Ellen's suspicions. It was once again a time of the month at which Bury was at his most vulnerable. The evening of Saturday the 29th again found him deep in the stews of Whitechapel.

In examining what took place over the next few hours, one is conscious of three people gyrating towards each other, and their destinies, with the same grim inevitability of the *Titanic* heading for the iceberg. At 8.30pm, Catharine Eddowes was lying drunk on the pavement in Aldgate High Street. When PC Louis Robinson picked her up, she simply fell down again, so he summoned assistance and took her to Bishopsgate Police Station.[36] Aldgate is just across the invisible boundary line between the East End and the City of London. The latter has its own separate police force, and Robinson was a City officer. Bishopsgate was and still is one of the City's two police stations and is situated opposite Liverpool Street railway station. Cathy was placed in a cell to sleep it off.

Elizabeth Stride was as fetchingly attired as her impoverished circumstances permitted. Her clothes, a black skirt, jacket and bonnet, were well worn and, in an attempt to add some lustre to her appearance, she had tied a chequered silk handkerchief around her neck to serve as a scarf.[37] It was Saturday night and she was, in East End vernacular, 'on the pull', hoping to find a man who would stand her drinks and then round the night off by paying her for sex. Since splitting up with her boyfriend, a waterside labourer named Michael Kidney, 'Long Liz', as she was known, had been living in a lodging house at 32 Flower and Dean Street.[38] Viewing her mortuary photograph – hardly the best time to look at somebody – it comes as a surprise to learn that she was fast approaching her 45th birthday. Abraham Hoshburg, a young Berner Street resident who saw her dead body *in situ*, told the *Evening News* that she looked 25 to 28.[39] In the photo, she does appear less than her real age and not unattractive.

Sometime between 8 and 11pm, Liz Stride picked up William Bury. Shortly before 11pm, they were observed by a group of labourers in a pub called the Bricklayers Arms in Settles Street, some five minutes' walk southeast from Spitalfields. The couple were getting rather amorous, and two of the labourers, 'J' Best and John

Gardner, began to take the mickey out of them. 'If he had been a straight fellow,' Best told the *Evening News*, 'he would have told us to mind our own business,' which means that, mob-handed, he and Gardner were looking for trouble. Bury knew enough about the environment he was drinking in not to respond to it, but, after Best called out to Liz, 'That's Leather Apron getting round you,' he ushered her out of the pub. Best described him as an Englishman, 5ft 5in (1.6 metre) in height, decked out in a morning coat over a black morning suit with a collar and tie and a tall, black billycock hat. He had a thick black moustache and no beard but, rather curiously, 'sore eyes without any eyelashes'.[40] Best summed him up as 'well dressed', and his description has the feel of a clerk out for the night. We shall see this reiterated by other witnesses.

Best told the *Evening News* that he was 'almost certain' that Liz was the woman he had seen. Gardner had no doubt: 'I told you the woman had a flower in her jacket, and that she had a short jacket. I have been to the mortuary and there she was with the dahlias on the right side of her jacket.'[41]

There is one problem with this description: according to the deputy of the lodging house where Liz resided and also one of her fellow lodgers, she was wearing a long, not a short, jacket when she went out that night. But eyewitnesses do often get minor elements like this wrong. What Gardner did get right was the important detail of the flower. It stuck in the minds of all who saw Liz out and about that night. Gardner, in fact, was the only one to call it by its correct name, a dahlia, in this instance a red rose set in white fern. According to the *New Oxford Dictionary*, a dahlia is a 'brightly coloured single or double flower'. Liz was wearing a red rose set in white fern – a double flower.

White and red somehow symbolised Liz's up-and-down life. She was a country girl born on 27 November 1843, and her maiden name was Gustaafsdotter and she came from Torslanda, a farming community near Gothenburg, Sweden, the city to which she decamped as a young woman to work as a domestic servant. But prostitution overtook her. Hospital records tell of a cruel life on the city streets: two courses of treatment for venereal disease and the birth of a little girl who was stillborn.

Liz never had another child but she did have the strength of character to begin a new life in London in 1866, marrying a carpenter named John Stride three years later. They opened a coffee house in Poplar, but in the long run their relationship foundered and by the time John died, of heart disease in 1884, they had been living apart for some time. Michael Kidney cared about her in a rough sort of way, but the last two years of her life were marked by frequent, and histrionic, appearances at Thames Magistrates' Court, charged with being drunk and disorderly.

It was raining when Bury and she left the Bricklayers Arms shortly after 11. The next sighting we have of them is in Berner Street at 11.45. The intervening 40 minutes were, likely, spent mainly in another pub, because, when her body was subsequently examined at 1.20, her clothing was dry to the touch.[42]

Berner Street, now called Henriques Street, is three minutes' walk from Settles Street, off the main thoroughfare of Commercial Road (not Commercial Street, which is different), on the left-hand side leading up towards the City from Stepney and set in the parish of St George in the East.

The rain had either ceased or tapered off into the lightest of drizzles when William Marshall, a labourer, of 64 Berner Street, came across them kissing again. Marshall could not see the man's face in the darkness, but thought he was about 5ft 6in (1.7 metre) and 'rather stout', dressed like a clerk in a black cutaway jacket and dark trousers with a round, peaked cap. He had the impression the man was middle-aged. Like Elizabeth Long, Marshall heard Bury speak and how soft and sinister his words were: 'You would say anything but your prayers.'[43]

Our next witness is somewhat controversial. Matthew Packer was an elderly man who sold fruit from the front window of his home at 44 Berner Street. At about 11.45, seemingly just after Marshall noticed the couple, Packer was approached by a 'man' and a 'middle-aged woman' who bought some black grapes off him. According to the fruiterer, the man addressed him as 'old man', just as Patrick Mulshaw's passer-by had done in Winthrop Street.[44]

Packer subsequently gave a description of the couple to the police:

> A young man 25–30 – about 5 ft 7 inches with long black (frock) coat buttoned up – soft felt hat, kind of Yankee hat; rather broad shoulders – rather quick in speaking, rough voice.
>
> A woman . . . dressed in black frock and jacket, fur round bottom of jacket, a black crepe bonnet, she was playing with a flower like a geranium white outside and red inside.
>
> I put the man down as a young clerk. He was about 1½ inches or 2 or 3 inches – a little higher than she was.[45]

Bury was 5ft 3½, Stride 5ft 2 (both approximately 1.6 metre).

Speaking to the press, Packer added that the man had a dark complexion.[46] As with Elizabeth Long in Hanbury Street, this was a good basic likeness of Bury.

Who ate the grapes has never been established. According to Packer, Bury bought them for Liz, and a handkerchief belonging to her was found to be stained with fruit juice. On the other hand, Bagster Phillips told her inquest, 'I am convinced that the deceased had not swallowed either skin or seed of a grape within many hours of her death.'[47]

But his use of 'I am convinced' implies that this was Phillips's opinion rather than something he was able to establish as a medical fact. A bloodstained grape stalk was in fact recovered from a drain near to where Stride's body was found by two private detectives named Batchelor and Grand on 2 October, following information from two women, Eva Harstein and her married sister, a Mrs Rosenfield, that they had noticed it at the murder site on 30 September.[48] The point is of some importance to the veracity of Packer's testimony. More of that later.

After the purchase, Packer saw them walk up the street to a club known as the International Working Men's Club, where they lingered for a while listening to the sounds of music and singing coming from inside. Then they crossed over to the other side of the street and stood outside a board school (a London County Council Schoolboard school), which also ran round the eastern corner of Berner Street into Fairclough Street. They were still there when Packer closed up at approximately 12.15.

Next to the club was Dutfields' Yard, formerly a carriage maker's premises. The gates were open and it was an ideal place for Stride to service Bury; equally, it was an ideal place for her murder, a fact she did not become aware of till it was too late. Why Bury did not then take her into the yard is unclear. The logical explanation is that there were too many people around at that point. According to Packer and a witness at Stride's inquest, the pubs in that vicinity turned out between midnight and 12.30 that night, so Bury was presumably waiting for the area to clear. Meanwhile, he was trying to keep Stride happy with the grapes.

But Liz grew unhappier by the minute. She had better things to do than stand about in the streets, especially if it started to rain again. What happened next made up her mind to ditch him.

PC William Smith paid the couple no particular heed as he passed them on his beat at 12.35. He did not see Bury's face clearly, although he noticed that he had a dark complexion, a small dark moustache and no whiskers. Smith gleaned little else about him other than that he wore a white collar and tie, a dark, hard-felt deerstalker hat, diagonal overcoat and trousers, stood about 5ft 7in (1.7 metre), appeared respectable and was carrying what looked like a parcel wrapped in newspaper, the first hint of another long-running Ripper myth: the infamous little black bag. Smith was almost spot on with Bury's age though – 'about 28'. The main thing he noticed about Stride was her flower.[49]

Bury must have tensed visibly as Smith went by because Liz now decided that she wanted out. Perhaps Best and Gardner had been right and he was Leather Apron – somebody had to be. When Liz was next spotted, she was trying to get away from him.

That was around 12.45, although James Brown, a docker who had gone out to get some supper, couldn't be sure about it. In 1888, Berner Street ran north–south from Commercial Road to Ellen Street, intersecting Fairclough Street on the way, and it was here, just around the corner from Berner Street with her back to the school wall, that Brown saw Stride talking to a man who was facing her with an arm against the wall, seemingly trying to hem her in. Very little about the couple conveyed itself to Brown: the man was wearing a long overcoat reaching down almost to his heels, was about 5ft 7in (1.7 metre) and 'stoutish'. But he heard Liz's rejection clearly enough: 'No, not tonight, some other night.'[50] She almost got away with it. But not quite.

What happened next is one of those incidents that make us grind our teeth in frustration, wishing we had more information about them. The occurrence is best described in Swanson's own words:

> 12.45 a.m., 30th. Israel Schwartz of 22 Ellen Street stated that at that hour on turning into Berner Street from Commercial Road and had got as far as the gateway where the murder was committed he saw a man stop and speak to a woman, who was standing in the gateway. The man tried to pull the woman into the Street, but he turned her round

and threw her down on the footway and the woman screamed three times, but not very loudly. On crossing to the opposite side of the Street, he saw a second man standing lighting his pipe. The man who threw the woman down called out apparently to the man on the opposite side of the road 'Lipski' and then Schwartz walked away, but finding that he was followed by the second man he ran as far as the railway arch but the man did not follow so far. Schwartz cannot say whether the two men were together or known to each other. Upon being taken to the mortuary Schwartz identified the body as that of the woman he had seen and he thus describes the first man who threw the woman down: – age about 30 height 5ft 5in [1.6 metre] comp. fair, hair dark, small brown moustache, full face, broad shouldered, dress, dark jacket and trousers black cap with peak, had nothing in his hands. Second man aged 35 ht 5ft 11 [1.8 metre] in compl fresh, hair light brown, moustache brown, dress dark overcoat, old black hard felt hat wide brim, had a clay pipe in his hand.[51]

In assessing the value of Schwartz's evidence, Swanson remarks, 'If Schwartz is to be believed and the Police report of his statement casts no doubt upon it', which strongly implies that he was considered to be a credible and competent witness. He goes on, 'The Police apparently do not suspect the 2nd man whom Schwartz saw on the other side of the street and who followed Schwartz.' This is reinforced in a separate report made by Abberline on 1 November. Commenting upon the seemingly abusive use of the word 'Lipski' by Stride's assailant, he says, 'I am of the opinion it was addressed to him [Schwartz].'

Abberline goes on to say of the second man, 'Whether this man was running after him [Schwartz] or not he could not tell, he might have been alarmed the same as himself and ran away.'

Israel Schwartz was never called to testify at the inquest. Why is one of the many annoying questions raised by his evidence. He may have been kept back deliberately, but Swanson's report also notes his belief that 'It is not clearly proved that the man that Schwartz saw is the murderer.'

In fact, the assault Schwartz witnessed was exactly the type of blitz-style attack that a 'disorganised' serial killer like Bury would launch on his victims.

One would particularly like to know which direction Bury appeared from. Schwartz was subsequently interviewed by the *Star*, and said that the man was swaying drunkenly in front of him as he, Schwartz, made his way along Berner Street from Commercial Road. This would suggest that Bury initially walked off down Berner Street following Liz's rejection, changed his mind and went back. But the *Star* article differs considerably from what both Swanson and Abberline say that Schwartz told them. The newspaper paints a vivid picture of the second man threatening Schwartz with a knife! Schwartz was a recently arrived Hungarian Jew who spoke no English. He gave both accounts through an interpreter and one fears that the *Star* failed to resist the temptation to embellish. Swanson's synopsis makes no mention of the direction Stride's attacker came from, so, equally, Bury may simply have followed her from Fairclough Street; however, because Schwartz did not give evidence at the inquest and important police documents are currently missing, we are left guessing.

What does seem clear is that, after Liz and Bury parted, she returned to Berner Street and was standing outside Dutfields' Yard trying to entice the man with the pipe. Bury's unwelcome appearance put paid to that – and to her. At 1am, Louis Diemshutz, steward of the International Working Men's Club, attempted to drive a horse and barrow into the yard. The horse suddenly shied to the left. Diemshutz dismounted and struck a match. Its flickering flame revealed the outline of Elizabeth Stride's dead body.[52]

One of the more fascinating aspects of life is the way in which seemingly unconnected events can impact upon, and even change, our own destinies without our knowledge. At the moment Diemshutz was bending over Stride, Catharine Eddowes was indulging in some good-humoured banter with PC George Hutt, who was discharging her from Bishopsgate Police Station: 'I shall get a damned fine hiding when I get home.' A little spitefully, she gave her name as Mary Ann Kelly, her partner's estranged wife.[53]

Eddowes has been described by crime historian Martin Fido as the most charming of the Ripper victims.[54] Mary Kelly has been posthumously endowed with glamour, Liz Stride provides pathos, Annie Chapman evoked a moving epitaph in the *Daily Telegraph*[55] and Polly Nichols makes us admire her cheerful fortitude. But Cathy Eddowes is indeed the one who makes us smile, albeit sadly. A tiny woman only 4ft 11in (1.5 metre) tall, she was a cockney-sparrow type who appears to have coped better with the downside of life than Bury's other victims did. Cathy was the only one in a stable, long-term relationship. She had lived with John Kelly, a labourer, for the past seven years, latterly in a lodging house at 55 Flower and Dean Street, very close to Liz Stride's last digs.

Catharine was born in Wolverhampton on 14 April 1842, one of 11 children sired by George Eddowes, a tinplate worker, with his wife Catharine, née Evans. Evans was the maiden name of William Bury's maternal grandmother, Jane Henley. Whether there was a family connection I have not been able to discover. Evans is hardly an uncommon name. Nor does the proximity of Dudley and Wolverhampton mean anything: there was a mass exodus from Wales to the West Midlands in the early years of the 19th century in search of work and prosperity.

On the available evidence, Cathy Eddowes lived only a small part of her life in Wolverhampton, anyway. Not long after her birth, George moved his growing family to Bermondsey, South London.

The borough of Southwark, as it is now, sometimes seems as important to the Ripper murders as the East End. 'The great social mill crushes and grinds,' wrote Hippolyte Taine, a French visitor to Britain in 1861.[56] William Bury's victims all too often appear to have been first crushed in Southwark before being ground in Whitechapel! The Eddowes family broke up in 1855 when her mother died of tuberculosis.

Catharine was sent back to Wolverhampton to live with her aunt, Elizabeth Eddowes, at 17 Bilston Street. Here we do have a tenuous link with Bury. Bilston Street is in east Wolverhampton, where Bury was residing from the mid-1870s to the 1880s. The 1851, 1861 and 1871 Censuses all record George and Elizabeth Eddowes living in Bilston Street and Elizabeth was still there in 1881, now a widow and running a boarding house. However, there is no provable link here between Bury and the Eddowes family, just as there is no known family connection. Wolverhampton was a rapidly growing township during the mid-19th century, no part more so than its eastern segment, which teemed with both the dispossessed of the countryside and those who sought greater opportunities in life.

On the last full morning of her life, Eddowes is supposed to have told the superintendent of the Mile End casual ward (where the homeless could sleep on a floor) that she thought she knew the identity of the murderer and intended earning the reward now being offered for his capture. 'Mind he doesn't murder you too,' cautioned the official. 'Oh, no fear of that' were her parting words. However, Philip Sugden, in *The Complete History of Jack the Ripper*, makes the point that this exchange of words is too close to her final conversation with John Kelly for us to feel comfortable that the former has not been juxtaposed with the latter.[57] Responding to a warning from Kelly that afternoon to beware of falling foul of the killer, Eddowes replied, 'Don't you fear for me.' Missing from this exchange was any suggestion that she might know the man the police were looking for.[58]

The point is of importance, because, unlike some of the literally clueless Ripper claimants trotted out in the past, Bury does not need far-fetched connections to endorse him as the culprit.

To return to Eddowes's upbringing, life with Aunt Elizabeth did not prove agreeable and she absconded to live with an uncle in Birmingham, where she likewise chaffed under family discipline. A rebellious imp, she saw her way out of the malaise as being one Thomas Conway, other times known as Quinn, an army pensioner who is said to have earned his living as a freelance writer of sorts, producing booklets of lives of famous people. Cathy took up with him around the age of 16, although he must have been considerably older than she. (Oddly, Liz Stride followed her down the same path: John Stride was over 20 years her senior.) Now calling herself Kate Conway, Catharine bore Thomas three children. There is no record of their ever marrying. This unconventional relationship nevertheless had a more conventional way of ending. The couple split up sometime around 1881. Conway blamed Kate's drinking; she claimed he used to beat her; the truth is lost in the mists of accusation.

What happened to Conway is unknown. Cathy made her commitment to Kelly and settled into East End life. If asked, she would probably have said it had its ups and downs. Truth is, the ups never got higher than lodging houses while the downs could be very decidedly out as well. Evidence of this can be discerned from the fact that John Kelly was treated for frostbite in November 1887.[59] Their most frequent lodgings were at 55 Flower and Dean Street, or 'Flowerydean', as the grim little East End thoroughfare was known. The lodging-house deputy, Frederick Williamson, remembered her as a 'very jolly woman' who earned her bread by hawking and charring and did not drink very much.[60] Although the autopsy noted signs of Bright's disease in her right kidney, it also states, 'liver itself was healthy'.[61] Williamson was adamant that Eddowes was not a prostitute: 'I never knew or heard of her being intimate with any one than Kelly.'[62] Although the police later assumed she was a street walker,[63] there is no firm evidence to gainsay Williamson. Her postmortem was the only one known to check for sperm, in both her clothing and body, and none was found. While not conclusive, this does suggest that Eddowes may have earned her drink money on the 29th from begging rather than selling herself.

The last days of Cathy's life were dreary and disheartening. On 27 September, she and Kelly arrived back in London from hop picking in Kent. It had not been a success. That night they slept in the Shoe Lane casual ward (twopence per night). On Friday Kelly earned sixpence. Cathy sent him to find a bed in a proper lodging house (fourpence) while she stayed at the casual ward in Mile End. The following night she would be in eternity.

Saturday morning, 29 September, the couple met up and pawned Kelly's boots for money to buy food, leaving him barefooted. Small wonder he had suffered frostbite in the past. They bought their necessities and by 2pm were penniless again. Cathy then went to beg money from her daughter Annie in King Street, Bermondsey, only to find she had moved to an address in, yes, Southwark Park Road. Somehow she made some money and by 8.30 was falling down drunk in Aldgate.

The City Police did not detain drunks any longer than they had to and at 1am 'Mary Ann Kelly' was on her way with a cheery 'Good night, old cock' to Hutt. Three-quarters of an hour later, another City Police constable, Edward Watkins, came across her in Mitre Square. Cathy was lying down again; this time she was dead.

On a September afternoon in 1998, I walked from the Harry Gosling junior school, where Dutfields' Yard used to stand, to Mitre Square. I started out at 2.49 and arrived in the Square at 3.06 – 17 minutes. Bury probably left Dutfields' at around 12.50. He was next seen again at 1.35, which leaves approximately 30 minutes unaccounted for. Euan Macpherson, a journalist who advanced

Bury's credentials as the Ripper in 1986, believes he may have kept a change of clothes on his cart. That is certainly not implausible, another lesson he may have learned from the Tabram murder. There could have been an added factor: it is conceivable that Bury injured himself while murdering Stride and, if he was to kill again that night, he would be more comfortable strangling the victim with a ligature rather than his hands. There would have been rope on the cart, which he used in his work.

A second victim was virtually a necessity. He had not been able to mutilate Stride and the lust was heavy upon him. When thwarted in their desires, serial killers will go in search of another outlet for them. Bundy is a case in point. Frustrated when one prospective victim, Carol Da Ronch, got away from him, he immediately embarked on a 30-minute drive to the next town and abducted and murdered 17-year-old Debbie Kent, even though he must have known that Da Ronch had raised the alarm.[64] William Bury and Ted Bundy were driven by the same elemental forces. When Bury turned the corner of Berner Street into Commercial Road, he was on course to commit his worse atrocity yet. Under the circumstances, he would probably have killed Cathy Eddowes anyway, but the name she was using that night, Mary Ann Kelly, effectively sealed her fate.

Behind him, he left a scene of swirling chaos. When Diemshutz arrived and discovered the body, his first thought was that it was his wife lying in the yard drunk! But he found her safe and well inside the club and, after enlisting help, returned and examined his find by candlelight. This revealed that the woman was lying in a pool of blood. Diemshutz then hared off to Fairclough Street shouting, 'Police, police!' Shortly afterwards, Morris Eagle, a club member, ran in the opposite direction, Commercial Road, and returned with PC Henry Lamb.[65] His lantern revealed that Liz's throat had been cut. Lamb sent to Leman Street Police Station for assistance and also summoned Dr Frederick Blackwell, who had a surgery in

Commercial Road. Blackwell's assistant, Edward Johnson, arrived first, followed very soon afterwards by Blackwell himself, at 1.10. The body was still warm and Blackwell decided that she had been dead between 20 and 30 minutes.[66] Dr Bagster Phillips turned up some 30 minutes later. Another visitor to Berner Street that night was Superintendent Thomas Arnold, the officer commanding 'H' division. Arnold had been on holiday during the earlier murders. He was still directing operations at Berner Street when, about 3.30, a message arrived asking him to go urgently to Goulston Street in Whitechapel, where another sensation awaited him.

In Constable Watkins's words, Cathy Eddowes had been 'ripped up like a pig in the market'.[67] His first, horrified, reaction was to stumble across the square to the Kearley and Tonge warehouse on the northeastern corner, diametrically opposite where the corpse lay. George Morris, the nightwatchman, was himself a former City Police officer. He was sweeping up when Watkins knocked at the door: 'For God's sake, mate, come to my assistance . . . there's another woman cut to pieces.' Morris had a quick look at the body himself and then dashed off to seek help. In Aldgate, he encountered PC James Harvey and told him what had happened. Harvey returned with Morris. Another constable, James Holland, went for a doctor and residents were despatched to locate more patrolling officers. The little square quickly began to fill up.[68]

Unlike the Metropolitan Police, who report to the Home Office, the City force are answerable to the Aldermen of the City of London. They are equivalent in size to no more than one of the Met's 25 divisions. But in theory, if not reality, the City Police enjoy equal status with the Met and the other 41 police authorities of Britain.

In 1888, the City Police Commissioner was Sir James Fraser. Like Anderson and Arnold, he was on holiday when Bury first came calling. Temporarily, command had devolved on his deputy, Major Henry Smith.

The City Police files were destroyed in the Blitz and only one of their reports has survived, a briefing to the Home Office by the head of the City's detective department, Inspector James McWilliam, which, as an official glumly notes, tells us little. It does confirm that, after Eddowes left Bishopsgate Police Station, nobody saw her except for three men. On their way home after a night out at a club a stone's throw from Mitre Square, Joseph Levy, Harry Harris and Joseph Lawende, a cigarette salesman, were headed towards Aldgate High Street at 1.35 when they came across Eddowes and Bury standing on the corner of Duke Street and Church Passage, an alley that led into the Square. Lawende, who was just behind the other two, turned to have a look at the couple.[69] He noted that the man was around 30, 5ft 7–8in (about 1.7 metre) tall, of medium build, with a fair complexion and moustache, shabbily dressed in a pepper-and-salt-coloured jacket, a grey cloth cap with a peak and a reddish handkerchief tied around his neck.[70] Lawende did not think he would be able to recognise him again.[71]

By 2.05, Mitre Square and its environs were a hive of activity. An Inspector Collard, several detectives and Dr William Sequeira were now on site. A little later they were joined by Major Smith and the City Police surgeon, Dr Frederick Gordon Brown. One of the detectives, Constable Daniel Halse, set out to search the surrounding streets in the direction of Spitalfields. He went up Middlesex Street and into Wentworth Street, where he stopped and questioned two men. Satisfied with their answers, he returned by way of Goulston Street, passing through it at 2.20. Clearly, the streets were almost empty. Halse makes mention only of the two men he spoke to and his instructions were to stop everyone.[72]

Cathy's body was removed to the City Mortuary at 2.30 accompanied by Halse and Collard. When the corpse was stripped it was discovered that a piece of an apron she was wearing was missing. On returning to Mitre Square, Halse learned that it had been found in Goulston Street.[73] It was not the only thing.

Constable Alfred Long was one of many officers the Met had drafted in from other divisions to beef up its foot patrols in response to the murders. His beat that night took in Goulston Street. The street ran north–south from Wentworth Street to Whitechapel High Street. At the northern end, on the right-hand side, stood a series of rather pretentious apartment blocks known as Wentworth Model Dwellings. Pausing just inside their main doorway, Long discovered the missing piece of Catharine Eddowes's apron, stained with blood and faeces. Shining his lantern on to the passage wall immediately above the piece of cloth, he discovered a message written in chalk. The bottom part of the wall was painted black and the upper part white. The chalked letters were on the black fascia brickwork that divided the two halves of the wall. In his notebook, Long wrote down the words as they appeared on the bricks (capitalised here as in the source):

> The Juwes are
> The men that
> Will not
> be Blamed
> for nothing[74]

Long noted the time as 2.55. He went into the building and made a search of the stairways and landings, thinking there may be yet another body, but found nothing.

News of Long's discovery sent Halse scurrying back to Goulston Street. Passing the doorway earlier, he had not spotted the apron, although, he said, 'I would not necessarily have seen it, for it was in the building.'[75]

Halse wanted the writing preserved till it was light enough to be photographed. Superintendent Arnold, on his arrival from Berner Street, decided to erase it, fearing an anti-Semitic riot. Wentworth, Middlesex and Goulston Streets housed the Sunday market and by the time it was light the traders would be setting up for business. Halse protested. Why not cover the writing up? Better still, erase only the top line or just the word 'Juwes'. Given that Halse represented a police force Arnold held no command in, he sent for Sir Charles Warren, who arrived shortly before 5am and concurred with his superintendent. The message in its entirety was sponged away without ever being caught on camera.[76]

Warren's action has generated more heated argument than virtually any other aspect of the East End murders. Among other things, it has stimulated a number of theories about who the Ripper was. In fact, the sole connection of the writing to the murders was that it appeared above the discarded piece of apron. Actually, there were many such messages chalked up around the East End at the time.[77] The simple truth, that Bury tossed the piece of apron into the doorway as he hurried past, was lost in the realms of fantasy. Long claimed that the apron was not there when he made his previous round at 2.20, but he did not perhaps want to admit that he had not really checked it. The coroner's jury implied by their questions that they did not think Long was a particularly zealous officer and he was in fact sacked for being drunk on duty the following year.

The chalkings were almost certainly made in the daytime. The idea that anybody would even attempt such a message in the pitch dark, let alone arranging it neatly line by line, defies common sense. Moreover, white chalk would not have shown up against white paint, which means that the writer deliberately stooped to scrawl it on the black fascia. This in turn means that he was able to distinguish between the white and black halves of the wall and, unless he was very familiar with the building, that distinction would have been apparent only in daylight.

The importance of where the piece of apron was found is that it enables us to plot a credible route from Mitre Square. The quickest way out and back to Whitechapel and Spitalfields was to exit the Square via

Church Passage into Duke Street, traverse Hounsditch, Gravel Lane, Ellison and Middlesex Streets into Goulston Street, and then turn east into Wentworth Street, which would bring him to Commercial Street, the heartland of his domain of terror, and where, one assumes, the pony and cart would be close at hand. Walking time – eight minutes. Wherever he spent the rest of that terrible night, he was long gone from Goulston Street by the time Halse first reached it. The subsequent claim of Halse's boss, Major Smith – 'I was within five minutes of the perpetrator' – was the posturing of a parade-horse policeman.[78]

It was a busy weekend for George Bagster Phillips. After turning out at Berner Street, he observed Eddowes's postmortem on behalf of the Met on Sunday afternoon, concluding that her murder was the work of an 'unskilled imitator', a view tentatively endorsed by Coroner Baxter at Stride's inquest and, arguably, Superintendent Arnold as well.

Phillips's attendance at the City Mortuary meant that Stride's autopsy took place on Monday, 1 October, Blackwell making the dissection. Their findings revealed:

> There was a clean cut incision on the neck. It was 6 inches [15cm] in length and commenced 2½ inches [6.3cm] in a straight line below the angle of the jaw, ¾ inch [2cm] over an undivided muscle, and then becoming deeper, dividing the sheaf. The cut was very clean and deviated a little downwards. The artery and other vessels contained in the sheaf were all cut through. The cut through the tissues on the right side was more superficial and tailed off to about 2 inches [5cm] below the right angle of the jaw. The deep vessels on that side were uninjured. From this it is evident that the haemorrhage was caused through the partial severance of the left carotid artery.[79]

There were no other incisions anywhere on the body but there was a massive bruise extending across the chest from shoulder to shoulder, especially on the right. The body had been found lying on its left side facing the right-hand wall at an oblique angle, the feet touching the wall just inside the gate, the head facing the wall 5 or 6 inches (12–15cm) away from it. Her left arm was extended and in the hand, which was 'partially closed', she clutched a packet of cachous (breath sweeteners). Her right arm was lying across her stomach, the inside and outside of the hand and wrist permeated with blood, 'smeared' according to Blackwell, 'clotted' said Phillips, while the police report uses the term 'dotted'. Blood was still issuing from the throat wound when the body was found, and was running into a gutter by the wall. Dr Blackwell, in his evidence at the inquest, stated, 'There was a check silk scarf round the neck, the bow of which was knotted to the left and pulled tightly.'[80]

Phillips gave the cause of death as loss of blood from the throat injury and Blackwell thought that Liz would have taken around 90 seconds to expire from the time the cut was inflicted. But this creates a puzzle because blood should not only have flowed from the wound but also *spurted* from the damaged artery while life was present. Accordingly, there ought to have been blood splashes on the wall next to her head. Yet there were none, as witness after witness confirmed.

Phillips: 'I could trace none.'

Reid: '[I] could find no spot of blood.'

Blackwell: 'There was no blood on the side of the house or splashes on the wall.'

Blackwell and Reid had examined the scene minutely by lamplight (presumably, Phillips, too, though it is not stated), Reid returning the following morning to inspect it in daylight. So could the doctors have been wrong? Was Liz dead *before* her throat was cut? The answer is that it is conceivable that she succumbed to what is termed reflex cardiac arrest. Professor Bernard Knight explains (in *Simpson's Forensic Medicine*):

> In strangulation and hanging, sudden pressure on the carotid structures can initiate rapid death before any congestive-petechial [dark red spots caused by bleeding into the skin] signs have time to appear, so the victim dies with a pale face.

This occurs at a time of what Knight calls 'tense emotion', an example of which would be restraint by the neck from behind (Knight uses deaths in police custody from armlocks around the throat as instances). As Blackwell noted, Stride was under attack, with her scarf being drawn tightly around her neck from behind. This could have led to the sort of pressure on the carotid, which would cause death. In what may be the clincher, the labourer Best noted that 'the face looks the same but a little paler', and Inspector Reid and an *Evening News* reporter both remarked on the pallor of Liz's features in death. Mercifully, she may never have been aware of the knife at her throat.

But why was she not mutilated? This, plus the use of a different knife, has caused some to question Elizabeth Stride's credentials as a Ripper victim. It is an argument I respect but do not agree with, although there were doubts among police officers at the time of the crime.

Let's get an expert opinion, Robert Keppel again, here talking about mutilation murderers in general: 'Unfortunately, a signature is not always recognised at the crime scene because of . . . interruption in the killer's routine, like the pressure of unexpected witnesses.'[81]

It has generally been suggested that the Ripper was interrupted by Diemshutz's arrival. Jack was certainly making preparations to carry out his usual depredations. In contrast to the other victims, Stride was found on her side. She was also very close to the open gateway and, even in the darkness, passers-by might have seen him. A little further into the yard there was a slight corner and it seems likely that he was preparing to drag her round there and turned her on to her left side to minimise contact with the haemorrhaging throat injury. It is at this point that he decided against it. Possibly this was due to Diemshutz, but my view is that Bury was already gone when the steward arrived.

I believe that Bury killed Stride in a blind fury after she spurned him. Bury was the last man who could have accepted rejection from a prostitute, especially one named Elizabeth who already brought to mind his imagined rejection by his family. So, seething with hate, he either followed or went back to her and in his anger assaulted her in front of the two witnesses. It is all too reminiscent of his attack on Ellen in the pub three months earlier. In the perversely self-centred way psychopaths have of looking at things, they are always the injured party. Thus, although Bury had not been home for three nights, Ellen had humiliated *him* by coming out to look for him and talking to Martin. Exactly the same paranoid self-image is on display at Dutfields' Yard. In Bury's distorted way of looking at things, Liz had no right to reject him, even though he intended killing her!

What Schwartz and the unknown second man witnessed was the opening stage of a serial murderer's 'blitz' attack. However, one or both could now be returning with a policeman. As Bury's anger began to subside, he realised that staying to mutilate posed too great a risk. There may also have been a second factor that, added to this, helped make up his mind for him. That we shall come to in its turn.

William Bury would do what he had wanted to do to Liz Stride elsewhere that night. But for the moment we stay with her murder to examine another bone of contention. Was Bury always the man seen with her that night? My own view has already been made clear. Objections to it centre on differences in detail in the various descriptions of Liz's beau. Such discrepancies are not the exception but the rule. Experience of criminal cases shows that eyewitness descriptions of the same man consistently alter from person to person, in many instances bearing little or no resemblance to the culprit when apprehended. We shall see in the next chapter that people who knew victim Mary Kelly differed quite radically about her looks.

The point was reinforced by the coroner, Wynne Baxter, during his summing-up at Stride's inquest: 'These discrepancies do not conclusively prove that there was more than one man in the company of the deceased, for everyday experience shows how facts are differently observed and differently described by honest and intelligent witnesses.'[82]

There were, he said, 'many points of similarity, but some of dissimilarity', in the descriptions tendered by Marshall, Smith and Brown. In my judgement, what is impressive – very impressive – is how minor the differences were. They convince me that the man the witnesses saw on every occasion that night was William Bury.

Several of the witnesses did not appear at the inquest. As well as Schwartz, Matthew Packer, the Harstein sisters, Grand and Batchelor and the two labourers from the Bricklayers Arms, Best and Gardner were excused testimony. Swanson later wrote scathingly that Packer 'has unfortunately made different statements so that . . . any statement he made would be rendered almost useless as evidence'.[83]

Had there been no blood-spattered grape stalk, no fruit-stained handkerchief, one might tend to be equally dismissive. But there were. So let us examine Matthew Packer's contradictions.

In an interview at Scotland Yard with Assistant Commissioner Bruce on 4 October, he put the purchase of the grapes at 11pm and his closing-up as 11.30. But elsewhere, to Batchelor and Grand, to an *Evening News* reporter on 3 October and in an earlier interview with the police on 4 October, Packer consistently maintained a later time: Batchelor and Grand, 11.45 and 00.10–15; *Evening News*, between 11.30 and midnight, and 11.30 and 'after midnight a little bit', respectively; police (Sergeant Stephen White), about midnight and half past midnight.

A second suggested contradiction lies exclusively between Packer and Sergeant White. The latter called on him during house-to-house enquiries on the morning of 30 September. According to White, four days later, Packer told him on the 30th, 'I saw no one standing about, neither did I see anyone go up the yard. I never saw anything suspicious or heard the slightest noise and know nothing about the murder till I heard of it in the morning.'[84]

But on 3 October Packer told the *Evening News*,

> A young man in plain clothes came in here on Monday and asked if he might look at the yard at the back of our house so as to see if anybody had climbed over. My misses lent him some steps. But he didn't put any questions to us *about the man and woman* [my emphasis]. *No detective or policeman has ever asked me a single question, nor come near my shop to find out if I knew anything about the grapes the murdered woman had been eating before her throat was cut* [*Evening News*'s emphasis].

So where's the contradiction? Of course White did not ask Packer about the grapes or about a man and woman. The police first learned of a couple buying grapes from the *Evening News*! They missed the grape stalk, which was not recovered by Batchelor and Grand till the Tuesday. Packer had no reason to associate the couple with the murder when White first called, at 9am on the 30th. They had purchased the fruit at least 30 minutes before he closed up. By the time Packer went to bed, nobody had been murdered and nothing suspicious was happening.

One might also add that White did not contradict Packer's assertion that he was chiefly interested in the backyard on Sunday morning.

The only issue on which Packer does, at first sight, appear to contradict himself concerns the dahlia. According to the *Evening News* of 4 October,

> There is one seeming discrepancy between the story of Packer and the facts as published. It has been reported that a red flower was found on the murdered woman's bosom and Packer states that she wore a white flower . . . Packer does not say the woman wore only a white flower but that the attention was particularly drawn to the white flower from it standing out against the black of her dress [author's note: he meant dress as a whole].

A further element of confusion is that Packer went on to say that she had the flower in her hand at that point. He subsequently told Bruce that she was playing with a flower red inside and white outside.

But, crucially, the seeming contradictions here are in Packer's favour and for one very simple reason: the flower, whether it was on her bosom or in her hand, or both, did have a surround of white fern. Packer was not only correct about this but *consistently* correct.

The flower likewise assists us in assessing the reliability of Miss Harstein and Mrs Rosenfield's observations. When they spoke to Grand and Batchelor on 2 October, they not only told the two investigators about seeing the bloodstained grape stalk on the 30th, but also some white flower petals close by.

Grand and Batchelor did not simply take Packer's story at face value. After listening to it on the 2nd, they told him they were taking him to the mortuary to identify Stride's remains. Instead, they took him to the City Mortuary and showed him Eddowes's body. Packer immediately said that she was 'not a bit like' the woman who had bought the grapes. Early on the afternoon of the 4th, the private detectives showed him Liz's body and he identified her as the woman he had seen. Somewhat humorously – there isn't much of that in the Ripper murders – White arrived after the identification, having been told to take Packer on the same errand. Later, while White was interviewing him at his shop, Grand and Batchelor turned up again and whisked Packer off to the Yard to see Bruce, leaving the obviously miffed detective sergeant staring ruefully after them.

There is an interesting footnote to Packer's story. Over the next few weeks, he was in the press again on Ripper-related topics, one literally when he recounted a meeting with a man who claimed his cousin was the murderer. Packer was obviously enjoying his 15 minutes of fame. But another report, in the *Evening News* of 31 October, is more interesting. Here, Packer claimed to have seen the man who bought the grapes again, on 27 October at the junction of Greenfield Street and Commercial Road. The man looked at him 'viciously' and jumped aboard a tram while Packer sent somebody to find a policeman. Packer doubters have dismissed this as attention seeking, but the fact is that Jack the Ripper did not exist in a vacuum between murders.

Ostensibly at least, he had business to attend to and that business took him to Whitechapel. We shall see that as time wore on William Bury became increasingly fearful of travelling into his murder haunts. We should remember that the boy who cried wolf eventually did get it right. In this instance, there is strong interlocking evidence that Packer was not just crying wolf in the first place.

The police should have kept an open mind about Packer, Harstein and Rosenfield. That they did not was arguably because they had not noticed the grape stalk, an embarrassing oversight. This has to be coupled with a degree of pique about Grand and Batchelor's appearance in the case, fostered in part by the *Evening News*, which was critical of the police for failing to unearth Packer and the Harstein sisters. No witness produced by that newspaper appeared at the inquest; these included Best and Gardner. Do we see a pattern of resentment emerging here? If so, then it has to be said that on this occasion the police were not at their best and that William Bury's path of crime was being smoothed for him.

Our scene now shifts to the City Mortuary at Golden Lane. Here, on Sunday afternoon, 30 September, Cathy Eddowes's autopsy was carried out by Dr Brown. In addition to Bagster Phillips, Dr Sequeira was in attendance, plus Dr William Saunders, the City analyst. After they had finished, Eddowes's frail little corpse was photographed for posterity.

Like that of Liz Stride, Cathy's death was attributed to her throat being cut: 'the cause of death was haemorrhage from the left carotid artery'.[85] There were two cuts, both running left to right. One, commencing 1½ inches (3.8cm) below the left earlobe and terminating 3 inches (7.6cm) under the right, was superficial. The other was deep enough to have penetrated to the bone, and had divided the big muscle on the left of the throat before severing the deep vessels and the larynx below the vocal cords. Bury's ferocity had tapered off as his knife reached the right side, merely opening the vessels and the jugular vein without dividing them. This wound had bled copiously, running off to the left and forming a pool beneath her head.

But, if loss of blood from the deep throat injury had caused death, then again there should have been spurting blood prior to death. There was not, which reinforces Camps and Cameron's view that the victim was strangled. As usual, the cuts had obliterated any marks to the neck, but the fingers of both hands were slightly flexed.

A chunk of Cathy's right ear had been completely severed (it fell out of her clothing), and there were a series of ghastly lacerations to her face. Here both eyelids were cut through and an attempt had seemingly been made to rip off her nose. There were several cuts, one of which extended from the bridge of her nose across the cheek to the angle of the jaw, while another had a tributary cut running off it, which had sliced through the upper lip to the gum. A second wound to the mouth arced downwards and ran under the lower lip. There were two rather curious triangular wounds, one on either cheek, which have given rise to a plethora of fanciful theories in the past.

Cathy's body was hideously mutilated. The injuries are more appropriately analysed in depth in a later chapter. For now, it is only necessary to say that, as with Annie Chapman, most of the uterus had been cut out and taken away, this time accompanied by the left kidney. There were two distinct stab wounds, to the left groin and the liver, plus two incised wounds into the liver. Dr Brown thought that the missing kidney had been taken because the murderer was seeking it, and he was therefore inclined to award him 'a good deal of knowledge as to the position of the organs and the way of removing them . . . such a knowledge likely to be possessed by one accustomed to cutting up animals'.[86]

Neither Saunders nor Sequeira endorsed this. They did not believe the killer possessed any great degree of anatomical knowledge, or that he had designs on any particular organ.[87] Sequeira later clarified this to *Star*: he did not mean the killer had no anatomical knowledge whatsoever, just very little.[88]

Nobody commented on the attack on the liver. In retrospect, it seems clear that Bury mistook it for a sexual organ. That being the case, then by extension he probably though the kidney was one too!

Viewed from this perspective, what we have is a 'cut-and-hope' strategy. Brown's 'good deal of knowledge' goes out of the window and we are left with a killer who has little or no familiarity with the human anatomy, at its highest a man whose past experience has been restricted to an activity like cutting up horsemeat for cats' food.

Catharine Eddowes had not slept in proper lodgings since returning from Kent and was carrying her entire household with her when she met her death. She was wearing her wardrobe: a black jacket and straw bonnet, three skirts – two of which are described as 'very old and ragged' – a linsey-woolsey bodice, petticoat, chemise, brown ribbed stockings and a man's vest and boots. She seems almost to have hoarded every old piece of rag she could lay her hands on. Like Annie Chapman, she was wearing pockets tied around the waist with string – three, no fewer. In them was the accumulated value of 46 years of hardship and poverty: bed tickets, a few items of cutlery, a ball of string, toiletries, pins and needles, two clay pipes and a variety of little boxes, two of which contained tea and sugar. Now, huge rents in her skirts bore mute witness to the savagery of the attack on her.[89] William Bury had not only taken her life but invaded her little walking home to do so.

He had started, as usual, to go through her possessions, cutting the strings to the pockets and removing from them three boot buttons, a thimble and a tin containing pawn tickets.[90] But at this point Bury seems to have left rather abruptly. Why? The obvious answer is that something or someone disturbed him, possibly the approaching Watkins, maybe Morris sweeping up. Or perhaps he had found himself a trophy among Eddowes's possessions. But this is pure speculation. Aside from the body parts, we have no knowledge of any other item taken away by Bury from Mitre Square. All we do know is that, as with Chapman, an attempt had been made to sift through Cathy's possessions, that serial killers often take small personal items to remind them of the victim and that theft was in this man's psychology.

There is an interesting postscript to the murder weekend. Shortly after midnight on Monday, 1 October, PC Joseph Drage was on fixed-point duty in Whitechapel Road opposite Great Garden Street, when a passing horse fell down. Drage went to assist in getting it back on its feet and thought no more about it till 15 minutes later, when he saw a man stoop to examine something in the doorway opposite where the horse had got into difficulties. Straightening up, the man, Thomas Coram, a warehouseman on his way home after a night out, beckoned to the constable and said, 'There's a knife down here.' Drage picked up a long-bladed instrument about 9 or 10 inches

(23–25cm) long with a rounded point. The knife and a handkerchief wrapped around the handle were both stained with blood. Drage handed the knife to Bagster Phillips that afternoon. The constable doubted that it had been there for very long before Coram discovered it: 'about an hour previously the landlady let out some woman, and the knife was not there then'. Drage thought it could have been left there while he was assisting with the horse. He was not asked whether the horse's owner would have had the opportunity of depositing it in the doorway. Nor did anyone ask if the horse had been pulling a cart.[91]

Bagster Phillips was unable to say whether the blood was human, only that it was 'similar to that of a warm-blooded being'. As to the knife:

> It has been recently blunted and the edge turned by apparently rubbing on a stone. It evidently was before that a very sharp knife. Such a knife could have produced the incision and injuries to the neck of the deceased [Stride] but it was not such a weapon as I would have chosen to inflict injuries in this particular place.

Blackwell was of the same mind:

> Although it might have possibly inflicted the injury it was extremely unlikely that such an instrument was used. The murderer using a sharp, round pointed instrument would severely handicap himself as he could only use it one way.[92]

This may account for the fact that Stride's carotid artery was only partially severed. The killer seems to have had to adjust the amount of pressure he used during the cause of the incision because the wound became deeper as it progressed, and, said Phillips, 'deviated a little downwards' before becoming 'superficial' and tailing off to about 2 inches (5cm) below the right angle of the jaw. At this point there was a tear in the handkerchief around Stride's neck. Phillips again: 'I have since ascertained it was cut. This corresponded with the right angle of the jaw.'

The impression is that Bury was indeed using an implement not entirely suited to the task, and that he was struggling somewhat to make the incision.

It is here that the unexplained bleeding on Stride's hand and wrist may have been caused. It clearly perplexed Phillips, who pronounced it 'a mystery'.[93] The blood is unlikely to have come from the knife: both sides of the hand and wrist were speckled with it. Moreover, a knife does not tend to pick up blood from a single incision because there is a slight delay before bleeding commences. The weapon will come into contact with blood when making subsequent cuts. So what we are left with is the distinct possibility that the blood was Bury's own. If that was the case, it happened something like this.[94]

As the cut tapered off to the right he tried to exert pressure on the knife again and his hand slipped down on to the blade. A spasm of pain shot through him, the knife veered downwards, tearing the scarf, and he let it slip from his grasp.

The weapon came to rest next to Stride's right hand. Blood from his injury dripped on to both the knife and the hand before he wrapped a handkerchief round it to staunch the flow. Some may also have dribbled on to the ground. Coroner Baxter asked Blackwell if he had seen any spots of blood and the doctor answered that some had been 'trodden about', meaning by club members clustering around the body. So, any from Bury's injury would not have been distinguishable. The blood on Stride's hand and wrist also became smeared on to the other side of them when he placed her hand on her stomach. Discomfort from the cut may also have played a part in his decision not to mutilate the body.

Why Bury used a different knife for the murder is a question that cannot be answered. A common, everyday error perhaps? On the other hand, it may have been a deliberate choice. I was struck by a comment made by Ted Bundy during his discussions with Robert Keppel about the Green River killings: 'Nobody's consistent. They don't do everything the same every time.'[95]

One thing we can be sure about: if it was the knife Coram found, injuring its user might explain why it was so battered and blunted!

It likewise explains why Stride's throat was not cut twice. Catharine Eddowes's was, and this time with his usual weapon. But, once again, there were differences with his normal MO.

The injury would have closed by the time he reached Mitre Square but there is a definite impression that something was hampering his cutting hand. The first incision on Eddowes's throat is described as being 'merely superficial', while the second, like Stride's, petered out towards the end. To reiterate, 'The sheaf of the vessels on the right was just opened – the carotid artery had a fine hole opening. The internal jugular was opened an inch and a half – not divided.'[96]

Contrast this with Nichols's, Chapman's and Mary Kelly's throat wounds. Nichols's neck muscles were deeply divided on both sides. Chapman's throat was cut right the way around to the extent that she was almost beheaded. Kelly's neck tissues were severed 'all round down to the bone', suggesting another attempt at decapitation.[97]

Similarly, the incision in Eddowes's abdomen ran laboriously upwards in a grotesque zigzag pattern, as though the perpetrator had to keep pausing. The effect was three wounds going in different directions, each starting from the previous one.

Police attached sufficient weight to Coram and Drage's discovery for them to testify at Stride's inquest. Obviously, the horse forges a potential link with William Bury. I will also reveal at this point that he was almost certainly away from home that Sunday morning, possibly the whole day, because the term 'suspiciously' was to be applied to one of his nocturnal absences, and Sunday, remember, was the one day of the week on which he never drank.[98] The incident with the horse and the finding of the knife and handkerchief happened that evening. Did tiredness and lack of nourishment cause the animal to stumble and fall? Something did. Did Bury hastily divest himself of his bloodstained accoutrements because he thought he might be questioned? Well, somebody felt he had to get rid of them. Peter Sutcliffe did much the same thing on the night he was taken into custody.

But what of the evidence of his even bloodier deed the previous morning – the knife used to eviscerate Catharine Eddowes? Provided he had cleaned it, it by itself could be explained as a work tool. It was *two* knives, one of them bloodstained, that could have aroused suspicion.

We will never know for certain whether the knife in the doorway was the weapon used on Liz Stride, or whether her killer injured himself with it. But the police thought the first part of this scenario credible enough to place it before her inquest.

NOTES

1. 28 August 1888. Warren himself was then holidaying in France.
2. Bruce visited both the Bucks Row and Hanbury Street murder sites.
3. Warren's internal memo of 15 September speaks of its being sent to 'division'.
4. Internal memo, 15 September 1888.
5. Robert Keppel, *The Riverman* (hbk), p. 164.
6. Draft letter to the Home Secretary.
7. Interview with the *Pall Mall Gazette*, 24 March 1903.
8. John Douglas and Mark Olshaker, *The Cases that Haunt Us* (hbk), p. 56.
9. Robert Anderson, *The Lighter Side of my Official Life*.
10. *Issues*, 18 February and 28 September 1888; William Fishman, *East End 1888* (hbk), pp. 151 and 154.
11. The so-called 'Swanson Marginalia', a series of pencilled handwritten notes that appear in Swanson's copy of Anderson's memoirs, both in the margin and next to Anderson's comments about the Ripper's being a Polish Jew, and then later on an end paper. Discovered by Swanson's grandson, *circa* 1980, they have been verified as being in his handwriting.

12. *Pall Mall Gazette*, 24 and 31 March 1903.

13. Ibid., 31 March.

14. *Northern Daily Telegraph*, 7 December 1888.

15. William Smith, statement to Metropolitan Police, 14 February 1889.

16. *Times*, 11 September 1888

17. Ibid.

18. Ibid.

19. Ibid.

20. Ibid.

21. Ibid., 13 September.

22. Ibid.

23. Ibid., 20 September.

24. Also referred to as 'Durrell' or 'Darrell'.

25. *Times*, 20 September.

26. Ibid., 11 September.

27. Ibid., 14 September.

28. Professor Bernard Knight (ed.), *Simpson's Forensic Medicine*, 11th edn, p. 21.

29. *Times*, 14 September.

30. Cadosch, inquest testimony, *Times*, 20 September; Swanson, police report, 19 October; Davis, *Times*, 11 September 1888.

31. *Times*, 11 September 1888.

32. Ibid., 20 September.

33. Ibid., 4 September.

34. Ibid., 20 September; *Lancet*, 29 September.

35. *Weekly News*, 26 October 1929.

36. *Times*, 12 October 1888.

37. Dr Frederick Blackwell, evidence at Stride inquest, *Times*, 3 October, otherwise referred to as 'striped'.

38. The term 'Long Liz' was originally thought to refer to her height, but this is now thought to be wrong. It is generally accepted that the nickname derives from her surname, Longstride.

39. *Evening News*, 1 October 1888.

40. Ibid.

41. Ibid. Best and Gardner went to the mortuary on 30 September. Gardner also noted that Liz appeared to be smiling, and Dr Blackwell testified at the inquest that, when he examined her, 'the face was quite placid and the mouth was slightly open'.

42. *Times*, 3 October.

43. Ibid., 6 October.

44. *Evening News*, 4 October.

45. Matthew Packer, police statement, 4 October.

46. *Evening News*, 4 October.

47. *Times*, 6 October.

48. *Evening News*, 4 October.

49. Composited from Donald Swanson's résumé of the murder, 19 October 1888, and Smith's testimony at Stride inquest in *The Times*, 6 October 1888.

50. *Times*, 6 October.

51. Swanson, résumé, 19 October.

52. *Times*, 2 October.

53. Ibid., 11 October.

54. *The Secret Identity of Jack the Ripper*, television documentary, 1988.

55. 6 October 1888.

56. John Carey (ed.), *The Faber Book of Reportage*, p. 364.

57. *East London Observer*, 13 October; Phillip Sugden, *The Complete History of Jack the Ripper*, 1st edn (hbk), p. 249.

58. Sugden, op. cit., p. 238.

59. Whitechapel Infirmary records, 1887; Sugden, op. cit., pp. 236–7.

60. *Times*, 5 October.

61. Autopsy report given at Eddowes inquest, 4 October 1888.

62. *Times*, 5 October.

63. Report to Home Office, Inspector James McWilliam, City CID, 27 October 1888.

64. He was subsequently convicted of her attempted murder.

65. *Times*, 2 October.

66. Ibid., 3 October.

67. *Star*, 5 October 1888; Sugden, op. cit., p. 176.

68. *Times*, 12 October.

69. Ibid.

70. Lawende's description of the man was withheld at the inquest but given in Swanson's résumé of 19 October.

71. McWilliam's report to Home Office, 27 October 1888; *Times*, 12 October; report by Donald Swanson, 6 November.

72. *Times*, 12 October.

73. Ibid.

74. Sir Charles Warren, report to Home Secretary, 6 November 1888. Warren and Halse both gave the spelling 'Juwes', whereas Long simply wrote down 'Jews' but admitted that he may have got it wrong, because his inspector said it was spelled 'Jeuws'. There was also some dispute as to whether 'not' appeared before 'be' or the second 'the'.

75. *Times*, 12 October.

76. Warren, op. cit.

77. Walter Dew, *I Caught Crippen*, autobiography.

78. Sir Henry Smith, *From Constable to Commissioner*.

79. *Times*, 4 October.

80. Ibid.

81. Keppel, op. cit., p. 341.
82. *Times*, 24 October.
83. Report, 19 October.
84. Stephen White, police report, 4 October 1888.
85. *Times*, 5 October 1888.
86. Ibid.
87. Ibid., 12 October.
88. Sugden, op. cit., p. 245.
89. Inventory of Eddowes's possessions given by Inspector Collard to the inquest, 4 October 1888.
90. Ibid.
91. *Times*, 4 October.
92. Ibid., 6 October.
93. Ibid., 4 October.
94. Knight, op. cit., p. 38.
95. Keppel, op. cit., p. 270.
96. Dr Frederick Brown, inquest deposition, 4 October.
97. Nichols, *Times*, 3 September; Chapman, Ibid., 14 September; Dr Thomas Bond's preliminary examination of Kelly, 9 November.
98. *Weekly News*, 26 October 1929.

CHAPTER EIGHT

SELF-PORTRAIT IN BLOOD

The events of a traumatic weekend left London in a state of panic unparalleled since the Black Death – a 'red terror' as the *East London Advertiser* termed it. That name, however, failed to catch on because on 1 October William Henry Bury acquired the hauntingly eviscerating nickname that still resonates with us today: Jack the Ripper.

It *may* have begun with a letter dated 17 September 1888:

> Dear Boss
>
> So now they say *I am a Yid* when will they lern Dear Old Boss? You an me know the truth dont we. Lusk can look forever hell never find me but I am rite under his nose all the time. I watch them looking for me an it gives me fits *ha ha* I love my work an I shant stop till I get buckled *and even then* watch out for your old pal jacky. Catch me if you can
>
> Jack the Ripper.
>
> Sorry about the blood still messy from the last one. What a pretty necklace I gave her.

The 'Lusk' referred to was George Lusk, a builder and decorator who on 10 September had founded the Whitechapel Vigilance Committee, a citizen action group set up to try to catch the murderer.

This strange, seemingly blood-smeared missive was not made public till 1997, when Paul Feldman included it in his book *Jack the Ripper: The Final Chapter*. Prior to that, its existence was known only to a handful of Ripper experts. The letter's history is as strange as the document itself.

Since 1988, the original Scotland Yard and Home Office files on the Ripper, as opposed to microfilm reproductions, have been available to viewers only by special request and with an official of the Public Record Office present. This followed pilferage of documents during the 1970s and 1980s.

A man called Peter McClelland was having difficulty reading the microfilm copies and asked to see the originals. While going through the Home Office files, he came across the 17 September letter tucked away in an envelope. McClelland subsequently brought the missive to the attention of crime historian Don Rumbelow, author of *The Complete Jack the Ripper*.

Opinion is divided on whether the letter is a genuine contemporary document or a modern-day hoax. If the latter, then it arguably emanates from three 1888 missives, all in the public domain for many years. The first is the letter that did actually christen the murderer with his garish *nom de plume*. This is dated 25 September 1888. It was received by the Central News Agency on the 27th and passed on to Scotland Yard two days later. It reads as follows:

> Dear Boss,
>
> I keep on hearing the police have caught me but they wont fix me just yet. I have laughed when they look so clever and talk about being on the *right track*. That joke about Leather apron gave me real fits. I am down on

whores and I shant quit ripping them till I do get buckled. Grand work the last job was. I gave the lady no time to squeal. How can they catch me now. I love my work and want to start again. You will soon hear of me with my funny little games. I saved some of the proper *red* stuff in a ginger beer bottle over the last job to write with but it went thick like glue and I cant use it. Red ink is fit enough I hope *ha ha.* The next job I do I shall clip the ladys ears off and send to the police officers just for jolly wouldnt you. Keep this letter back till I do a bit more work then give it out straight. My knife's so nice and sharp I want to get to work right away if I get a chance.

Good luck.

Yours truly

Jack the Ripper

Dont mind me giving the trade name

A postscript reads: 'wasnt good enough to post this before I get all the red ink off my hands curse it. No luck yet. They say I'm a doctor now *ha ha*'.

The handwriting is markedly different from the 17 September letter, although the tone and tenor of both letters is very similar with shared expressions such as 'buckled', and the 'ha ha' underlined. But then one would expect this if the letter of the 17th is a modern-day hoax based on it.

The consensus is that the 25 September letter was itself a fake, written by an enterprising journalist to keep the pot boiling.

In 1998, I submitted a copy of William Bury's *original* marriage certificate to handwriting expert Sue Iremonger for analysis of Bury's signature (the only example of his handwriting then in my possession) against both letters. She replied as follows:

It is always preferable to compare like with like. By this I mean comparing a signature with another of the same name or, at least against another signature. Even taking into account the difficulties of not being able to compare like with like I have looked for any possible signs of common ownership and I am afraid I have not found any.

I know that you are particularly interested in the style of the capital letter 'B'. However, this is a particular style of 'B' that would have been used by the majority of writers at that time as it was the style taught in schools.

It is *possible* [Sue's emphasis] that the letter of 17th September is disguised, however, without more extensive handwriting samples of W H Bury it is difficult to make any judgement on this.

I would not, however, necessarily recommend taking this further as I would deem it unlikely to throw up any similarity.

This would certainly tend to exculpate William Bury as being the author of either missive. The Ripper profile prepared by the FBI states that the killer would shun publicity and not inject himself into the case, and, as previously stated, the majority view of the Ripper historians, myself included, is that *all* the Ripper correspondence was fake.

Perhaps more intriguing is the fact that the hoaxer who penned the 25 September letter unwittingly produced a very accurate pen portrait of William Bury. The letter appears to come from an uneducated man but at times the writer gives the game away, correctly putting apostrophes into 'knife's' and 'I'm'; Bury had received a good education for a man of his birth.

The phrase 'look so clever' is echoed in a remark Bury made later in the death cell. The writer says he is 'down on whores'; Bury had previously been injected with venereal disease. 'I shant quit ripping them till I do get buckled' reminds us that a horse has a saddle buckled on it, and a horse had been responsible for Bury's father being ripped up. 'Real fits': Bury's sister had died during epileptic convulsions. The word 'work' is used four times and 'job' twice; one of Bury's previous jobs was as a horsemeat butcher. He promises to 'clip the ladys ears off'; Bury did subsequently cut off part of Catharine Eddowes's right ear. Finally, the correspondent jokes about giving the trade name; apparently Jack the Ripper was a nickname sometimes given to horse slaughterers!

A hoaxer, yes, but a very prescient one for all that. He was probably a journalist who had covered the crimes. As he profiles the real killer so adroitly, it is fitting that our hoaxer should have also provided him with his nickname.

The letter was published in the newspapers on 1 October and immediately produced the second of the three documents from which the 17 September letter may be derived, a postcard posted on 1 October in which the writer, claiming to be the killer, refers to himself as 'Jacky'. So does the writer of the 17th letter. Here, too, there is no similarity between the handwriting.

The name Jack the Ripper caused an immediate sensation, quickly replacing the somewhat lacklustre 'Leather Apron' to become the symbol of silent butchery in the night the world over. London, however, needed terrifying imagery like a hole in the head. The Ripper scare itself had already claimed one victim, a Mrs Mary Burridge, who died of heart failure after reading an editorial in the *Star* that proclaimed the murderer to be 'a nameless reprobate, half beast, half man . . . a pawnee Indian simply drunk with blood and he will have more'.

A letter to the *Daily Telegraph* gives some idea of how the Ripper seemed to take London over that autumn: 'Can nothing be done to prevent a set of hoarse ruffians coming nightly about our suburban squares and streets yelling at the top of their hideous voices: "Whitechapel! Murder!"'

Robert Anderson, about to be recalled to arms by the angry sentinels of the press, later wrote of the furore he found on his return: 'When the staid English go in for a scare they take leave of all moderation and common-sense . . . the nonsense that was talked and written about these murders would sink a dreadnought.'[1]

Staid people may have been panicking but others found the murders a ghoulish outlet for sick fantasies. As the autumn of fear wore on, so the police found themselves deluged by imitators of the 25 September letter. The sickest was the individual – possibly in the plural – who wrote to George Lusk enclosing what was claimed to be the missing Eddowes kidney. This constitutes the third of the missives that could have inspired the 17 September letter. Beginning 'From Hell', it ends with a near-identical signing-off phrase: 'Catch me when you can'. The kidney was human, but there are no grounds for thinking it was Eddowes's. The handwriting, again, matches none of the others.

The police, under immense pressure, which, as we have seen, included Queen Victoria, also found themselves dealing with an imitation murder, in County Durham of all places.

Jane Beetmore was 28 and considered 'flighty', whatever that meant in Victorian England. On the evening of Saturday, 22 September, she set out for a pub called the Oxclose at Birtley in Durham. She never reached it and her body was found next to a railway line the following morning, just 200 yards (183 metres) from her home. She had been stabbed three times, once through the right cheek, once behind the left ear running down to her spinal cord, and finally in the lower abdomen, the death wound, which left her entrails protruding.[2]

The apparent similarity to the murders of Polly Nichols and Annie Chapman caused a panic among local people. On 24 September, Inspector J Roots of Scotland Yard accompanied our old friend Dr Bagster Phillips up to Birtley, where they viewed the body and announced that Beetmore was not a victim of the East London murderer. Subsequently, a man named William Waddell, who seems to have been a suitor of Beetmore's (he actually claimed to be her husband), was convicted and hanged a week before Christmas. He may have attempted to imitate the Ripper in a crude attempt to avert suspicion, but it is one of many unexplained factors in the case, and there is a faint, lingering doubt about his guilt. There is no doubt, however, about the man who put Waddell to death, and, not many months hence, William Bury would be making executioner James Berry's acquaintance too. When Berry hanged Waddell, he executed a man believed to be a Ripper imitator; he would take a diametrically opposite view about William Bury.

The importance of the Beetmore case is that the Metropolitan Police had wasted time and money on what had turned out to be a fool's errand. As the police files make clear, they had enough false leads in London to occupy them without traipsing round the countryside after them as well. This was to have an important bearing on their attitude towards William Bury.

There was also the continuing problem of their belief that the man they were looking for was a Polish Jew. In a sense, every time an English, non-Jewish suspect proved to be either quite innocent or a harmless loony, it reinforced this view. There was the misogynist sometime publican William Piggott, who was visited by delirium tremens, not homicidal mania;[3] Billy Bull, so drunk he would probably have confessed to being Jack the Ripper, Spring-Heeled Jack and Sweeney Todd all rolled into one;[4] another, probably tipsy, fantasist called John Davidson, who confessed in order to bum a free meal out of a temperance devotee;[5] John Lock, whose paint-smeared jacket was mistaken for blood;[6] and yet another John, surname Langan, down and out in London and Boulogne, who excited the attention of the British Consul there because he resembled a newspaper sketch of Matthew Packer's customer.[7] Lastly, the pick of the bunch, an army general named Brown, whose nefarious racetrack activities so upset a rather sensitively inclined lady that she thought him capable of operating on fast women as well as fast horses.[8] Interestingly, this came to the police's attention through a communication retrieved from the Post Office's dead-letter file.[9] By a quirk of fate, this was how Peter Kurten, Düsseldorf's version of the Ripper, was apprehended in Germany 40 years later. Kurten was a disciple of the London Ripper but, alas, the Düsseldorf Police's London counterparts were not as fortunate with their multicide.

It was almost a freak show in a circus tent, and obviously no discouragement to the literary 'Jacks' from joining in what they perceived to be fun. The *Bradford Daily Telegraph* records that 21-year-old Maria Coroner, described as 'a pleasant-looking girl of good figure . . . never appeared to regard the proceedings with any gravity but frequently smiled' as she was bound over by Bradford Magistrates for sending two letters signed 'J. Ripper'.

Into this wretched little whirlpool of caricatures strode Robert Anderson on 5 October, summoned back from holiday and demanding to know why the killer had not been laid by the heels during his absence. He spent the next 36 hours closeted with his senior detectives 'reinvestigating the whole case' (his words). Now of course we cannot be flies on the wall at those conferences, and if we were then we would be very old flies indeed, but there can be no doubt that the belief that the murderer was a Polish Jew was anointed with holy oil. That term is not out of place when discussing Robert Anderson. Even by the standards of the 1800s, he was a religious zealot, with a belief in literal concepts of good and evil, which found expression in the stern way he regarded the sad little women who had fallen under Bury's knife.

At a subsequent meeting with Commissioner Warren and Home Secretary Matthews he professed to be astonished at the 'wholly indefensible and scandalous measures I found in operation; for these wretched women were plying their trade under definite police protection'(!). He urged that known prostitutes abroad in the area after midnight be either locked up or warned that the police would not protect them.[10] One can well imagine Warren and Matthews shifting uneasily in their seats at this pearl of wisdom. It was in fact a variation on the infamous Contagious Diseases Act (1864), happily repealed by 1888, in which women out alone after 9pm within a three-mile radius of a military barracks could be arrested and forcibly examined for venereal disease upon a magistrate's order. Anderson would certainly have needed little persuasion, if any at all, that nobody of the Christian religion could harbour within his soul the murderer's 'unmentionable vices'[11]. Anderson could be flexible and innovative, as he showed when bringing in outside assistance, but on the other hand his moral beliefs tended to reflect the obstinate side of his nature and had a tendency to get in the way during this investigation.

Back in Bow, William Bury felt no elation at the mayhem he was causing. Bury was the sort of killer who shrinks from his own infancy. As with the population on whom he preyed, the overriding emotion he felt was fear. And remorse. Not for his victims, though, but himself. The victim, as Dennis Nilsen chillingly reminds us, is the dirty platter after the feast. When the mother of one of John Wayne Gacy's 33 victims exclaimed that he should be executed 33 times over, Gacy sneeringly advised her to take 33 Valiums. William Bury's anguish was for the turmoil *he* was enduring.[12]

His fear now extended to his appearance. Even allowing for the vagaries of eyewitness identification, he had good reason to be concerned. Too many people had seen a William Bury clean-shaven but for his moustache in Berner and Duke Streets; PC Smith, and with less certainly William Marshall, had made a point about his having no whiskers. If Bury did encounter Matthew Packer again at the end of October, it would have given him even greater impetus to change the way he looked. The William Bury who turned up three months later in Dundee sported a beard and side whiskers to go with the moustache.

The end of the first week of October came and went without incident. So did the end of the month. Once again, if Packer did see him it would have reinforced the existing dread of recognition. This has to be coupled with another major factor: a fog that shrouded London during much of these weeks. In one sense this lessened the chances that somebody would recognise him late at night, but this was not a significant enough factor to offset the fog's greatest drawback.

He had a working knowledge of the maze of streets, alleys and courts that made up Whitechapel and Spitalfields, but was not confident of finding his way around in the dense mist that now hung like a cloak over the East End. This should have led Scotland Yard to an important conclusion: the killer was not a native of the area. But it didn't, so the man they were seeking remained safe in his lair, the twin terrors of recognition and the fog holding in check the demons inside him. For the moment.

In October, Bury committed his worst attack on Ellen yet – at 6am on a Wednesday morning, he knocked at Margaret Corney's door saying that his wife was very unwell. When Margaret went round to see her, she discovered that Ellen was

> very ill in bed. She [Ellen] said that her illness was on account of his ill treatment of her on the Monday before; he came home and struck her on the nose and on the mouth [which] was very much swelled. I saw there was blood in the passage where he had struck her.[13]

It was either on this occasion, or one very close to it, that Ellen confided to her sister that Bury slept with a knife under his pillow.

William Smith confirms the brutal treatment Ellen was enduring at her husband's hands: 'He frequently assaulted his wife and on one occasion about three months ago I heard her screaming and had to interfere to prevent him further assaulting her.'[14]

This may have been 8 September, when, on returning home after killing Annie Chapman, Bury behaved like a 'madman', but it could equally have been the same assault described by Margaret. No firm date is given for the latter, except that it was in October. It may actually have been on Monday, 1 October, if that was the day Bury returned home after the double murder, which in turn could link with PC Drage's encounter. But this is all sand shifting around the rock, the assault itself. Something made Bury explode even more violently than usual against his wife. Fear engendered by a near miss with the law? Frustration? Whatever the cause, it is another building block in the case against him.

Another question: how much by now did Ellen suspect? The brutality, the knife, the absences at the times of the murders – all of these must have been beginning to add up. She would have tried to thrust them away, telling herself not to be silly. But they kept coming back. *Somebody* had to be Jack the Ripper.

Mary Jane Kelly. Or so she was called. one hundred and twenty years of protracted research has not brought historians any closer to her real identity.

This is how Mary's partner, Joe Barnett, describes what Mary told him about herself:

> She was born in Limerick – she was 25 years of age – and from there went to Wales when very young. She came to London about 4 years ago. Her Father's name was John Kelly. He was a gauger (or foreman) at some iron works in Carmarthen or Carnarvonshire. She had one sister, who was a traveller with materials from market place to market

place. She also said she had 6 brothers at home and one in the army, one was Henry Kelly, serving in 2nd Battn, Scots Guards, and known among his comrades as Johnto, and I believe the regiment is now in Ireland. I never spoke to any of them. She told me she had been married when very young in Wales. She was married to a collier named Davis or Davies, I think Davies. She was lawfully married to him till he died in an explosion. She lived with him 2 or 3 years up to his death . . . she was married at the age of 16 years she first went to Cardiff after her husband's death and was in an infirmary there 8 or 9 months and followed a bad life with a cousin while in Cardiff. She came to London [and] was first in a gay house in the West End. A gentleman there asked her to go to France. She did not like the part [and] did not stay there long, about a fortnight. She did not like it and returned. She came back and lived in Ratcliffe Highway for some time, she did not tell me how long. Then she was living near Stepney gas works. Morganstone was the man she lived with there . . . in Pennington Street she lived with a Morganstone, and with Joseph Fleming, she was very fond of him. He was a Mason's plasterer. He lived in Bethnal Green Road. Fleming used to visit her. I picked up with her in Commercial Street.[15]

None of this can be verified prior to the mid–1880s. Some very able researchers have spent years attempting to piece together Mary's life history before she arrived in the East End of London, entirely without success. The reason may be fiendishly simple: all she needed to do was change her name to 'Kelly' and we are left chasing shadows. Some of the actual details of a very mundane family background are probably true. The brother in the Scots Guards, however, is doubtful. Barnett originally gave the details about 'Johnto' in his statement to the police on 9 November; there is no mention of him in his inquest testimony three days later because police enquiries with the Scots Guards had failed to throw up a 'Henry Kelly'.[16] There is evidence, from Mary's landlord, John McCarthy, of her receiving letters from Ireland, and, according to one newspaper report, the mysterious brother had been known to visit her in the East End, although whether this was a guise for a clandestine meeting with Joseph Fleming is another matter.

In all probability, the story of her husband's being killed in a mining accident was also a piece of fiction to account for her descent into prostitution. Research has not yielded any record of either the marriage or the accident. Or perhaps – two words that seem to prefix almost every statement you can make about Mary Kelly's antecedents – they happened but under a different name.

Popular history, particularly the celluloid version of it, traditionally portrays her as being a vivaciously attractive young woman. Here again, the evidence is conflicting. The *Daily Telegraph*, ostensibly quoting Kelly's landlord John McCarthy, calls her 'tall, slim, fair; of fresh complexion and attractive appearance', as does *The Times*, albeit in slightly different terms.[17] Mary's neighbour, Elizabeth Prater, agreed with McCarthy: 'tall and pretty and as fair as a lily'.[18] But others tended to qualify their judgements somewhat. Walter Dew says simply that she was 'quite attractive',[19] while Elizabeth Phoenix, sister of a previous landlady, endorsed McCarthy's and Prater's comments about Mary's height, giving it as 5ft 7in (1.7 metre), but told the *Star* (12 November) that she was 'rather stout'. The rest of Phoenix's description – 'blue eyes and a very fine head of hair which reached nearly to her waist' – also contained a sting, or rather a bite, in the tail: 'two false teeth which projected very much from the lips'. Maurice Lewis, whom we will meet again, is quoted in the *Illustrated Police News* (17 November) as saying that Kelly was 'short, stout and dark and about 5ft 3 inches' (1.3 metre). Finally, we hear from

Caroline Maxwell, another witness who crops up again: 'a pleasant little woman, rather stout, fair complexion and rather pale'. Different eyes, and in Caroline Maxwell's case perhaps slightly condescending ones.[20] Mary apparently enjoyed the nicknames of 'Fair Emma' and 'Ginger' among her friends. 'Ginger' may have been an allusion to her fondness for ginger beer, nine empty bottles of which were later found in her room.

Kelly's own preferred name was 'Marie Jeanette', at least according to Barnett. None of her friends mentioned this sobriquet, which is supposed to have emanated from a brief stay in France. Barnett appears to have been the only one who used it, claiming that Mary returned to London because she did not like what she had to do there. The story is, however, supported by Elizabeth Phoenix's sister, a Mrs Carthy, whom Mary lodged with in Pennington Street, just off John Williams's stamping ground of the Ratcliffe Highway (see Chapter 1). Kelly allegedly told Carthy that she had made a number of trips to France before taking up residence in the East End with a Mrs Buki, also near the Ratcliffe Highway. Buki, said Mary, had accompanied her to Knightsbridge in West London, where she retrieved some expensive clothes from a French woman in a house.

This is all highly anecdotal and we are asked to believe that, in one fell swoop, Mary descended from France and the West End to the surroundings of the most squalid, crime-ridden street in London, truly a fall of quite spectacular dimensions. We must be very careful of taking it on trust: Carthy never appeared at the inquest and her story was printed in only one newspaper, the not overly reliable *Star*, on 12 November 1888. There was never any confirmation of it, even from Buki. But it does broadly slot in with Barnett's recollections and he confirmed that Mary had stayed at Carthy's, describing it as 'a bad house', i.e. brothel. There was, in the second half of the 19th century, a flourishing cross-Channel trade in girls bound for the brothels of France and Belgium, and it is feasible that Mary was either taken to

France to work in one, or assisted in escorting other girls there. There were complaints of girls being drugged or intimidated into going, which may explain why Mary found it onerous and put as much distance between herself and the procurers as possible. It would also make sense of a remark made by Barnett at the inquest that she 'seemed afraid of someone'.

Exactly how long Mary stayed with Carthy is difficult to gauge. Carthy described her as a terror in drink but very likeable when sober and good at drawing. Back to Barnett: Mary left Pennington Street to live with a man called Morganstone 'near Stepney gas works'. Ripper historians Stewart Evans and Nick Connell have tracked down two brothers of Dutch origin named Morgenstern whose occupations are listed in the 1881 Census as 'gas workers'. They were then living in Fulham but moved sometime after that.[21]

The evidence for Mary's next boyfriend is likewise anecdotal, but seems reliable enough. He was Joseph Fleming, a plasterer who lived in Bethnal Green Road. Mark King, an indefatigable researcher into the Ripper murders, has traced a man by this name who died in an insane asylum in 1920, aged 60 or 61. Carthy adds weight to the relationship, stating that Mary went to live with a man in the building trade who she (Carthy) thought would marry her. Unfortunately they split, but, according to Barnett, Fleming was still involved with her after he and Mary took up together. A friend of Mary's, Julia Venturney, bears this out: 'She told me she was very fond of another man named Joe, and he had often ill used her because she cohabited with Barnett.' Venturney later spoke of a Joe who visited Mary and gave her money, adding that she (Venturney) thought that he was a costermonger. One assumes that Venturney was referring to the same man on both occasions and that this was Barnett's Joseph Fleming, despite the different occupations.[22] But we cannot, of course, be 100 per cent certain. From the assumption, we may deduce that Mary and Fleming's relationship was one of 'can't live with each other; can't live without each other', a dilemma that William Bury was to resolve, homicidally, for them.

Finally, to Barnett himself. Mary picked him up in Commercial Street on Good Friday 1887. They had a drink together, presumably followed by sex, and the following day decided to give living together a chance. Possibly they were drawn together by mutual sympathy: Barnett suffered from echolalia, a condition in which the sufferer repeats the last few words spoken to him, while Caroline Maxwell said that Mary herself had a speech impediment.[23]

Their relationship was to last for the next 18 months. Barnett was a fish porter employed at Billingsgate Market. His porter's licence described him as 5ft 7in (1.7 metre) tall with fair hair and blue eyes. Although he was working for most of this time, the couple flitted from address to address generally leaving without paying the rent.

Early in 1888, they set up their final home together, 13 Miller's Court, a 12-by-10-foot (3.5-by-3-metre) room in a cul-de-sac off Dorset Street in Spitalfields. Dorset Street, now a multistorey car park, also had an unenviable reputation, which means that Mary had not progressed very far from Ratcliffe Highway. In 1888, it was home to a plethora of lodging houses totalling an estimated 600 beds. One of them, number 35, called Crossinghams, was opposite Miller's Court, and Annie Chapman had lived there up to her death.

Dorset Street was a very short thoroughfare running east–west from Commercial Street to Crispin Street. To give some idea of the area's wretchedness and squalor, Crispin Street carried on into Bell Lane, which by 1888 had been officially declared as unfit for human habitation for the past 11 years!

Miller's Court was situated on the north side of Dorset Street. The Court's western corner housed a grocer's shop owned by John McCarthy, landlord of the properties in the Court. McCarthy has a tiny claim to fame as the great-grandfather of Kay Kendall, star of the 1950s film *Genevieve*.

Continuing down the west side of the Court were four tenements, mainly occupied by prostitutes. Coming back the other way, on the opposite side, were three more dwellings, followed by an aperture with a communal tap, and then, obliquely opposite McCarthy's shop, number 13, which had previously been the back parlour of 27 Dorset Street and was now partitioned off from it. In the room above, 20 Miller's Court, lived Mrs Elizabeth Prater, separated from her husband and without doubt earning her living from prostitution.

Mary Kelly had built up a circle of friends in and around Miller's Court. She was clearly well liked. So what if she did get roaring from time to time and was a bit free with her language? She was always ready with her 'sorrys' and looking for a forgiving hug the following morning. The impression that comes down to us is of a gregarious person with a certain style about her. Even McCarthy seems to have felt this: as autumn arrived she drifted into arrears with the rent but he made no move to evict her. Barnett had lost his porter's licence in July and could no longer work at Billingsgate. Author Bruce Paley, the main authority on him, surmises that it was withdrawn for theft. It took Joe till 1906 to get it back.[24]

Mary was forced to return to the streets, a life she clearly despised. Towards the end of October she allowed a prostitute friend to sleep at number 13.[25] The resultant row with Barnett led to a window being broken and his moving out to a lodging house in Bishopsgate. Mary's philanthropy may have had the additional motive of easing Barnett out of the picture. She confided to Julia Venturney that she could no longer bear him,[26] and it is fairly certain that she still had feelings for Joe Fleming.

Even so, Barnett was not giving up without a fight. He continued to visit Mary, giving her small sums of money when he could afford to. He popped into Miller's Court on the evening of Thursday, 8 November, and found Mary with 'a female friend'.[27] There is some dispute over who this was. Twenty-year-old Lizzie Albrook told the press it was her, but at the inquest another friend, Maria Harvey, laid claim to being Mary's companion. Perhaps everybody wanted to be in on the death of Mary Kelly. One would dismiss it anyway as the minutiae of murder but for the poignancy with which Albrook endows their final conversation.[28] As she prepared for another soul-destroying night of selling herself – the rent was due tomorrow and she was six weeks behind – Mary advised her young friend to steer clear of the arid path she was about to tread.[29] The events of the forthcoming hours would bring that warning home in the most terrible manner possible.

Mary's movements during the remainder of that evening are best described as shadowy. At one point she seems to have stopped for a brief chat with Elizabeth Prater, although the latter makes no reference to it in either her police statement or inquest testimony.[30] *The Times* of 10 November observes her twice in Commercial Street, the first time at 10pm accompanied by a man, then on her own at 11.30. No sources are given. But, in between, the picture is very confusing indeed. According to some newspapers, on the 10th, an unnamed woman told the Press Association that *circa* 10.30 she had encountered a clearly depressed Mary who spoke of suicide before going off with a respectably attired man. But from the rest of the report it appears likely that the source was confusing Mary with another of the local 'daughters of joy', one Lizzie Fisher. Issue clarified, or rather not, because two days later the clouds reappear in the shape of a woman referred to only as 'Margaret', who approached the Press Association with a similar story of Kelly talking about doing away with herself and then attending to business with a shabbily dressed client. Make of all this what you will.[31]

The scene now shifts indoors. There were pubs at both ends of Dorset Street: the Britannia on the corner with Commercial Street and the Horn of Plenty at the juncture with Crispin Street. A report that appeared in the *Star* on 10 November says Daniel Barnett, brother of Joe, also met up with Kelly that evening. This is corroborated by Maurice Lewis, a tailor living in Dorset Street, who claimed acquaintanceship with Mary going back five years. Lewis spoke of seeing her in the Horn of Plenty with 'Dan' and 'Julia'. The latter was not Venturney, who said that she retired to bed at 9 that night, but it may have been the prostitute whom Kelly had put up in Miller's Court in October. Lewis said that Mary left with a respectably dressed man.[32]

At around the same time, 11pm, Mary pops up at the other end of Dorset Street in the Britannia with a man described as young, respectable, well dressed and sporting a black moustache. However, this sounds suspiciously like a man she was allegedly seen with on the night of the 7th, so whether the report is a mistake, whether it was the man she left the Horn with or whether it was another new client altogether is lost in the bewildering hall of mirrors that was Mary Kelly's last night on earth. Since we know neither her real name nor what she really looked like, one has to say that it is in keeping with the rest of her short life.[33]

Walking the little cluster of streets, she was never too far from home, or the welcoming glow of the pub and a drink to take the edge off the nip in the air, because cold weather had now set in chasing the fog away. But that also meant that the Ripper was out of his lair, and, as *The Times* perceptively noted two days later, 'There is also . . . a striking similarity in the period of the month in which the crime has been committed.'

Mary had clearly fortified herself with several winter warmers. Mary Ann Cox, herself a prostitute living at 5 Miller's Court, described her as 'very drunk' and attired in a red knitted shawl when she saw Kelly take a client into number 13 between 11.45 and midnight. Unlike the previous sightings, Cox gave her testimony at the inquest. The client she described as 5ft 5in (1.6 metre), stout and shabbily dressed in a black billycock hat and a dark, longish coat. He was about 36 with a fresh complexion, carroty moustache, small side whiskers and no beard, but the main points that registered with Cox were his blotchy face and the fact that he was carrying a beer pail. After Mary and he had gone into number 13, Cox heard her singing, 'A violet I plucked from my mother's grave'. Cox went in and out again, before returning home a second time at 1am. Mary was still singing, much to the annoyance of one of her friends, Catherine Picket, who lived further down the Court. Cox, who plainly had not prospered that night, again went out shortly after 1am, before finally calling it a day at 3. By now, Mary had stopped singing. Cox lay down on her bed fully clothed but was unable to sleep. She heard men going in and out of the Court, including one at 5.45.

The next sighting has divided Ripperologists for years as to its veracity. George Hutchinson was a 28-year-old unemployed labourer living at a lodging house in Commercial Street. At 2am he was accosted by Mary, whom he claims to have known, in Commercial Street. Having no money, he had to disappoint her. He then saw her get picked up by a man near Thrawl Street. Hutchinson heard some of their conversation. Mary said, 'All right,' and the man replied, 'You will be all right for what I have told you.' They walked past him together and he and the man exchanged looks. Hutchinson followed them to Miller's Court, where Mary and her client stood on the corner talking. She told the man, 'Come along, you will be comfortable,' and then complained that she had lost her handkerchief. He produced a red one and gave it to her. They kissed and then went into the Court. Hutchinson stood outside for about three-quarters of an hour and then went off.

Hutchinson provided a very full description of the client – too full for most people's liking. He rounded it off by saying the man was of 'Jewish appearance'.[34]

The first problem with Hutchinson is that he didn't come forward till the evening of 12 November, *after* the inquest had been concluded.

This does not by any means invalidate him as a reliable witness, no more than it should Maurice Lewis, who likewise never gave evidence at the inquest. But it may be significant that Hutchinson provided his statement only after another witness, Sarah Lewis, told the coroner of seeing a man standing outside Crossinghams at 2.30am.

Hutchinson's statement was submitted to Abberline, who interviewed him the same evening and announced: 'I am of [the] opinion his statement is true.'[35] Possibly the *basics* are, but this leads on to the main objection to Hutchinson's credibility. His description of the man he saw is so detailed – even down to white buttons on his boots – that no one can really take it seriously.

In all probability Hutchinson was the man outside the lodging house, and upon hearing at the inquest that he had been noticed went to the police with an embellished version of what he had seen in order to avoid suspicion falling on himself. Ironically, it has had the opposite effect in recent years.[36]

The middle of the night is not the best time to have a row with your husband but Sarah Lewis (no relation to Maurice Lewis) managed it in the early hours of 8 November. She stormed out of their home in Great Pearl Street and walked round to Miller's Court to stay the night with a couple named Keyler, who lived at number 2, the first-floor room opposite number 13. En route she passed Crossinghams and noticed a man, Hutchinson, standing outside 'looking up the Court as if waiting for some one to come out'. It was a somewhat fraught journey for Mrs Lewis, who also claimed at the inquest to have passed a man in Commercial Street who had accosted her in a rather frightening manner two days earlier.

Lewis reached the Keylers' home at 2.30am and passed the rest of the night sitting in a chair. Shortly before 4am, she heard a woman scream 'murder' once, loudly. The sound seemed to come from across the Court. She took no notice of it then, but she did later that morning.[37]

The same scream was heard by Elizabeth Prater in the room directly above Kelly's. Prater had been woken by a kitten just beforehand. The cry was in a 'faint voice'. She then went back to sleep.[38] Eight o'clock and daylight. Catherine Picket knocked at the door of number 13. There was no answer; Picket went away.[39]

Also around 8am, Maurice Lewis saw Mary come out and go back.[40]

Caroline Maxwell was the wife of Henry Maxwell, the lodging-house deputy at 14 Dorset Street. That morning, at 8.30, she came across Mary on the corner of Miller's Court. Maxwell was not an intimate of Kelly's – they had spoken together only twice before – but she asked, 'What brings you up so early?' Mary replied that she had the 'horrors of drink' on her: 'I have been drinking for some days past.' Maxwell suggested she go to the Britannia for a half-pint of beer. Pointing to some vomit on the pavement, Mary said, 'I have, and brought it all up again.' Maxwell left her with the comment that she pitied her feelings. But she was not through with seeing Mary that morning. At around 9, Maxwell was returning from buying milk in Bishopsgate when she saw Kelly outside the Britannia in conversation with 'not a tall man – about 5ft 5in (1.6 metre), aged about 30, stout, dressed like a market porter in dark clothes and a sort of plaid coat'. Kelly was wearing a maroon shawl. Maxwell added in a newspaper interview that the man was 'dark'.[41]

A report in *The Times* on 12 November backs Maxwell up. An unidentified woman – she is described merely as 'young', although the newspaper adds somewhat cryptically that her name 'is known' – told them that she too had seen Mary Kelly between 8 and 8.45 on the morning of the 9th and that she had informed the police of it.

We move on an hour, to 10 o'clock, at the Britannia, and three more sightings of Mary. One has her drinking with Barnett at around this time, a second talking to a man half an hour later, and the third involves Maurice Lewis again, who says that she appeared to be in company with a group of people.[42] There are problems with all three statements. Barnett makes no mention of such an encounter, Mary was certainly dead by 10.30, and, as Lewis makes no claim of seeing her twice that morning, we must assume that this was an amplification of his previous sighting. But these difficulties pale into insignificance beside the one they posed for the authorities: according to them, by 10am, Mary Kelly had been dead for at least six hours!

Tom Bowyer was John McCarthy's rent collector. That morning he had specific instructions to get some money out of Kelly. He knocked on the door of number 13. No answer, so he stepped round to the side window. Two of the panes had been broken during Barnett and Kelly's last row, on 30 October, and an old coat was hung across them to prevent a draft blowing in. Bowyer pulled it aside and peered into the dingy little room. The thing that hit him most was the blood.

Lying on the bed was what appeared to be a butchered animal. They were the remains of Mary Jane Kelly. Her face no longer existed. The nose, ears, eyebrows and cheeks had been largely slashed off and lay in a sickening little pile next to her head. The rest of her face had been cut to pieces, the lips virtually torn off. Only the eyes, two terrified orbs in a ruined head, remained undamaged.

Mary's throat had been cut right the way through to the spinal column. Below that the injuries almost defy coherent description. Both breasts had been cut off, one placed by her right foot, the other under her head, where it had been joined by the uterus and both kidneys, a dreadful butcher's display of bloody organs. Her liver lay between her feet and her spleen by her left side. On the other side of the body were her intestines. Part of her right lung had been hacked through, her heart removed in its entirety and seemingly taken away. Next to the body on a bedside table, congealing in their own blood, were the flaps from her abdomen and thighs.

The nightmare was unrelenting. The police photograph makes it appear that she is wearing britches. In fact, the thighs have been stripped of skin, the right torn away to the bone, partially damaging the buttock. The left was savaged down to the knee and the calf gashed through to the deep muscles, the wound extending downwards to 5 inches (12.7cm) above the ankle.

Not even her arms had been spared, as several deep gashes testified. Abrasions on the back of Mary's right hand and a lacerated thumb bore mute evidence of a struggle, but it must have been pitifully brief.

In this instance, the throat had been cut from right to left; Kelly's bed was almost hard against the wall on her right, leaving no room for her killer to operate on that side. Judging from the defence wounds, she was alive and conscious before the knife cut through her carotid artery. Blood splashes on the wall by her head suggested blood had spurted; it could have winged its way off the weapon but the positioning makes spurting more likely. The injury had bled profusely on that side, saturating the pillow, sheet and bedspread in the top right-hand corner.

After death, said Bagster Phillips at the inquest, the body had been pulled 'two thirds' over the left side of the bed, although Dr Bond said 'the middle' in his examination notes. It was then that the mutilations were made.

As with Stride, one of Mary's hands, the left, had been placed on what remained of her stomach. Why Bury did this with some victims – Chapman's left hand was placed on her breast – and not others, since Nichols's and Eddowes's arms were by their sides, is a puzzle. Even more interesting is the position of Mary's head, which had been turned to the left.

Robert Keppel views the positioning of the face as a 'hallmark' of this type of murderer. Once his anger has cooled the killer will try to keep the victim's countenance away from him. In death she has become his accuser, her eyes reproaching him, and he cannot meet her gaze because, for a while, he feels ashamed of what he has done to her.

Polly Nichols was left staring up at the sky but, as his crimes progressed, Bury began to leave their heads turned to one side. Chapman's was to the right, which indicates that, although he cut her throat from the right side, he ended up on her left, a point possibly substantiated by her left arm being placed on her breast. Stride's and Eddowes's heads were both turned to the left, like Mary Kelly's, but in those cases their faces – their accusing eyes – were away from him. Mary's, on the other hand, confronted him, at least at some point. In all probability he mutilated her face and upper body from the left and the lower part from the front. It is certain that, when he put the various skin flaps on the bedside table and placed the organs under her head, Mary would have been looking right up at him. She would likewise have appeared to be observing his leaving, a point Keppel regards as a no-no: 'He will not walk away with her facing him . . . some killers have even placed plastic bags or pillows over the head so the victim cannot watch him walk out.'[43]

One would have thought that Bury would have turned her head to the right, facing the wall like Stride. It is as though he wants her to see him going about the business of dismantling her and then walking out of the door. This impression is heightened by the fact that her eyes were the only uninjured part of her head. It has been argued that he enjoyed the look of terror in them, and perhaps up to a point he did. But, as Keppel observes, from the vantage point of many similar investigations, this should not have lasted. However, it did. Why? The answer that suggests itself is that William Bury knew Mary Kelly and, unbeknown to her, harboured some sort of grudge against her.[44]

Most accounts have Tom Bowyer stumbling into John McCarthy's premises in a state of near collapse. In fact, Bowyer was an ex-soldier and veteran of India, and he walked quietly into the shop and told the landlord what he had seen. McCarthy went to see it for himself: 'The whole scene is more than I can possibly describe,' he later told the press with feeling, but he followed Bowyer to Commercial Street Police Station calmly enough. Inspector Walter Beck returned with them, accompanied, according to his own account, by Walter Dew. Beck, said Dew, looked through the window and immediately drew back, saying, 'For God's sake Dew, don't look'. Inevitably, Dew did look; what he saw would remain with him as a harrowing memory for the rest of his life.[45]

The police sealed off both ends of Dorset Street and refused to allow the inhabitants of Miller's Court to leave their houses till gone 5pm. Unfortunately, the proceedings were tinged with farce. In October, the police had tried out bloodhounds as a means of tracking the murderer when he struck again. They were found to be unsuitable for use in the densely packed streets of London and returned to their owner. However, nobody had told Abberline and his men, who now waited outside number 13 for the dogs to arrive. Not till Superintendent Arnold turned up at 1.30 did they make preparations to enter the room, McCarthy breaking the door down with a pickaxe, an unnecessary exercise because it could be opened by the simple expedient of putting a hand through the window and operating the latch (the door had a spring lock and the key had been missing for some time). Even then it was still another 30 minutes before anybody went into number 13, possibly because the police were waiting for Anderson to arrive, which he did at 1.50.

There were almost as many medical men as detectives: the omnipresent Bagster Phillips and his assistant, Dr Brown, representing the City; a police surgeon named William Dukes, who had been alerted by Beck and was first on the scene; Anderson's star turn Dr Bond; and Dr John Gabe, a gynaecologist presumably called in because of his expertise with female reproductive organs. Whatever report Gabe made is one of the legion of documents presently missing. That, happily, is not the case with Bond's findings. He was then an assistant surgeon at Westminster Hospital and police surgeon to that district's 'A' division. Bond's CV included service with the Prussian Army in 1866, which suggests that he helped tend the wounded at the battle of Sadowa during the Austro-Prussian war.[46] In practice, though not in theory, Bond was superseding Bagster Phillips.

At 2pm, he commenced a preliminary examination of Kelly's remains. This took two hours, after which the corpse was removed to Shoreditch Mortuary, where it basically had to be reassembled in human form for the formal autopsy the following morning. Bagster Phillips later said that the whole operation took six and a half hours.[47] On Saturday afternoon, he returned to 13 Miller's Court along with the coroner, Dr Roderick Macdonald, and they sifted through the ashes of a fire that had burned in the grate at some point during the night of the 8th/9th. Precisely when it burned out has always been a matter of speculation – we have no way of knowing exactly – but Bagster Phillips implies that it was no longer alight when he arrived at 11.15 on the morning of the 9th.[48] Exactly what Phillips and Macdonald were looking for that Saturday afternoon has never been divulged, but the likelihood is that they thought that the killer may have thrown the dead woman's heart on the fire.

Bond did not attend the inquest on Monday, 12 November. Here, Bagster Phillips was allowed to give the cause of death only, technically a breach of the statute governing inquests, but a good decision under the circumstances. The reason for this was given, obliquely, by Macdonald during his summing up: 'There is other evidence which I do not propose to call, for if we at once make public every fact brought forward in connection with this terrible murder, the ends of justice might be retarded.'

The 'other evidence' consisted of specific details of what the killer had done with Kelly's body parts, her possessions and possibly some other factors that we still know nothing about. Withholding these from the public meant that the police had information otherwise known only to the killer or his accomplice. The thinking was sound enough but unfortunately the plan contained two major flaws, one of which no police force in 1888 could have been aware of. The second was more fundamental: it was badly executed.

Any pie that Home Secretary Matthews had his finger in was likely to become contaminated by error, and this was no exception. On 10 November, the Cabinet authorised him to offer a free pardon to any accomplice 'not being a person who contrived or actually committed the murder'. This, however, applied only to Mary Kelly's murder. Asked if he intended to make the offer retrospective to the earlier crimes, Matthews told the House of Commons on 23 November that he did not, adding, 'In the case of Kelly there were certain circumstances which were wanting in the earlier cases, and which made it more probable that there were other persons who, at any rate after the crime, had assisted the murderer.'[49]

What these 'certain circumstances' were remains unknown. It is possible that Matthews was referring to information that today we have no knowledge of, but the greater likelihood is that they were bound up with Anderson's pet obsession about Polish Jews. To recap on what the assistant commissioner wrote in his memoirs: 'the conclusion we came to was that he and his people were certain low-class Polish Jews, for it is a remarkable fact that people of that class in the East End will not give up one of their number to Gentile Justice.'

Whatever the truth, by not making the pardon retrospective Matthews was effectively defeating its purpose. Presumably, he meant that there was no evidence that could be used against an accomplice in the earlier crimes, but, unless this was self-evident to the person concerned, the possibility of being charged as an accessory to the previous murders remained a very real fear.

The plan was hindered, anyway, by the first flaw. Lone serial killers do not have accomplices. They operate strictly by themselves, trusting nobody. For the idea to work they had to catch the actual perpetrator and get him to confess.

Nor did the police fare well in their bid to withhold the information that a body part had been taken away. Dr Gabe was the culprit telling the press that a 'certain organ' was missing.[50] This conflicted with the Yard's official statement that all the body parts had been accounted for. *The Times* on 10 November carried both versions. In Column 1: 'The lower portion of the body and the uterus had been cut out and these appeared to be missing.' (This report has the heart left on the bedside table with the kidneys and breasts.) In Column 3: 'The latest account states upon what professes to be indisputable authority that no portion of the murdered woman's body was taken away by the murderer.' Neither *The Times* nor the *Telegraph* believed the denials. 'Notwithstanding reports to the contrary it is still confidently asserted that some portions of the body are missing,' reported the former on 13 November.

However, Scotland Yard did better with its disinformation on where Kelly's breasts had been left. For the next 99 years, we students of the Ripper crimes would repeat as holy, or rather unholy, writ the canard that they were on the bedside table. The police were even able to spoon-feed this deception to John McCarthy because what he thought he saw at number 13 and what he did see were two very different things.[51]

The inventory that Abberline took of Mary Kelly's possessions[52] is missing today from the files. A few items were, however, subsequently placed in Scotland Yard's 'Black Museum'. They were seen there in February 1891 by a reporter from the now defunct *Globe*, whose brief was to write an article on 'criminals and their tools', which was published on the 16th of that month. Next to artefacts from the Lipski case, the journalist discovered a minor treasure trove of items relating to the Kelly murder:

... that hatchet by the door was used by the Whitechapel murderer to hack and disfigure the body of the first [sic] poor girl who fell a prey to his fiendish fury in Dorset Street. Close to it is the end of the cigar he smoked that evening, together with the chignon and earrings the girl was wearing.

Even though William Bury was a smoker, I really do doubt that anyone could say for sure that the cigar belonged to him and not some other client. The earrings and chignon (hair pad) are more relevant in that they show which items, if any, he did not take away as personal possession trophies. In Chapter 11, I will draw attention to two items that may conceivably have come from Miller's Court.

But what is really interesting is the hatchet, because we now have reliably based evidence that the killer did use one on Kelly. This was certainly one of the things the police held back.

In the mid-1990s, N P Warren, editor of *Ripperana* and a practising surgeon, assessed a photograph of Kelly's thighs and abdomen that first came to light in November 1987. He noted that the left thighbone had been split longitudinally from the hip downwards, a wound that could only have been inflicted with something like a hatchet, certainly not a knife.[53]

The truncated photograph was clearly taken for a specific purpose, which can only really have been to preserve the evidence of the hatchet being used.

Warren is also of the opinion that Mary's facial injuries were chops rather than slashes, although on this point he is more equivocal than with the thigh wounds. Whether a specific photograph was taken of the face we do not know. Dr Gabe told the press that, despite poor conditions for photography, the police had 'succeeded in securing several negatives',[54] and it is conceivable that more were taken in the mortuary.

Perhaps the biggest question mark hanging over the murder of Mary Kelly is when it actually took place. Here is Doctor Bond's estimate:

> In the Dorset Street case the body was lying on the bed at the time of my visit, 2 o'clock, quite naked and mutilated as in the annexed [postmortem] report.
>
> *Rigor mortis had set in, but increased during the progress of the examination.* From this it is difficult to say with any degree of certainty the exact time that had elapsed since death as the period varies from 6 to 12 hours before rigidity sets in. *The body was comparatively cold at 2 o'clock* and the remains of a recently taken meal was found in the stomach and scattered around about over the intestines [author's note: fish and potatoes]. It is therefore pretty certain that the woman had been dead about 12 hours and the partly digested food would indicate that death took place about 3 to 4 hours after the food was taken, so one or two in the morning would be the probable time of the murder [my emphasis].[55]

The first point, though a small one, is that Bond was mistaken about the body being naked. Mary was, in fact, wearing a chemise, a point verified by Phillips at the inquest. Part of it can be seen in the full-length photograph of the corpse. However, rather more serious in terms of being challengeable are the criteria that he used in fixing the probable time of death.

First, the digestion rate. In Bond's era great claims were made for its efficacy in pinpointing when someone had died, but not any more, Professor Bernard Knight going as far as to use the word 'discredited'. Professor Knight does qualify this somewhat by stating that, where it is possible to identify the constituent parts of a meal, that may indicate that death has occurred soon after consumption, but overall the rate of digestion is now considered to be of very limited value.[56]

Likewise, a good deal more is known about rigor mortis than in 1888. I shall stick to citing two of the many experts, Professor Knight and Dr Peter Dean, another eminent forensic examiner of the present era. Knight writes that rigor will commence in the features 1–4 hours after death and from 4–6 will begin to spread to the limbs. It will carry on increasing till the cadaver is completely stiff, probably 8–12 hours.[57] Dean is in harmony with this, stating that rigor will begin 2–4 hours after death and be completed 9–12.[58]

Superficially, Bond appears to be in agreement: 'the period varies from 6 to 12 hours before rigidity sets in'. But what exactly is he saying – that rigor *commences* 6–12 hours after death or is *complete* by this stage. If he meant the latter and he was right about the time of death, Mary should have been as stiff as a board by 2pm. But this was not the case. 'Rigor had set in but *increased* during the examination' (my emphasis). Moreover, according to the forensic evidence given to the 1977 Fisher Inquiry into the death of Maxwell Confait, the actual terminology Bond uses here would normally be taken to mean a body at the *outset* of rigor.

So, overall, what he appears to be saying is that rigor *begins* 6–12 hours after life has left the body, and his use of the term 'sets in' in both sentences would seem to confirm this. This too would be in keeping with the time of death he proffers. He also found the remains only 'comparatively cold at 2 o'clock', suggesting that they were cold for a body in that stage of rigor. The reason why they were thus cold is given in *The Times* of 12 November 1888:

> There is no doubt that the body of a person who, to use Dr Phillips' own words, was 'cut all to pieces' would get cold far more quickly than those of one who had died simply from the cutting of the throat, and the room would

have been very cold, as there were two broken panes of glass in the windows. Again, the body being entirely uncovered would very quickly get cold.

In fact, although it has generally passed unremarked, Bond's assessment of the time of death was not universally accepted at the time. Walter Dew wrote, 'There were differences of opinion as to the actual time of the Kelly murder.'[59] One of the dissidents was Bagster Phillips, who put it at 5–6am.[60] The City Police files were destroyed in the Blitz but there is a tantalising little hint that their police surgeon, Dr Frederick Brown, also disagreed with Bond, and substantially so. On 3 December, the *Philadelphia Times* published an article by a 'thoroughly reliable source' who was clearly a City detective, possibly even its most senior detective, Inspector James McWilliam. Certainly, the Met attached sufficient importance to the article to preserve it among their files.[61] The piece concludes:

> The last murder, on November 9th, came as a complete surprise to them [the City force] but it was *skilfully timed*, as that being Lord Mayor's day, on which the City is *thronged with sightseers, every available City detective and policeman was on street duty* [my emphasis].

Which can be interpreted to mean that, by contrast with their Met counterparts, the City Police thought that the murder had been committed late in the morning while the police were engaged with the crowds lining the route of the procession. If so, then that opinion could only have emanated from Dr Brown.

Now of course we need to be careful. Professor Knight makes the general point that rigor mortis is a variable process and should never be used alone to determine a time of death.[62] The cooling rate of the body is a far more reliable meter. Unfortunately, however, here we have no alternative but to fall back on rigor and see where it takes us. Taking the averages provided by Professor Knight and Dr Dean and the state of rigor at 2pm, Mary Kelly probably died between 10 and 10.45am, when the body was discovered. In fact, had Mary expired between 1 and 4am, as the police/Bond thought then, even allowing for the mutilated state of the corpse and the cold air seeping through the broken windowpanes, rigor would conceivably have progressed even a little faster than normal because of the fire burning in the grate during the early hours.

Once the police had Bond's estimate of the time of death they ignored any witnesses who reported having seen Mary alive later on the morning of the 9th, with, of course, the splendid exception of Mrs Maxwell, who had already made a statement and would not be dissuaded from it. Caroline Maxwell is normally the sort of firm, reliable witness who comes as manna from heaven to the police. Dew, in *The Hunt for Jack the Ripper*, describes her as 'sane and sensible and with an excellent reputation'. But, because she did not slot into the scenario of Mary's dying in the early hours of the morning, she was treated as obdurate and subjected to some almost intimidating remarks by Coroner Macdonald: 'You must be very careful; your evidence is different from the rest.'

At first sight, 'the rest' seem to confirm Bond's estimate of the time of death, give or take a couple of hours. But do they?

Sarah Lewis in the tenement opposite heard a loud cry of 'murder'; Elizabeth Prater in the room immediately above Mary's heard it only faintly. Prater should have heard it more loudly than Lewis if it came from just below her: the floorboards were very thin and, as Prater confirmed at the inquest, she would have been able to hear anyone moving about down there. Logically, she should therefore have heard the murderer. Yet she heard 'nothing else whatever'.[63] Significantly, Prater also told the police in her original statement, 'I did not take much notice of the cries as I frequently hear such cries from the back of the lodging house where the windows look into Miller's Court.'[64] The latter part of this statement, giving the specific direction of the previous screams, was not repeated at the inquest. Here, too, 'the two or three screams' of her original statement were compressed into one: 'I did not hear it a second time.' In other words, her testimony was tailored to fit Lewis's and to get round the inconvenient fact that she had thought at the time that the cry came from elsewhere. Julia Venturney, who also lived opposite Mary at number 1, said, 'I could not sleep all night; I only dozed, I heard no screams,'[65] although here we must caveat that the probative value of her evidence is somewhat diminished by the fact that she also did not hear Kelly and Cox at midnight, nor Kelly singing. Mary Ann Cox, however, was more specific about being awake all night, and she was adamant about not hearing any cries: 'I should have heard any cry of murder; I heard nothing.'[66] This was echoed by a market porter living at number 3 who likewise heard nothing.[67]

On balance, therefore, the scream came not from 13 Miller's Court, in fact not from the Court at all, but an upper storey of the lodging house, and more in line with Lewis's room on the western side of the Court than Prater's on the opposite side.

Elizabeth Prater got up at 5.30 and went for a drink at the Ten Bells on the corner of Fournier and Commercial Streets. There was no noise from Mary's room, nor when she returned. Prater went back to bed again and slept soundly till she was awoken by police activity downstairs at 11.

Catherine Picket knocked on the door of number 13 at 8 o'clock. She got no answer but, then, if Caroline Maxwell's statement is accurate, Mary was likely to have been in the Britannia at this point.

Which brings us on to Mrs Maxwell. Nobody has ever been able to pick holes in her testimony. On 10 November, she told *The Times* that the maroon shawl Mary had worn was a 'woollen crossover I have not seen her wear for a considerable time'. Along with her interview, the newspaper told its readers, 'The crossover was found in Kelly's room.'[68] This ties in with the crossover shawl noted by Mary Ann Cox, except that she merely termed it as red.

Maxwell was likewise able to verify that she had indeed been out and about between 8 and 9am on the 9th. She either borrowed or returned some crockery and then went shopping in Bishopsgate, where the shopkeeper recalled that she had not been in of late prior to that morning. She came forward as soon as the body was discovered and her statements were wholly consistent throughout. She spoke of Mary's vomiting up her drink, which is obliquely confirmed by the negative value of the autopsy evidence. Tellingly, she also stated that Mary said to her, 'I have the horrors of drink on me as I have been drinking for some days past.'[69] This too can be verified, at least in part, by the fact that Mary had been drinking with Maria Harvey the previous afternoon before going out again in the evening.[70]

Slipstreaming along in Caroline Maxwell's wake, we have Maurice Lewis and three unidentified sources, each one claiming to have seen Mary Kelly alive and well several hours after she was supposedly dead. The impression that the official line was seriously awry is perhaps best summed up by the *Manchester Guardian* on 12 November: 'This conclusion conflicts with the statements made today by people in the neighbourhood.' For good measure the *Guardian* added one itself: 'One person stated that the woman was seen to purchase milk for breakfast.' As this sounds like a misattributed version of Maxwell's errand, we can probably discard it. Probably, but not definitely. Even allowing for possible duplication and error in the other sightings we are still left with a significant body of evidence too powerful to be ignored. In particular, it has not been appreciated how Maxwell's and Lewis's sightings draw water from each other. Weave all this evidence together and the tapestry it creates is similar to that woven in Hanbury Street by the combined statements of Cadosch, Richardson and Long, who confounded Bagster Phillips's original estimate of the time of Annie Chapman's death. Although it can never be said with absolute certainty, on the balance of probabilities, Mary Kelly was likely murdered sometime around 10 o'clock that morning.

The time of her death is not an issue that affects the case against William Bury either way, for the simple reason that we now know that he was out all night on the 8th/9th. The latter was the day of the new Lord Mayor of London's inauguration celebrations, preceded by a parade through the East End to the City. In those days it was a holiday for Londoners. The previous morning Mary had told Elizabeth Prater that she would be one of the anonymous thousands thronging the streets to watch the so-called great and good pass by.[71] When people have so little, little means much.

If the East End had thought the murders had ended, it was greatly mistaken: broken by fog and fear, yes, but nobody was aware of the inner forces that drove this driven man. When he met Mary Jane, he succumbed completely to them. The hatred is evident in the extent of the atrocity. Previously he had concentrated on the reproductive organs; this time he tore out the heart as well, symbolic of the way he saw women: heartless creatures who had brought him into the world and then left him, and who had inflicted a nightmare childhood on him. Symbolic too of the way he saw himself: a worthless, heartless creature. When we look at the appalling photographs of Mary Kelly, we are looking at William Bury's self-image.

Not content with just practising his ritualistic slaughters with the knife, Bury used the hatchet he found at number 13 to turn the tiny room into an insane replica of the cat-meat shop. 'Butchery' is the word that springs most readily into the minds of those who have written about the carnage at Miller's Court. This was a man who had at one time cut up animals with society's approval. Now he was ripping up women he regarded as animals. What he could not see, or, if he did, turned away from seeing, was that he was also well advanced along the road to his own destruction.

NOTES

1. Robert Anderson, *The Lighter Side of my Official Life*.

2. *Newcastle Daily Journal*, 25 September 1888.

3. Phillip Sugden, *The Complete History of Jack the Ripper*, 1st edn (hbk), pp. 147–8.

4. *Times*, 4 October.

5. *Newcastle Chronicle*, 2 October 1888; report, Inspector Abberline, 10 October.

6. *Morning Advertiser*, 4 October 1888.

7. British Consulate, Boulogne, reports to Home Office, 10 and 12 October 1888.

8. Sir Charles Warren, confidential memo to Home Office, 17 October 1888.

9. Home Office correspondence, 15 October 1888.

10. Anderson, op. cit.

11. Ibid.

12. *Serial Killers – John Wayne Gacy*, Channel Five, 1999.

13. Margaret Corney, evidence at Bury's trial, 28 March 1889, and statement to Procurator-Fiscal, 15 February 1889.

14. Statement, 14 February 1889.

15. Statement to Metropolitan Police, 9 November 1888; inquest testimony, 12 November.

16. Nor subsequent research.

17. Both of 10 November.

18. *Star*, 10 November.

19. Walter Dew, *I Caught Crippen*, autobiography.

20. *Daily News*, 10 November.

21. Nick Connell and Stewart Evans, *The Man Who Hunted Jack the Ripper*, p. 59.

22. Julia Venturney, inquest testimony, 12 November, and Venturney police statement, 9 November 1888.

23. *Daily News*, 10 November 1888.

24. Bruce Paley, *Jack The Ripper, The Simple Truth* (pbk), pp. 34–5 and 173.

25. Said to have been a German woman named 'Julia' by Barnett in press interviews. Julia Venturney was of German origin, but lived at 1 Miller's Court with her boyfriend, and there is no confirmation of her being the woman Barnett was referring to.

26. *Evening Standard*, 13 November 1888.

27. Inquest testimony, 12 November 1888.

28. From the various accounts, it seems likely that Harvey was there when Barnett arrived and left almost immediately afterwards and that Albrook turned up during his visit.

29. *Lloyd's Newspaper*, 11 November 1888.

30. *Star*, 10 November 1888.

31. Paul Begg, *Jack the Ripper: The Uncensored Facts* (pbk), p. 152.

32. Lewis told *Lloyd's Newspaper* (10 November) that Mary was in company with 'Julia' and 'Dan', an orange seller with whom she had recently been living. He was clearly mistaking Daniel Barnett for his brother Joe, a point confirmed by Joe himself, who was the source of the *Star's* information that Mary had a drink with his brother Dan on the night of the 8th. For good measure, the *Daily News* of 10 November records that Joe was selling oranges in the street in November. Lewis's story also appears in the *Illustrated Police News* of 17 November.

33. John McCarthy, statement given second hand to the *Daily News*, 10 November. Its original source is unknown, but Thomas Bowyer is supposed to have seen Kelly with the man on the night of the 7th. There is no confirmation of this in either Bowyer's police statement or inquest testimony.

34. Statement to police, 12 November 1888.

35. Report, Inspector Abberline, 12 November 1888.

36. Bob Hinton, *From Hell . . . The Jack the Ripper Mystery*; Stephen Wright, *Jack the Ripper: An American View* (both nominate Hutchinson as the Ripper).

37. Inquest testimony, 12 November 1888. The usual confusion attends Lewis's evidence in that it is almost identical to that of a woman dubbed 'Mrs Kennedy' by the press. The only difference of note is that 'Kennedy' speaks of arriving at Miller's Court at 3.30am very shortly before the scream and of observing a woman without a hat talking to two men inside the court as she, 'Kennedy', entered her parents' home there. The seemingly trivial point of the woman's being bareheaded assumes importance here because, unlike most females of that era, Mary Kelly is said to have never worn a bonnet or hat. However, the rest of 'Kennedy's' story is so indivisible from Sarah Lewis's that Ripper historians have concluded that they were one and the same person, a view I do not dissent from.

38. Inquest testimony, 12 November 1888.

39. Begg, op. cit., p. 157.

40. *Times* and *Daily News*, 10 November 1888.

41. Police statement, 9 November; inquest testimony, 12 November; *Times*, 12 November, 1888.

42. *Star, Times, Daily News*, 10 November; *Illustrated Police News*, 17 November 1888.

43. Robert Keppel, *Signature Killers*, pp. 99–103.

44. In all probability she had rebuffed him on some past occasion when she was not prostituting herself. In his mind, when he left the room she was no longer belittling him: now she was looking up to him.

45. Walter Dew, *The Hunt for Jack the Ripper*, p. 144.

46. Paul Begg, Martin Fido and Keith Skinner, *The Jack the Ripper A to Z*, 1st edn (pbk).

47. *Times*, 13 November 1888.

48. Such may be inferred from the 12 November comments in *The Times* about the body being exposed to the cold, based on their interview with Bagster Phillips. See also Abberline's evidence at the inquest, in which he uses the past tense in relation to the fire when he arrived on the scene. Walter Dew, who calls it a 'drizzling morning', is specific that 'there was no fire in the grate but there were signs that there had been a big blaze'. Dew (op. cit., pp. 146–7) also says that the 'atmosphere in the room was stifling in spite of the broken window'.

49. Hansard, 3rd series, Vol. 331, p. 16.

50. *Halfpenny Weekly*, 10 November 1888.

51. McCarthy's account in *Times*, 10 November 1888.

52. Inquest testimony, 12 November 1888.

53. *Ripperana*.

54. Ibid.

55. Report to Robert Anderson, 10 November 1888.

56. Professor Bernard Knight (ed.), *Simpson's Forensic Medicine*, 11th edn, p. 25.

57. Ibid, p. 21.

58. W D S McLay (ed.), *Clinical Forensic Medicine*, 2nd edn (pbk), p. 273.

59. Dew, op. cit., p. 146.

60. *Times*, 12 November 1888.

61. Metropolitan Police files – Mepo 3/140.

62. Knight, op. cit., p. 21.

63. Inquest testimony, 12 November 1888.

64. Police statement, 9 November 1888.

65. Inquest testimony, 12 November 1888.

66. Ibid.

67. *Daily Telegraph*, 10 November 1888.

68. *Times*, 12 November 1888.

69. Police statements, 9 November 1888.

70. *Daily Telegraph*, 10 November 1888; inquest testimony, 12 November 1888.

71. Sugden, op. cit., p. 311.

CHAPTER NINE
POPLAR INTERLUDE

Police Commissioner Sir Charles Warren was already out of a job as Mary Kelly lay dead in her Spitalfields hovel. He was the scapegoat for London's terror and the government's image. Henry Matthews, the Home Secretary, was the weakest link in Lord Salisbury's Conservative administration, but high politics dictated Matthews's survival, just as it had propelled him into the job in the first place.

For both Warren and Matthews, the 1886 general election was a watershed in their lives. Warren, a soldier and an unsuccessful Liberal candidate in the November 1885 election, had been handed the job the following May. He hardly had time to find out where the Scotland Yard loos were before the Liberal government fell over Irish Home Rule and Salisbury's Tories were returned to power with the support of the Unionist wing of the Liberal Party. Salisbury had no constructive policy on Ireland, but he did have maverick Randolph Churchill as the party's leader in the House of Commons. Henry Matthews was Churchill's protégé; he was also that rarest of birds in the Conservative party of his era, a Roman Catholic, and had once advocated self-government for Ireland. The new government's initial strategy has been described as 'platitudes and rosewater' and in every direction Matthews was the ideal platitude. As Home Secretary he became the first Catholic to hold a Cabinet position since the early years of Elizabeth I's reign. That he was both in temperament and ability wholly unsuited for high office was not regarded as important.[1]

Except, of course, to those who had to work under him. Relations between Matthews and Warren were never satisfactory. Making things worse for Warren was the fact that the Permanent Undersecretary, Godfrey Lushington, also disliked him. Jack the Ripper compounded a situation that was increasingly untenable. Early in November, Warren published an article in *Murray's Magazine* in which he responded to criticisms of policing policy. He was then rebuked by the Home Office for not seeking their approval beforehand and offered his resignation, which was accepted. It is difficult to avoid the conclusion that this was the outcome Matthews and Lushington wanted. But not their sovereign: 'the Queen fears this resignation will have a bad effect in encouraging the lawbreaker to defy the Police, who under Sir Charles Warren, have always done their duty admirably'.[2]

Victoria then went on to berate the detective department for their failure to catch the Ripper. The implication here is that the Queen did not hold her now ex-commissioner responsible for that failure. One of the problems Warren had always faced was the detective branch's belief that, while administratively under the commissioner's control, operationally they should be autonomous. This had been at the heart of the clash between Warren and Anderson's predecessor, James Monro. Matthews had done nothing to put a stop to this internal wrangling; indeed, Anderson and Swanson had been consulting Monro about the murders throughout October at the Home Secretary's instigation![3] If the Queen's words were meant to imply that the fault rested with Matthews or Monro, their import was either ignored or misunderstood, because Monro was now named as Warren's successor. Interestingly, his belief that the CID should be autonomous seems to have disappeared with the early-morning dews of his appointment.

None of this mattered very much to William Bury. What did matter was the nightmare reality of his crimes. The transcendent brutality of his latest murder acted as a catharsis throughout the next few weeks and London endured no end-of-November atrocity. There was, however, an attack on a woman named Annie Farmer inside her lodgings at 19 George Street (Martha Tabram's last address). On 21 November, Farmer brought home a client who stayed the night and then ostensibly cut her throat in the morning. She was not seriously hurt and the alleged culprit made his escape.[4] I use the words 'ostensibly' and 'alleged' because it is possible that Farmer inflicted the minor injury on herself when the man caught her trying to bilk him. According to one witness, he called out 'what a cow' to bystanders as he fled down George Street[5] and it transpired that he was a previous client of hers. Certainly, after an initial flurry of activity, the police appear to have completely lost interest in the matter, a point confirmed by the *East Anglican Daily Times* on 26 November: 'the Police are inclined to believe that the affair was only an ordinary brawl'.

The newspaper's brief report has, however, been carefully preserved among the police papers on the Ripper, not, arguably, for its mention of the Farmer case but of two other, unconnected, incidents that occurred over the weekend of the 24th/25th. In one, a Ripper-hunting vigilante was questioned by the police for carrying a gun. But it is the second incident that is of real importance:

> Two of the men who described at the time the man believed to have committed the Berner Street and other murders, today reported that they have again seen him, but that though they followed him he disappeared suddenly down an unfrequented turning.

Infuriatingly, we have no further details, not even the names of the two witnesses, although the fact of their being together makes Best and Gardner the likeliest candidates. Whoever it was, the sighting coincided with a major change in Bury's behaviour. He ceased to operate his sawdust business, a fact confirmed by Ellen to her sister in December: 'He would let some one else do his work while he stayed in the public house.'[6]

Clearly, he was now too frightened to be out and about in the streets of the areas in which he had previously made his rounds, Whitechapel, Spitalfields, Aldgate and St George in the East. This despite the fact that Ellen's resources had been depleted to merely a 'very few pounds', as Christmas approached, so much so that Bury was threatening to pawn her jewellery, causing her to carry it around with her in a little white basket.[7]

Next he sold the horse and cart. Margaret Corney puts this at around the end of the first week of December.[8] The timing – the end of the first week of the month – is rich in significance. He hoped, in vain, that by removing the means by which he travelled to and from his murder zone he could control the demons inside him – 'magical thinking', as psychologists term it. His horse and cart had provided a measure of safety, enabling him to come and go as he pleased. Interestingly, Walter Dew subsequently reminisced that the police were now stopping respectably attired pedestrians late at night, but not, apparently, anyone using a conveyance. One thing is certain: after William Bury sold his, Whitechapel and Spitalfields were never troubled by Jack the Ripper again.

Catherine Mylett was a woman of many aliases. She was born on 8 December 1859 at 13 Thomas Street, Whitechapel, the daughter of Henry Mylett, a labourer at a starch works, and Margaret Mylett, née Haley.[9] Both parents originated from Ireland, Henry from Loughton and Margaret Ballingbough, in the mid-1820s. As far as is known, they had only one other child, a son named William, listed as a clerk in the 1881 Census and living with his parents at 46 Thomas Street.

For the rest of Catherine's story – and there isn't much of it – we have to rely on what few records there are of her existence. According to her mother, she married an upholsterer named Davis at the beginning of the 1880s and bore him a daughter, Florence (or Florrie). Later they split and by December 1888 the child was enrolled at a school in Sutton, South London.[10]

There is no record of any such marriage either at the Family Record Centre or the London Metropolitan Archives, but there is evidence of a child named Florence. The records of Poplar Workhouse show that 'Rose' Mylett, alias Davis, and her daughter Florence were admitted on 19 January 1888. The following day 'Rose' was discharged to Bromley Sick Asylum, where she stayed till 14 March.[11] She had been treated there several times previously during the 1880s each time for the same, unspecified, illness. The latter information was supplied to the police by the hospital matron on Christmas Day 1888.

Florence was discharged to Stepney Workhouse on 20 January. The next sighting we have of her is at the Brighton Road School, Sutton, on 26 February 1889. Her place and year of birth are given as Stepney 1882 in both the Poplar Workhouse and school records.[12]

'Rose' was one of a number of aliases used by Catherine Mylett including 'Fair Clara', 'Alice Downey' (or 'Downe') and 'Elizabeth Davis'.[13] That by 1888 she was living a life of prostitution was obliquely confirmed by her mother. A report appearing in the *Daily Chronicle* of 28 December 1888 has Margaret telling the police that she had 'frequently remonstrated with her daughter about her mode of life, but without avail'. She last saw Catherine on Sunday, 16 December. At this point (possibly unbeknown to Margaret), Catherine had just broken up with a man named Goodson, with whom she had been living at the lodging house, 18 George Street, from which Emma Smith had been admitted to hospital in April.[14] Here Mylett was known as Elizabeth Davis and it is at this point that the alias becomes very interesting indeed. Of course it may be entirely coincidental – both 'Elizabeth' and 'Davis' were such common names – but the 1881 Census lists an Elizabeth Davis living with her family at 16 George Street. This would be around the time Florence was conceived. Elizabeth Davies had four daughters and two sons, Wallace age 25, and Alfred, 18. Was one of them Florence's father, and did Catherine Mylett adopt her putative mother-in-law's name when it suited her? Both Wallace and Alfred are candidates. Ostensibly Catherine was older than Alfred, making Wallace more likely to have been her lover. But, whether through ignorance or design, she gave her year of birth as 1862, the same as Alfred's.[15] Neither brother was employed in the upholstery trade, at least not in April 1881, but then according to the Census – which is not wholly reliable – no Davis was then employed in this trade in London.[16]

If Catherine Mylett did indeed use Elizabeth Davis's name by deliberate rather than random choice, then astonishingly both the Catherines in our story may have died because they chose to assume the identity of somebody connected with their boyfriends.

We can add two more little twists to this. The real Elizabeth Davis had a daughter named Alice, and another of Mylett's aliases was 'Alice' Downe or Downey. Then there was another daughter, Agnes, aged 11 at the time of the 1881 Census. Why Agnes is interesting is something we will pick up on later.

Very likely, however, little Florrie 'Davis' was the product of an unintentionally catadromous coupling in the dockland area Catherine Mylett ended up in on the night of Wednesday, 19 December 1888. It was the last evening of her life but she didn't know this. What she was aware of was that a cheerless, penniless Christmas was almost on her. But her life was not about enjoying it, anyway, just surviving. Her luck in that direction was about to run out, too.

The area bounded by Poplar High Street and the East and West India Dock Roads was a good place for a prostitute to earn money, provided she was not too fussy about whom she went with. Merchant seaman of all nationalities and tastes swarmed ashore as soon as their ships hit port. Most were coarse; some were brutal.

At 7.55 that evening, Charles Ptolemy, a night attendant at the Poplar Union, was on his way to work when he came across a woman and two sailors in Poplar High Street. One of the men was evidently propositioning the female while his companion paced up and down nearby. Ptolemy heard her say 'no' several times. Later he would identify Catherine Mylett's corpse as being that of the woman.

We move on in space and time to 2.30 on Thursday morning in Commercial Road, where Alice Graves, a woman who knew Mylett, saw her outside a pub with two sailors, apparently drunk. Graves was perhaps an appropriate name because she was the last person to lay claim to seeing Catherine alive.[17]

At 4am back in Poplar High Street, a young girl identified only by the surname of Green encountered two more sailors who asked her the way to West India Dock Road. One of them told his companion, 'Make haste Bill and we shall be in time to catch the ship.'[18]

At 4.15, Sergeant Robert Golding and Constable Thomas Costello were on foot patrol in the High Street. They paused to check out Clarke's Yard at number 108, directly opposite the spot where Ptolemy had earlier spotted Mylett. Inside they came across her still-warm body lying on the ground. The outward appearance of the corpse gave no indication of foul play. Nor was there any sign of a struggle. The only discordant note in an otherwise perfectly tranquil scene was that one of Catherine's earrings was missing.[19] The two policemen, who between them had almost 50 years' experience of police work,[20] came to the conclusion that she had died of natural causes.

The autopsy then came as something of a shock. The first medical man to examine the body was a Dr Harris, assistant to the local police surgeon, Dr Matthew Brownfield. Harris had it removed to the mortuary and the following morning, Friday the 21st, assisted Brownfield with the postmortem. Both doctors concluded that Mylett had been strangled with a 'Four Lag cord (equal to packing string of very moderate thickness)'.[21] Their report states,

> Blood was oozing from the nostrils and there was a slight abrasion on the right side of the face . . . on the neck there was a mark which had evidently been caused by cord drawn tightly round the neck, from the spine to the left ear . . . there were also impressions of the thumbs and middle and index fingers of some person plainly visible on each side of the neck . . . The brain was gorged with an almost black fluid blood . . . The marks on her neck were probably caused by her trying to pull the cord off . . . the murderer must have stood at the left rear of the woman . . .[22]

What particularly convinced the doctors was congealed blood under the skin where the ligature mark was.

The inquest was scheduled to begin at 11am that day. Brownfield spoke, seemingly briefly, to the police beforehand, but did not apprise them of his findings. It thus came as an unwelcome surprise and the inquest was adjourned for the time being.

Wheels spun into motion at the Yard. Swanson was briefed to overview the investigation in case it was Ripper-related and Commissioner Monro attempted to contact Dr Bond, only to find he was out of town. He turned instead to the police surgeon general, Dr Alexander MacKellar, who went himself to Poplar to examine the body and reported back that he agreed with Brownfield and Harris.

While all this was in progress, Bond's assistant, Dr Hibbert, took it upon himself to make an examination. He too endorsed strangulation, as subsequently did Bond after reading Hibbert's notes and seeing the body for himself. Meanwhile, upon receiving Dr MacKellar's opinion, Monro reported to the Home Office, 'There is therefore no doubt that the case was one of murder – and murder of a strange and unusual type.'[23] It is fair to say, though, that Monro was not without reservations.

One man was having none of it, however. 'I undertook the distasteful task of going to the mortuary and examining the body myself,' wrote Robert Anderson in a subsequent report to Monro.[24] Anderson's assessment was that Mylett had choked to death on the stiff collar of her tight-fitting jacket while in a state of intoxication.

Having thus convinced himself, Anderson summoned Bond and Hibbert. A 'long conference in which I pressed my difficulties and objectives' ensued. It seems clear that both men initially declined to alter their opinions because Anderson ended up by referring them to Monro. That afternoon Bond paid a second visit to Poplar and returned to tell Anderson that strangulation had occurred by accident, not 'homicidal violence'.[25]

This conclusion was in turn supported by the coroner, Wynne Baxter, at the resumed inquest on 9 January. But not by Bagster Phillips, who regaled the jury with an exposition on the similarity between the technique used in strangling Mylett and that of the thugee cult in India. How Phillips came to have a cameo role at this inquest in unclear. He was an 'H' division police surgeon and Mylett had been murdered on 'K' division's ground. Despite Baxter's promptings, the jury returned a verdict of murder, following which Superintendent Steed of 'K' division asked Anderson what course of action he should take. Anderson reiterated his personal opinion of accidental death, meaning 'don't bother'. So they didn't!

There are two questions to be asked: was Catherine Mylett murdered, and, if so, by whom?

There can be no real doubt that the answer to the first question is yes. Five police surgeons examined the body and each concluded that she had been strangled with a ligature. One, Bond, later changed his mind, but it is plain that he was not of a view to change it of his own accord. Enormous pressure was exerted on him to do so. Under these circumstances his original judgement must be preferred.

Two caveats were inserted against Dr Brownfield's postmortem report. One is that he found no trace of alcohol in the body, yet Mrs Graves's impression at 2.30am was that Mylett was drunk. This really is hardly an objection at all: what Graves *thought* she saw cannot be given precedence over the clinical findings of an autopsy. The second was that Brownfield and Harris concluded that Mylett had never given birth. This has more weight, but the question they were being asked to determine was the cause of death, and here they gave clear and cogent reasons for their verdict, which was endorsed by three subsequent examinations. Had they not been so powerfully supported, their error might cloud the issue, but they were, and it doesn't.

Anderson's assessment was worthless. It was based on no medical evidence whatsoever, and has all the hallmark of believing what you want to believe no matter what the facts say. He was very influenced by Sergeant Golding, 'an exceptionally safe and reliable witness',[26] who was commended by the coroner's jury both for his zeal and for returning of his own accord to the murder site to search for more evidence. However, that was two days later. Crime scenes were not then preserved for any length of time and this was not even thought to be such prior to the autopsy, so Golding's revisit, while laudable, was perfectly useless. Anderson should have separated in his mind Golding's quite reasonable deductions on finding the body from the medical examinations that brought to light evidence not discernible to the sergeant at the time.

Which brings us to the second question: who killed Catherine Mylett?

December was a nightmare month for William Bury. Getting rid of his means of transport would have done nothing to assuage the worm of murder wriggling inside his head. Financial constraints added to his frustration. About 10 December, there was another major row over money, accompanied by more violence, when Ellen refused to give him the funds to attend a smoking concert. It ended with Bury simply taking the money from her purse and giving it back to her empty, not the first time this had happened according to Margaret.[28] As the festive season approached, the Bury household was anything but a haven of goodwill.

Poplar is due south from Bow. In September 1998, it took me 24 minutes to walk from Spanby Road to Poplar High Street. Bury had no need to make the outward half of the journey on foot. Trams were now available. Coming back could probably have been accomplished by a man of his age on foot in 20 minutes, without the journey being made fraught by the same police presence existing in Whitechapel.

Ironically, 'Elizabeth Davis' was from the very East End heartland where Bury had committed his previous crimes. One explanation of why she was operating so far from Spitalfields is that she deemed herself to be safe from the Ripper's attentions in Poplar. It cannot have escaped her notice that she was living in the same lodging house as Emma Smith; or that Martha Tabram had lived opposite the house where Annie Farmer had had her contretemps a month earlier.

But, if Bury had the opportunity then, on this occasion, he certainly did not have the ferocity. Mylett's killer strangled her from behind with a rope. Here the murder itself was an exact replica of the way in which he killed Ellen seven weeks later, a very definite link between the two crimes. But Ellen's body was then mutilated in the same fashion as his victims' in Whitechapel, Spitalfields and Aldgate. Mylett's was intact. As we have noted, there were differences in all the Ripper crimes, but none so great as in this one, if it *was* his handiwork.

Is there an explanation that will pass muster? Yes. As with Liz Stride, he was in the confined space of a yard. On the earlier occasion, his overweening fear of capture prevented the mutilation.

Nobody saw the couple enter Clarke's Yard, but there were people in the vicinity, a point made by Anderson on 11 January, when he referred to 'people who are known to have been close at hand'.

So fear may have got the better of him, just as it did with Peter Sutcliffe on two occasions between his penultimate and final killings. In the first he attempted to garrotte the victim but was disturbed by a passing police car and on the second he was interrupted after hitting a teenage girl over the head.

There was no attempt to ransack Mylett's pockets, again suggestive of a hurried departure. Coins amounting to one shilling and twopence were found on her, indicative of her having serviced a couple of genuine punters that night. The missing earring could have been taken as a trophy but there is no mention of any tear in the earlobe. We shall look at this aspect again in Chapter 11.

There is one item that could inextricably tie William Bury to the murder of Catherine Mylett. Here we hark back to the possible link between Mylett and the family of Elizabeth Davis. As we saw, the name of Davis's youngest daughter was Agnes. Among the Burys' possessions, the police later found 'a book entitled "child of Jesus" ("To Dear Agnes with best love from Vicky, Agnes Davis with best love from Vicky") written on front page in ink and pencil'.[29]

The inhabitants of East End dosshouses learned by experience to keep any valuables and mementos with them. Catharine Eddowes was carrying virtually an entire household in her pockets! Mylett, at 29, was already a veteran of the lifestyle. Was the book, then, a treasured keepsake of her possible association with the Davis family, which fell out of her pocket when she hit the ground?

Alternatively, was it taken from 13 Miller's Court, a memento of Mary Kelly's relationship with her late husband? That is the problem with this type of clue: it can run off in so many different directions. And they all have their different objections. If Mary was married to a Welsh collier, his name was more likely to have been spelled 'Davies' than 'Davis' and the link between Mylett and the Davis family of George Street is entirely conjectural. Adding to the buts is the fact that other, similar, items were found among the Burys' possessions with no discernible link to either of their families, and we also have no way of knowing which of the two of them, Ellen or Bury, *Child of Jesus* belonged to.

So many ifs and buts. Whichever corner we turn in the hunt for Catherine Mylett's killer, we find one of them staring us in the face. Typical is the fact that, whereas her alias was one of Bury's trigger names, the night of 19/20 December was outside the time zones at which his inner frenzies were at their peak. Yet even here a pro emerges from the cons. It may explain that his inner tensions were not sufficient to risk mutilating the body with people walking past the yard.

This welter of points and counterpoints really does sum the matter up. There is a 50 per cent chance of Mylett's being Bury's victim but no more. Catherine was doing business in a rough part of town; who knows what evil came ashore that night? The proximity of Poplar to Bow, the strangulation and the silent and sinister way in which the crime was accomplished may point to Bury, but they do not firmly indict him for it.

Anderson's obduracy curtailed any effective police investigation. Not till Christmas day did they as much as locate Mylett's mother, arriving while the family were tucking into Christmas dinner and causing one previously merry old soul to have a fit.[30] Even then, the death certificate was made out in the name 'Elizabeth Mylett'. Her real forename does not receive its first airing in police records till 11 January, with Mylett misspelled 'Millet'. She had been buried four days previously in Bow Cemetery, attended by only her mother and a female cousin.[31]

Whether or not Bury killed Catherine Mylett, her fate determined his. We have seen how fear was now his predominant emotion, that the terror of being caught so governed him that it had, step by step, led him first to alter his appearance, then progressively to dispense with both his business and his transport so that he did not have to set foot west of Bow. Now, as police argued with doctors over the corpse in Poplar Mortuary, something happened that caused him to take the next, perhaps inevitable, certainly irrevocable, step, and flee London altogether.

In the police files it forms a rather sad little tiff between the police and Dr Brownfield. Over the weekend of 22/23 December, the doctor was interviewed by the *Star*. Later he was to deny to the surgeon general, although none too emphatically, responsibility for what appeared in the newspaper next day, saying, 'I hope you do not think me responsible for their reporters' articles',[32] followed a week later by: 'I deny that portion marked with blue lines and shown to me in your *Star* and further was most careful not to state to anyone more than what I had said at the inquest.'[33]

Whether or not Brownfield did make the remarks attributed to him, or whether some of the interview was a reporter's interpretation of what the doctor told him, makes no difference to the import of what was said in his name, at least not as far as William Bury was concerned.

The relevant portions of the *Star*'s article of 24 December run as follows.

> The suggestion is this: – 'Was the Poplar murder another of the series of Whitechapel and the work of the same man? If so, has the murderer changed his methods, or is it not possible that the deed of Clarke's Yard is a new revelation of his old methods – that in the other cases partial strangulation was first of all resorted to, and that when the victims were by this means rendered helpless, the knife was used in such a manner as to obliterate the traces of the act?'

The article then delves into Mylett's murder before switching back to the Ripper in general:

> 'The Question is', he [Brownfield] said, 'whether there is not another and still more striking point of resemblance. If the murder was the work of the same man the question is whether strangulation is not the beginning of all his operations. Does he strangle or partially strangle them first, and then cut their throats afterwards?'
>
> Then Doctor Brownfield went on to explain why this was likely. 'If his object is mutilation', he said, 'he could cut their throats so much more cleanly and deliberately. And this would explain too, how the murderer would be able to do his work without getting covered with blood.'
>
> But if the other victims had been first strangled would there not be post mortem indications? – 'If he cut the throat along the line of the cord he would obliterate the traces of partial strangulation.'

Whatever opinion the police may have held about tabloid journalism, the *Star's* reporter was nothing if not thorough, because he then looked up Bagster Phillips's testimony about suffocation at Annie Chapman's inquest, and part of Phillips's evidence at Elizabeth Stride's, before concluding with some hearsay comments from the good doctor himself:

> Dr Phillips was disinclined to express any opinion on the matter to a newspaper man, but from another source [author's note: possibly Brownfield again] our reporter ascertained that Dr Phillips, as soon as he knew of the Poplar discovery, expressed the opinion that it was the work of the same man. He also recalled at once the fact of the strangulation in the Hanbury Street case. With respect

to the other murders Dr Phillips points out that the retraction of the skin immediately upon severance of the throat would immediately destroy the marks of the cord supposing it first to have been used.

Bagster Phillips's opinion of the murderer's surgical skill then gets an airing before the article ends by posing a rhetorical question that must have caused Bury's blood to run cold: 'Does not this new theory open out a vista of possibilities which, being followed, may lead to the identification of the murderer?'

It certainly should have done seven weeks later. That it did not was a tragedy that the police had already inflicted on themselves.

Ironically, the *Star's* prescience failed to find an audience. Nobody was interested in 'Jack the Strangler' and the public took not a blind bit of notice. Had more then been known about sexual murderers, the police would have been aware that strangulation is a form of perverted foreplay used as much to heighten the killer's sexual arousal as it is to control and kill the victim. But they didn't know, and the fact that Bury first throttled or garrotted his prey remained in the shadows behind the myth for the next hundred years. No police report – not even Chapman's – mentions it, and no Ripper author was aware of it prior to the late 1980s. Up to then the public thought that the Ripper was just that, a killer wedded to his knife who simply cut his victims' throats before mutilating them.

But one place in which the truth was known was 3 Spanby Road, and, because Bury was the only one to know that the *Star's* report was accurate, he alone was influenced by it. Whether he killed Catherine Mylett or not, her death acted as a catalyst. Fear of being caught already clutched at his heart. Now a hidden part of his killing technique had been revealed. He could feel his little world getting smaller by the minute. From his controlling it, *it* was now constricting *him*, fuelling his paranoia, bringing the spectre of the gallows into sharp relief. The only solution that presented itself was flight. The situation is summed up for us by Colin Wilson and Donald Seaman in their book *The Serial Killers*:

> Statistics show that such offenders . . . have left the area because the publicity generated by their murders has made them increasingly nervous of arrest. When this happens the move will probably have been planned to avoid arousing suspicion.
>
> Had the Ripper felt constrained to quit England in November 1888 for fear of arrest – because of the hue and cry – he would still have been unlikely to be able to resist killing again: homicide is the serial killer's *raison d'être*.[34]

'When this happens,' they continue, 'the move will probably have been planned to avoid arousing suspicion.' Which is precisely the way Bury organised it. On 12 January he sat down and concocted a letter, supposedly from Malcolm Ogilvy & Co., jute merchants, of Dundee, the industry in which Ellen had once worked. He wrote:

> January 12/1889
> We Messrs Malcolm Ogilvy & Co Lim Dundee do here by agree to take into our employ W H & E Bury of number 3 Spanby Road London E for a period of 7 years
> Wages for W H B £2 per week
> Wages for E B £1 a week
> To enter on duty as soon as possible.
> Travelling expenses will be allowed after 1 month from date of entering employ
>   Messrs Malcolm Ogilvy & Co
>   Dundee
> W H Bury (signature)
> pro tem Ellen Bury[35]

He then witnessed it himself in the name 'William James Hawkins'. Margaret Corney would later confirm that she had never heard of anyone by that name.[36]

It was a crude enough forgery but it sufficed to deceive the poorly educated Ellen. How Bury came to select this particular company is a question that was never fully resolved, but the Whitechapel jute works where Ellen had been employed sometimes exchanged staff with Ogilvy & Co. There had also been an announcement in the London newspapers in January confirming the acquisition of some property by the Scottish firm.[37]

Viewed with the benefit of hindsight, these acts in themselves – the sudden flight and the bogus reason given for it – were admissions by Bury about who he was. There was just no cause for either action other than guilt.

Had it been possible to leave Ellen behind, he would have done so. The marriage that wasn't had served its purpose. He had had her money. But simply to walk out on her was fraught with danger. It is clear from what happened less than a month later that she had her suspicions. There can be no doubt that he was aware of this. If he simply ran out on her, he was not only leaving behind an embittered woman, but by doing so giving her the final piece of the jigsaw to send her running to the police.

Whether it ever occurred to him that she would make that last connection anyway when she discovered he had lied about their having jobs in Dundee, we don't know. It is unlikely: multicides especially disorganised ones, are not given to thinking about the long-term consequences of their actions.

The news that they were going to Scotland was dished out strictly on a need-to-know basis, which in this case meant just Smith and the Corneys, and, only the day before their departure in the case of the Corneys: 'On the afternoon of 18 January 1889 my sister and accused came to see me at my house and I then for the first time heard of their intention to go to Dundee.'[38]

For Smith, Bury had a different story altogether, saying that they were going to Brisbane, Australia. When the landlord asked which dock they were sailing from, Bury answered, 'Oh that's what you want to know like a lot more.'[39]

A lot more? Was this an oblique reference to the police?

At Bury's request, Smith knocked together two packing cases for their possessions. The larger of the two, Smith noted, was almost empty when they left Spanby Road, Bury telling him that he would have more things to put into it at the docks. As we shall see, both trunks had plenty in them in Dundee. Did William Bury also have some other bolthole in the East End?

He sold the furniture to a dealer before taking Ellen to Stratford to break the news to Margaret. He did not show his sister-in-law the phoney agreement and fended off queries about how Ellen and he had got their newfound jobs with the reply 'by inquiries'. Margaret did not have the opportunity of speaking to Ellen alone.

The Burys slept that night at Clements Coffee House in Bow. The following morning they boarded the steamship *Cambria* for Dundee. Margaret went to the docks to see them off. Here she was finally able to snatch a brief conversation with Ellen on their own in the cabin: 'She appeared as if she did not wish to go and was sorrowful. I am sure she was in the belief that he had got the situation in the jute factory and but for that she would not have gone'.[40]

As Margaret watched the steamer sail away, she little realised that in less than four weeks she would be identifying Ellen's body in the mortuary.

NOTES

1. R F Foster, *Lord Randolph Churchill: A Political Life*, pp. 273–4 and 338; Paul Begg, Martin Fido and Keith Skinner, *The Jack the Ripper A to Z*, 1st edn (pbk), pp. 289–91. This author has not discovered any contrary views to challenge the repeated assertions of Matthews's unsuitability. However, it should be noted that Matthews

himself wished to exchange his office for a judgeship and was prevented from doing so by Salisbury for reasons of political expediency.

2. Draft letter from Sir Henry Ponsonby, the Queen's private secretary, to the Home Secretary, 13 November 1888.

3. On 22 September, Matthews minuted his private secretary: 'Stimulate the Police about the Whitechapel murders. Monro might be willing to give a hint to the CID people if necessary.' It is not clear what 'hint' actually means, possibly simply advice, but it is known that a Ripper suspect, arguably Francis Tumblety, was involved with the Fenian movement, and Monro's interim job at the Home Office was in countering Fenian activities. See also in this context Douglas Browne and Ralph Straus, *The Rise of Scotland Yard*, pp. 205–9. The authors enjoyed official access to Yard files.

4. *Times*, 22 November 1888.

5. *New York Times*, 23 November 1888.

6. Margaret Corney, evidence at Bury's trial, 28 March 1889.

7. Ibid.

8. Margaret Corney says in her statement to the Forfar Procurator Fiscal (15 February 1889) that the pony and cart were sold six weeks before the Burys left London on 19 January, i.e. *circa* 8 December.

9. Birth certificate.

10. *Daily Chronicle*, 25 and 28 December 1888.

11. London Metropolitan Archives, Microfilm X20/121.

12. London Metropolitan Archives Microfilm X20/414.

13. *Daily Chronicle*, 26 December 1888.

14. Ibid.

15. 1881 Census and Register of Births Marriages and Deaths. As with any census, individuals have been missed – Charles and Margaret Corney and our Ellen Elliot, for example.

16. *Daily Chronicle*, 26 December 1888.

17. Ibid.

18. Report by James Monro to the Home Office, 23 December 1888.

19. Ibid.

20. *Ripperologist*, February 1998.

21. Monro, op. cit.

22. Postmortem report, 21 December 1888.

23. 23 December.

24. 11 January 1889.

25. Ibid.

26. Ibid.

27. Margaret Corney, statement, 15 February, and trial evidence, 28 March 1889.

28. Margaret Corney, Bury trial evidence, 28 March 1889.

29. Dundee Police Inventory of Possessions, 12 February 1889.

30. *Daily Chronicle*, 28 December 28th.

31. Ibid., 8 January 1889.

32. Brownfield to MacKellar, 30 January 1889

33. Ibid., 7 February 1889.

34. Colin Wilson and Donald Seaman, *The Serial Killers* (pbk), pp. 72, 74–5.

35. List of Crown productions in the case of William Bury.

36. The name appears to have been entirely made up by Bury.

37. David Malcolm of Malcolm, Ogilvy & Co., evidence at Bury's trial, 28 March 1889.

38. Margaret Corney, statement, 15 February 1889.

39. William Smith, statement, 14 February 1889.

40. Corney, op cit.

CHAPTER TEN
DUNDEE

The SS *Cambria* arrived in Dundee on Sunday evening, 20 January. The Burys stayed on board that night, leaving the ship between 7 and 8am on Monday. The young steward and stewardess, William Grimond and Jane Guild, spoke to them from time to time during the voyage but had no specific reason to recall the couple. It would come as a shock when, three weeks later, they were asked to identify the woman's dead body.[1]

Once ashore, Bury quickly found them a room upstairs at 43 Union Street let by a Mrs Jane Robertson at 8 shillings a week. He engaged a carter to collect their cases from the dock and they moved in at around 10am.[2] That afternoon 'Ellen' sat down and wrote to her sister:

> 143 [sic] Union Street
> Dundee
> Monday afternoon
> My dear sister
>
> According to promise I will just send you a few lines to let you know that we have arrived and also to give you our present address.

Our journey was without anything occurring to mar our pleasure – till Saturday night about 8.30 when the ship began her games of pitching and tossing and rolling which she did not leave off doing till about 7 o'clock on Sunday night. I remained in bed all day on Sunday till about 8 o'clock. In fact I had all my meals in bed. I was very [author's note: the word 'sick' deleted] queer but not a bit sick and had all my meals as usual. But poor Will he got paid out sick from about 9 o'clock Saturday night till he landed. Eating nothing of course. We got in about 8.30 Sunday night but having no place to go to we arranged to remain on the ship all night and got a room this morning.

I think I shall like the place as it is a very clean town and seems a busy one too. Kind regards to all my relations – not forgetting yourself and Charley.

I beg to remain your affectionate sister

Ellen Bury

P.S. You must please excuse this being so short. The post leaves here so early for London and we are tired.

Write *before Friday*.³

The letter was actually written by Bury himself. Nothing too significant should be read into this, a point well made by the judge at Bury's trial. The letter needed to be written in a hurry and it made sense for Ellen to allow her much better-educated husband to write it. She, by contrast, was only semiliterate. According to Margaret, her sister could write but 'not very much . . . she never had much schooling'.⁴

Rather more interesting is what Margaret had to say about Bury's handwriting. He 'could write [in] several hands'.⁵ Here she was referring to the forged Ogilvy letter, which was not in his normal hand bar the signature. Nobody ever asked Margaret to explain how she knew her brother-in-law wrote in different hands. The obvious answer is that Ellen told her.

Perhaps the most intriguing point about the Union Street letter is that the real Jack the Ripper was subconsciously imitating his literary impostor. The 'Dear Boss' letter referred to 'funny little games' while Bury writes that the ship 'began her games'.

The overall importance of the communication is that it shows that Ellen's murder was not premeditated. Bury was quite happy to let the Corneys know where they were staying. He made a small error with the number, '143' instead of '43', but enclosed an addressed envelope apparently bearing the correct number. He also urged Margaret to reply 'before Friday', underlining these two words. She received it on Tuesday the 22nd and had plenty of time to respond (she didn't),[6] because the Burys did not move on from Union Street till the 29th.

On taking up residence with Mrs Robertson, Bury confessed that he had no job to go to.[7] Exactly when Ellen found this out we do not know, but, given her husband's track record, it probably did not come as much of a surprise. But it would certainly have left her fearful. They were at the end of her funds, possibly existing now on the sale of their Spanby Road furniture. Destitution was just around the corner.

Of course, with a glass in his hand Bury painted a very different picture of their fortunes. To John McIntyre, manager of the wine-and-spirits bar on the ground floor of number 43, he boasted that Ellen and he both had private incomes and that they were currently living off hers because it had been her idea to move to Dundee. By way of 'proof' he brandished Ellen's now defunct share certificates.[8]

On Monday the 28th, Bury made what appears to have been a calculated attempt to deter Mrs Robertson from collecting the rent.

He said that he had seen lodgings advertised in the papers
for six shillings and asked if I would not let my room to
him for that sum. I replied that I would not, when he
turned his eyes on me and gave me a look which
frightened me.[9]

Jane would have been utterly petrified had she known of the fate of
the last few women her lodger had looked at so malevolently! As it
was, she asked her daughter Margaret to take over dealing with the
Burys: 'My mother asked me to attend to them as she was afraid of
the man owing to him looking so wickedly at her.'[10]

The following morning, their last at Union Street, Bury's fantasy
world was back in place. Ellen, he told Margaret Robertson, had now
commenced working at a local factory. This part was actually true,
but Bury went on to claim that he was starting there also, in the
office, the next day. This was pure fiction.

Along with this, Bury imparted the news that they had taken two
unfurnished rooms in the Milltown district. Not exactly – at least not
as far as the letting agent was concerned. In fact, Bury had found
them a squat.

Early that afternoon, the 29th, two labourers, Henry Fay and
David Dick, turned up with a barrow to transport the Burys'
belongings to the new address. Peering out of the window, the
inquisitive Margaret saw that their now ex-lodgers had purchased a
bed that was already loaded on to the barrow. She also noted that the
box, which had been almost empty at Spanby Road, was now, like its
counterpart, being utilised for their possessions: 'The man [Bury] . . .
packed the unlocked box with their clothing and other articles.'[11]

The couple's new lodgings were a basement apartment at 113
Princes Street. It is clear that Bury intended only a short sojourn here.
Formerly a tailor's workshop, the basement flat was advertised to rent
at 2s 6d a week by E Shepherd, housing agents. Bury had looked it

over on the 28th. He returned at noon on the 29th, took the key on the pretext of showing it to his wife, and never returned. The agent knocked twice during the next four days but received no answer.[12]

While not exactly a hovel, number 113 represented downward steps for the Burys, irreversibly so. The two-roomed apartment was at the bottom of a four-storey building and reached by entering through a gate at street level and then descending a 17-step staircase to a small kitchen with crimson curtains. A white screen, probably cardboard, had been placed across the lower half of the window to cover a broken pane, and two of the upper panes were likewise cracked. The *Dundee Advertiser* would later describe this exterior as 'dirty and squalid'.[13]

The kitchen led through to a living room-cum-bedroom, which had a back door exiting on to another stone stairway. This wound its way up to the rear of the premises to ground level, where the tenants burned their rubbish in an ash pit.

On 29 January 1889, Dundee was a week away from receiving its charter as a city. However, slum clearance was a main priority. In an occasional series entitled 'The Dens and Hovels of Dundee', the *Dundee Advertiser* and its *People's Journal for Dundee* highlighted parts of the city that remained a blight on its honour. For example, the area bordered by the aptly named Dudhope Street to the north contained a collection of single-room hovels known as 'Beef can Close', so called because their original inhabitants – rural families who had migrated to Dundee to work in the jute factories – had had to make do with empty beef cans to serve as both cooking and eating utensils. The close was

> entered with difficulty. There are two short flights of steps at the entrance and both are very much worn and dirty. The close itself is filthy in the extreme. When I saw it it was covered with filth, and the whole locality presented a most ruinous and miserable appearance.[14]

For the most part Princes Street was far superior to dens such as Beef can Close and populated by what the *Advertiser* termed respectable, working-class people. But, said the newspaper, 'The rooms beneath are occupied by those of a much poorer class.'[15]

This description now included William and Ellen Bury, reduced to existing only one remove from Beef can Close. The last days of a serial killer's freedom are often marked by squalor and degradation (witness John Christie's decline at Rillington Place); things beginning to slide as weariness and apathy set in – an ennui of the soul. The only inclination that Bury showed during the following 12 days was to drink, and even here his days were beginning to be numbered by approaching penury. Looking for work was nothing more than pretence. One person whom he sought to take in was the Reverend Edward Gough, minister of St Paul's Episcopalian Church, which the Burys visited while they were at Union Street. Bury recalled to Gough that he, Gough, had once been a minister in Wolverhampton, claiming in return to have been a Sunday school teacher there. Oddly enough, it may even have been true. For Ellen's benefit, he asked Gough to help him find a job, but the reality was that drink and murder had destroyed what little will he had once possessed.[16]

For Ellen, it was an appalling situation. Her husband had squandered and drunk his way through her once proud little nest egg. One tangible thing that comes down to us about this so reticent young woman is that she set great store by appearances. All sources describe her as a neat, well-dressed person. Within her means she liked nice clothes and little pieces of jewellery to wear when the occasion merited it. In Bow, we remember, she had rented a furnished room, which she hardly ever used, to mask the fact that she was a prostitute. Now, almost penniless, she was reduced to living in a near-slum in a strange city with a violent drunk about whom she certainly had suspicions of far worse. Here again, there is a comparison with Christie, whose wife's suspicions grew to the point where he had to kill her. Now that William Bury was not even pretending to provide for her, Ellen had less and less reason to quell the nagging questions inside her head. And the more she allowed them free rein, the more she would have realised that, if her husband was Jack the Ripper, she could claim the private rewards on offer for his capture back in London.

One of the Burys' respectable ground-floor neighbours at 113 Princes Street was Marjory Smith, who kept a licensed broker's shop there with her husband Alexander. He helped the newcomers to move in. Afterwards they went up to the Smiths' shop and purchased some bedding and a candlestick. By way of introducing themselves, Bury went out and purchased a pot of beer for the four of them.

While he was gone, Ellen confided to the Smiths that her husband had got into bad company in London, staying out late at night.[17] On Bury's return, the talk turned to Whitechapel and the murders. Ellen remarked, 'Oh, Jack the Ripper is quiet now.'[18]

The Smiths were not to know that Ellen was uniquely qualified to make this statement. As for her husband, Marjory was later to tell the *Dundee Courier*, 'On this subject the prisoner [Bury] seemed to have no desire to speak.'[19]

We shall see this pattern repeat itself.

After leaving the Smiths, the Burys went for a drink at their new local, the Prince Regent bar, at 129 Princes Street, where Bury had a glass of bitter and Ellen a port.[20] Later Marjory Smith told her that it was not the done thing in Scotland for women to go into pubs. Ellen responded, 'Oh, indeed. The woman of Scotland will drink on the sly.'[21] But she was not seen in the Prince Regent again.

Ellen also seems to have steered clear of Marjory Smith after this encounter – and the other females in the neighbourhood. Only one other, Mary Lee, a middle-aged woman who lived next door, recalled passing the time of day with her and that was limited by the fact that Lee found Ellen's English accent difficult to understand. Bury's was more comprehensible but overall both kept their distance. Lee remembered that for the first two mornings they had employed a boy to knock them up. This presumably was in connection with Ellen's job cleaning at a local mill.[22] But she quit this after a day, Bury telling Marjory Smith that such work did not agree with her.[23]

Mary Lee also noticed something that nobody else did. When Bury went out in the mornings he wore his slippers.[24] This tends to add to our picture of Bury's decline into slovenliness.

According to Alexander Patterson, manager of the Prince Regent, Bury visited the pub on an 'almost daily' basis, sometimes coming in several times during the course of a day. He invariably drank bitter and bought drinks for those he fell into conversation with, always refusing one in return. This was typical Bury, posing as a man of means on the last few pounds of Ellen's money. Patterson noted, as had the Smiths, that he wore expensive rings on both his little fingers, gold on one and a 'jet' ring on the other (wedding gifts, he told the Smiths). When he left the pub he sometimes bought a bottle of beer as a takeout, saying that it was for his 'old woman'. These aside, he made little impression on Patterson. Just as in Whitechapel, he was a nobody, coming and going in his own anonymous way.[25]

But he did strike up an acquaintance of sorts with David Walker, a decorator employed on painting the pub. Walker seems to have been the sort of naïve young man who is easily flattered by someone with a tall story to tell and the money to wash it down with. The Procurator-Fiscal was to describe him as being 'considerably reluctant' to give evidence,[26] and at Bury's trial the judge took him to task for being evasive. Walker was not as observant as Mary Lee, otherwise he might have noticed that his newfound friend had feet of clay.

On Friday, 1 February, Bury purchased the ribs of a grate for the fire from Marjory Smith. He also asked for the loan of a chopper. Smith asked light-heartedly, 'Surely you are not Jack the Ripper?' Bury responded, 'I do not know so much about that.'

He did not return the chopper and Smith had to retrieve it herself the following day. The Burys were at tea, he 'much the worse for drink'.[27] Smith subsequently told the Procurator-Fiscal that this was the last time she saw Ellen, but in the immediate aftermath of her death she was to say something quite different.

The prosecution was to claim that Monday, 4 February was the last full day of Ellen Bury's life. This tied in with what Bury himself said. Indisputably, he obtained the rope he later strangled Ellen with on the 4th.

Typical of Bury, it was a freebie. Since moving into number 113, he had purchased such daily items as bread and firewood from Janet Martin's provision shop at 125 Princes Street. Martin recalled Bury as a furtive little man who avoided eye contact and was forever whingeing about her prices. Ellen had come into the shop only once, Bury remaining outside, although he called from the doorway, demanding to know if Ellen was buying the whole shop. His parsimony with women makes a striking contrast to his bonhomie towards his fellow males in the pub. Martin noted that he was often the worse for drink. She did not charge him for the rope, which had a double knot in it and was, she said, the type of cord 'generally used in roping boxes'.[28] Given the fact that he obviously intended only a short stay in the Princes Street basement, this was undoubtedly the use he originally intended it for.

That morning, David Walker encountered the Burys in King Street, the second time he had seen them together. Bury, he noted, was dressed in a tweed suit.[29]

After Walker saw him, Bury went on alone to the Dundee Magistrates' Court, where he slipped into a seat in the back row of the public gallery and sat watching the cases as they were heard. He was, remarked the *People's Journal* on 16 February, 'a most attentive spectator'.

In the early hours of the following morning, Tuesday the 5th, David Duncan, a labourer lodging at 101 Princes Street, heard a woman screaming in terror from the direction of 113. Duncan's landlady, Ann Johnston, who slept in the same room, heard nothing, although it is unclear whether she was then awake. Duncan did not make a note of the time. He had gone to bed shortly after 10pm, at which point the fire in the room was 'burning brightly'. When he awoke, shortly before hearing the screams, it was out.[30]

That afternoon, Mary Lee noticed that the blinds were down in the rear window of the basement of 113. Thereafter, they remained drawn, and Bury, who she said had previously left the door open when he went out, now took care to lock it after him. Lee had last seen Ellen on Wednesday, 30 January; thereafter, she had neither sight nor sound of her.

At least that is what she said in her statement to the Procurator-Fiscal on 16 February. It differs from what she told the *Dundee Courier* five days earlier. Here she said that she had last seen Ellen on the 4th and there is no mention of the blinds continually remaining drawn. Moreover, her statement that the door had previously been unlocked was contradicted by the letting agent.

Lee, in fact, did not actually see Bury on Tuesday the 5th. But David Walker did, at 9am, when Bury called in at the Prince Regent. He was dressed differently from the previous day, a dark suit under a brown overcoat. From then on, Walker was in his company several times a day.[31]

On Thursday morning, Bury was again a spectator at the Magistrates' Court. The court officer, a police constable named McKay, recalled him from three days earlier. By the time another three days had elapsed, McKay would have seen Bury yet again, but this time at Dundee Central Police Station.[32]

Bury admitted, but never explained, these visits to the police court. The *Dundee Courier*, on 12 February, implied that he was familiarising himself with the Scottish judicial system, while the *People's Journal* speculated that on the Thursday he may have been contemplating giving himself up for Ellen's murder.[33] Neither suggestion is very convincing and the latter is bedevilled by the likelihood that Ellen was still alive on 7 February.

In fact, there is another, much more credible explanation, one entirely in keeping with this furtive, secretive little man. He was lured there by the sight and sound of Dundee's lowlife being paraded in front of him, the women in particular engaging his fantasies. These were the sorts of people he had mixed directly with in London's East End. Now he was indulging in a form of voyeurism, similar to Peeping Toms or underwear fetishists. But it was nearing the end of the first week of the month, and, although he did not know it, his next explosion was just around the corner.

On Saturday, 9 February, Bury appeared to Marjory Smith to be in a 'very dirty' state as he hurried past her in Princes Street that morning, his customary polite 'Good morning' replaced by a tersely mumbled 'Morning'. His demeanour indicates a mind in turmoil.[34]

That evening, Bury made his final visit to Janet Martin's shop, where he bought candles and matches. She noted that, as usual, he had been drinking, but it did not stop him trying to get his goods on credit till the next day. 'Tomorrow's not ours,' Janet replied prophetically. She noticed that his jet ring was broken.[35]

Bury then joined David Walker for a drink at the Prince Regent. After leaving the pub, they walked back to number 113 together, Bury parting company with the decorator at the top of the steps. He was 'a little under the influence', Walker recalled, but his speech was still 'quite sensible'.[36]

It was the last time William Henry Bury would ever go out for a drink. As he makes his way down the stone staircase, we can see in our mind's eye the ghosts of his victims standing in silent vigil over his descent. The last one in the line is Ellen.

At noon on Sunday, 10 February, David Walker was lying in bed at his lodgings in Crescent Lane, 250 yards (230 metres) or so from Princes Street, when Bury suddenly turned up unannounced.

Walker later told the Procurator-Fiscal, 'On his entering we spoke a few words and I afterwards handed him the "People's Journal" which I had been reading.'[37]

The *People's Journal* was published every Saturday. The issue of 9 February contained several stories about elopements and suicides.

But it was one particular suicide story that really grabbed Bury's attention. Under the heading 'Tragic Suicides in Dundee', it told how Janet Murray, a widow anxious about her health, had killed herself a week before:

> She was last seen on Friday night, and her absence on Saturday led the neighbours to call the Police, who, on forcing open the door, found Mrs Murray hanging by a rope fastened to a knob on the door of a press [cupboard].

Walker, in his statement, juxtaposes these three stories, saying that Bury 'read aloud a paragraph relating to an elopement which ended in suicide'. He made his statement over a week later and, as we have noted, was not inclined to be too helpful anyway. Nor was Walker's imagination fired up by these particular tragedies. It was the one recently played out on the streets of London that he wanted to hear about. 'I said, "Never mind elopement and suicides, look and see if there is anything about 'Jack the Ripper', you that knows the place."'

Bury responded as though the newspaper had suddenly caught fire, immediately throwing it down. Walker changed the subject. Hearing the sounds of an English couple who lived upstairs making preparations for their lunch (and probably hoping to get rid of his uninvited guest), he hinted that 'English people feed high on Sundays'.

Bury took the cue, remarking that Ellen and he would not be very happy if they did not have their Sunday roast. She was preparing a rabbit and a piece of pork and he was expected home at 1.30, otherwise he would not get any.

He was right about the latter part: all that awaited him at home was Ellen's dead and mutilated body. To that he now returned. Mary Lee said that she later saw him go out up the stairs at 1.30.[38] She must have been mistaken about the time, because he returned to Walker's lodgings at about 2.30, having been away approximately an hour.

Walker noted that his newfound friend was very restless. The pair of them went for a walk down by the shore, where Bury gazed wistfully at the tall ships riding at anchor and asked if they sailed to Hull, Glasgow or Liverpool. What he had in mind was cramming Ellen's body into the larger of the two trunks and disposing of it at sea, either over the deck rail at night or through a porthole, as ship's steward James Camb was to do with actress Gay Gilson's body 60 years later. Then he switched tack and spoke of taking a 'run' to London to see his old pals there. The Dundee press were to speculate that he could have loaded the trunk on to a train for London and simply left it 'to be called for'. Here Bury would have presaged Tony Mancini, the Brighton Trunk Murderer, by nearly half a century.

Yet in the end Bury was to choose neither of these options. Nor did he simply flee Dundee and leave the body to be found when the letting agent repossessed the property. As his advocate pointed out several weeks later, Bury 'could possibly have been in the wildest parts of America by the time the murder was discovered'.[39]

Why, then, wasn't he? Well, he had tried flight once and it had all gone wrong. Now, the discovery of his victim was likely to end with his being unveiled as Jack the Ripper. He would be a hunted man for the rest of his days.

Was there a way out of this deadly maze? By the time he parted from David Walker that Sunday afternoon, a wild gamble was forming in his mind, one based on the newspaper stories he had read in Walker's room earlier that day. Nobody would possibly expect Jack the Ripper to stay and brazen it out. If flight this time was an admission of guilt, then staying would be a demonstration of guile, a way of making his crimes work in his favour. He would go to the police and tell them Ellen had killed herself. His luck had always held in Whitechapel – why not Dundee, too?

William Bury was what we call a present dweller, a pathological liar who not only built castles in the air but wanted to move into them! All who came to know him attested to this. It is one of the commonest traits in a serial killer, a fatal flaw that was always going to undo Bury one day. Simple common sense should have told him that flight was his only viable option, even if it did unveil him as Jack the Ripper.

But something else now had the better of common sense. When a multicide reaches the end of his tether, it manifests itself in the deteriorating appearance we noted with Bury earlier, alongside erratic, often seemingly inexplicable behaviour. Deep inside, he is sickening of his repetitive slaughters and wants to stop but knows he cannot. Bobby Joe Long provides us with a graphic example. He raped his penultimate victim but then let her go:

> I knew when I let her go that it would only be a matter
> of time . . . I just didn't care any more and I wanted to stop.
> I was sick inside. *Doesn't the fact that I could have run and
> didn't count for something?* [my emphasis].[40]

Author Joel Norris remarks of Long that 'his fantasy world had exploded and his skein of rapes and murders was coming to an end'.[41]

This is exactly what was happening to William Henry Bury, a.k.a. Jack the Ripper. 'For heavens sake catch me before I kill more. I cannot control myself,' Chicago multicide Williams Heirens scrawled above one of his victims. Similarly, Bury had not been able to control himself, although now his depredations sickened him. It is a subject we will examine further in the next chapter. In the meantime, unlike Heirens, he could not broadcast it to the world – that was not in his psychological DNA – so his semiconscious took over and embarked him on a death ride to the gallows.

Things would change after his capture. They always do with multicides, once they have ensured the authorities will stop them killing – it is axiomatic that they cannot do it themselves: witness Heirens – the pressure subsides, equilibrium returns, and they most emphatically do not want to die, so they bend every cunning bow they can think of to avoid execution. We saw this in the opening chapter with 'Warren', Ted Bundy and Henry Lee Lucas. Add to them Heirens, who confessed to save his life, and Long: 'I realised I could be fried for what I was saying, so I asked for a lawyer.'[42]

The man who led them on tiptoe down this path was William Bury, but that later. For the moment there was only the risk that he had decided to run. Winds howled and gaslights flickered in the bleak Dundee streets as Bury made his way to the Central Police Station in Bell Lane. Snow, long promised, had arrived with a vengeance and crunched like gravel beneath his feet.

He arrived at the station at 6.50. The senior uniformed officer on duty was Lieutenant James Parr. At Bury's request, Parr took him into a private room. There he told the policeman a story that Parr certainly did not believe at the time. On 4 February, said Bury, he and his wife had been drinking. They had gone to bed and when he awoke the following morning Ellen was lying dead on the floor with a rope around her neck.

What Bury said next has, down through the years, been the subject of distortion and exaggeration. It has him blurting out dramatically that he was Jack the Ripper. Not quite, although what he actually did say was as revealing as it was evasive. He used the age-old technique of lying with the truth. Parr's version of their conversation – and his is the only one that counts – runs: 'He said he then became afraid as he might be arrested as "Jack the Ripper". He added that he had cut up the body and concealed it in a large box in the house.'

Clearly unimpressed, Parr asked him if he had been drinking lately and Bury replied that he had, although he now appeared 'quite sober'. He added that he had continued to stay in the house with the body but that it was affecting his peace of mind. Had he used the old chestnut, 'It's a relief to get off me chest, guv,' Parr would probably have burst out laughing. One suspects that there was indeed a smile on his face when he marched Bury into the detectives' office with the words, 'This man has a wonderful story to tell you.'[43]

The officer Parr handed Bury over to was Lieutenant David Lamb, chief of Dundee's detective department. To him, Bury repeated his story, adding that he had stabbed Ellen's body only once.

Like Parr, Lamb decided that he was 'quite sane and collected and sober'. Rather curiously, Bury took a bankbook out of his pocket, studied it for a moment and then tried to put it back again before Lamb confiscated it, along with his house key. Possibly he was weighing up whether his funds would allow him to have a drink because he seemed genuinely surprised when Lamb told him he would have to remain in custody while they checked out his story.[44] Then Lamb and Detective Constable Peter Campbell set off into the windswept night for Princes Street.

After they had gone, Parr took Bury into the orderly room and searched him, discovering a small knife. That done, they sat back and awaited Lamb's return.

NOTES

1. William Grimond and Jane Guild, statements to the Procurator-Fiscal for Forfarshire, 12 February 1889.
2. Margaret Robertson, statement to Procurator-Fiscal, 14 February 1889.
3. Scottish Public Records Office, Ref. JO 26/140/1.
4. Margaret Corney, Bury trial evidence, 28 March 1889; *Dundee Courier*, 29 March.
5. Ibid.
6. Margaret Corney, statement to Procurator-Fiscal, 15 February 1889.
7. Robertson, op. cit.
8. John McIntyre, statement to Procurator-Fiscal, 18 February 1889.

9. *Dundee Courier*, 12 February 1889.

10. Robertson, op. cit.

11. Ibid.

12. *People's Journal for Dundee*, 16 February.

13. 12 February 1889.

14. *Dundee Advertiser*, 12 February 1889.

15. Ibid.

16. Reverend Edward Gough, Bury trial evidence, 28 March 1889; *Dundee Courier*, 29 March.

17. *Dundee Courier*, 12 February 1889; Marjory Smith, statement to Procurator-Fiscal, 18 February 1889. There are inconsequential differences in Smith's accounts as to the days on which various items were bought.

18. *Dundee Courier*, 12 February 1889.

19. Ibid.

20. Ibid.

21. Ibid.

22. Ibid.

23. Ibid.

24. Ibid.; statement to Procurator-Fiscal, 18 February 1889.

25. Ibid.

26. David Walker, statement to Procurator-Fiscal, 18 February 1889.

27. Smith, op. cit.

28. Janet Martin, statement to Procurator-Fiscal, 22 February 1889; *Dundee Courier*, 12 February 1889.

29. Walker, op. cit.

30. David Duncan, statement, 18 February; Ann Johnston, statement to Procurator-Fiscal, 19 February 1889.

31. Walker, op. cit.

32. *Dundee Courier*, 12 February 1889; *People's Journal*, 16 February 1889.

33. 16 February 1889.

34. *Dundee Courier*, 12 February 1889.

35. Ibid.

36. Walker, op. cit.

37. Ibid.

38. Mary Lee, statement to Procurator-Fiscal, 16 February 1889.

39. Trial evidence, 28 March 1889.

40. Joel Norris, *Serial Killers: The Growing Menace* (pbk), p. 187.

41. Ibid., p. 189.

42. Ibid., p. 202.

43. James Parr, statement to Procurator-Fiscal, 13 February 1889.

44. David Lamb, statement to Procurator-Fiscal, 18 February 1889.

CHAPTER ELEVEN

THE SCORPION AND THE FROG

T he Scorpion needed to cross the stream, so he asked the Frog to carry him. The Frog said, 'But if I do then you'll sting me.' 'Of course not,' said the Scorpion. So they set off with the Scorpion on the Frog's back, and halfway across the Scorpion stung him. 'Why did you do that?' gasped the Frog. 'Now we'll both die.' The Scorpion replied, 'I couldn't help it: I'm a Scorpion.'

Sunday, 10 February had been another ordinary day in the ordinary lives of Mary Lee and her husband John, but it was not to end that way. At about 8 o'clock, there came a knock at the door and on opening it John was confronted by the majesty of the law in the dual shape of Detectives Lamb and Campbell. They did not wish to alarm him, but could he bring a candle and some matches and assist them next door?

Thus equipped, Lamb unlocked the door of the basement of number 113 and the three men stepped into its darkened kitchen. Nothing appeared amiss, so they went through into the backroom and lit the candle. Here, too, all seemed normal, but it was in fact an illusion. Viewed retrospectively, Princes Street was eerily reminiscent of another number including a 13: Miller's Court. There were the broken window panes, what were to prove charred remains of woman's clothing in the grate and a mutilated body naked save for a chemise.

The backroom was sparsely furnished, just a bed in the northwest corner and two chairs. Dominating the room were the two packing cases, one padlocked, the second, and larger, now with items of women's clothing heaped on top. Next to it, on the floor, was another pile of garments, chiefly more women's clothing and household linen such as curtains and tablecloths. At the foot of the bed was an open portmanteau, which likewise contained clothing.

Not then immediately apparent in the dinginess – the police were to discover them during the course of the next few hours – was the piece of rope that Bury had obtained from Janet Martin, which was now lying on the floor near the bigger trunk, and a large penknife on the back windowsill. Hairs from Ellen's head were to be found intertwined with the strands of the rope. The knife was bloodstained and had a piece of human flesh clinging to the blade.

Lamb and Campbell ignored the padlocked box and concentrated on its companion, which stood in the centre of the room.

Lamb gave it a gentle push but did not move it; clearly there was something heavy inside. Beneath the pile of clothes were two white, unfastened boards (although Lamb recalled only one at the trial) and under the boards was a dirty white sheet, which the detectives peeled away. What they then discovered is best left to Lieutenant Lamb to describe:

> We found protruding part of the right leg and foot.[1] The leg was [drawn] upwards till it came to the brain, and then it was broken in two and placed underneath the lid of the box . . . the left leg was drawn right over the body and rested on the right shoulder.[2]

In cramming Ellen's body into the trunk in this fashion, Bury had broken her right leg in two places.[3]

Leaving Campbell in charge, Lamb hurried to the Eastern Police Station, where he telephoned the chief constable to arrange for the police surgeon, Dr Charles Templeman, to be sent for. Lamb then returned to Princes Street. Templeman arrived at 8.40 and after a preliminary examination decided that he would like the assistance of another medical man, so Lamb returned to the Central Police Station to summon Templeman's colleague, Dr Alexander Stalker. His journey was twofold because at Bell Lane he charged Bury with the murder of his wife. Bury contented himself with a simple 'no' in response, but he must have felt the ground shifting under his feet. His high-risk strategy was beginning to go awry, as it was always destined to do.

After charging Bury, Lamb and another inspector, Dunn, searched him. His pockets yielded up the better pieces of Ellen's jewellery:[4] her wedding, eternity and two gold rings, two brooches – one inset with a five-shilling piece and the other four sixpences – a pair of earrings in the shape of shilling pieces, two pairs of gold earrings, a brace of gold lockets, a necklet and a lady's silver watch and chain.[5]

Bury was then escorted to the cells and Lamb sent a cab for Dr Stalker and the two returned with Chief Constable Dewar to Princes Street. Later, they were joined by the Procurator-Fiscal for Forfarshire, Alexander Agnew.[6] The body was eventually extricated from the box, laid out on a stretcher and taken away to the mortuary at Constitution Road. At 1am on the 11th, Templeman and Stalker commenced the autopsy.

Back at Princes Street, there was little more the police could do that night. A painstaking examination of the crime scene would have to wait till the morrow and daylight. But, before locking up the premises and leaving an officer to stand guard over them, Lamb and his colleagues took a look out back. What they found should by rights have written '*finis*' to the entire mystery of Jack the Ripper. Had his crimes occurred today with our more detailed knowledge of serial killers and their behaviour, it would have done, but in 1889 Dundee and William Bury might as well have been on the moon as far as the Metropolitan Police's purview was concerned. By the time the blinkers came off, the opportunity had all but passed.

In the quarter-light cast by the flickering candle, two bizarre messages, written in white chalk, could dimly be made out. One was scrawled on the back of the rear door of the apartment:

> Jack Ripper
> is at the back
> of this door

A little further on, at the turn of the stairwell leading up to the ash pit, was a second garish little missive:

> Jack
> Ripper
> is in this
> seller [*sic*]

Chilling signposts on the way to dusty death.

By the time Lamb and Campbell returned the following morning, news of the murder had swept through the locale like a tidal wave. A crowd of sightseers thronged Princes Street, virtually laying siege to number 113. Dundee's two daily newspapers, the *Advertiser* and the *Courier*, both had their reporters *in situ*. It is clear from the *Advertiser*'s coverage that it had the inside track with the police. During the course of the day, the *Advertiser*'s reporter was taken down the back steps of number 113 to photograph the two Ripper

Top: Facsimile of the message chalked on the rear door of the basement flat at 113 Princes Street. (*Dundee Advertiser*)

Bottom: Facsimile of the second message at the rear of 113 Princes Street, chalked on the wall leading down to the basement. (*Dundee Advertiser*)

messages. Facsimiles appeared in the newspaper the following day.[7] The page cutting is carefully preserved among the Police files on the Bury case.[8]

While the *Advertiser* toured with the force, the *Courier* was forced to tour, which was lucky for posterity, because the latter carried out a series of in-depth interviews with the Burys' neighbours and comprehensively covered the Sheriff's Court hearing that afternoon. The *Courier* also conveyed the excitement that built up during the day as rumours spread throughout the city that Jack the Ripper had been apprehended there. The evening brought more snow, mirroring the frostiness with which Scotland Yard greeted the news when Chief Constable Dewar telephoned them.

Meanwhile, inside the basement apartment, Lamb and Campbell quietly went about the task of examining the backroom and its contents. Lamb found a spot of blood 'the size of a penny' on the floor near the box that had contained the body.[9] Among clothing found in the box was a woman's brown Ulster jacket, which, in Lamb's words, was found to be

> in a considerable number of places covered with recent blood. We also saw that left wrist of the Ulster was much covered in blood both outside and inside as if the Ulster had been worn at the time the blood came upon it. There were rents on each side of the Ulster as if a considerable amount of violence had been used.[10]

Next, Lamb and Campbell turned their attention to minutiae lying in the fireplace, 29 buttons, 20 hooks, 11 hairpins, seven eyes and a button hook, two sides of the back of a corset and the steels of a dress improver. On the 15th, Margaret Corney verified ten of the buttons and the hooks and eyes as belonging to a brown dress trimmed with velvet owned by her sister, and five more buttons as coming from a second brown dress. Another six of the buttons she recognised as being from an old grey pair of trousers worn by her brother-in-law. She shook her head at the remaining buttons and the button hook, but noted that a black dress trimmed with satin was now missing from her sister's possessions along with the other items listed above and her corsets and a black quilted petticoat.[11]

We may reasonably infer that Bury burned the trousers, one of the brown dresses, the petticoat, corsets and dress improver because they had blood on them. But what of the other dresses? Here we go back to the articles found on top of the trunk and the bundle of garments lying next to it. Lamb surmised that these had been removed to make way for the body,[12] and it would seem that Bury had begun to burn them as surplus items that he no longer had room for.

Other bric-a-brac discovered in the fireplace were two small lock keys, part of a watch chain, a portrait frame, three metal umbrella rings (the ribs for two of them were found in the trunk) and three brooches and an earring, seemingly discarded as being of no value. Bury had also burned Ellen's two purses, her handbag and a woollen muffler. On the mantelpiece the officers found yet another knife from his collection, this one a twin-bladed pocket knife.[13]

We need not examine in detail the items found in the two trunks, both of which were – or rather had been – full. In the trunk with the padlock (it was unlocked when the police arrived), Lamb discovered a yellow belt with what looked like bloodstains on it. The stains were not, however, recent. Those on a handkerchief in the trunk seemingly were, and Bury's advocate, William Hay, was to claim its retention as a point in his client's favour.

The jury appears to have taken the view that it meant nothing either way.

But perhaps, like the belt, there were two articles that did – not to the Dundee murder but those a few months earlier. Among a collection of mostly male items, the police found what their inventory terms 'articles of jewellery of very inferior metal'. They included two finger rings. As nothing in this little miscellany was relevant to Ellen's murder, Lamb paid them no heed, which means we have no way of knowing what types of rings they were. Could they have been Chapman's? This is a question we shall return to.

Finally, from the trunk with the padlock, two felt hats described as 'old'.[14] A little younger in Whitechapel perhaps.

Delving into the open portmanteau, Lamb came across what appears to have been the suit jacket to the old grey trousers Bury had burned (the inventory describes the jacket as 'well worn'). In the inside pocket, he came across the forged Ogilvy letter, which was to become one of the Crown's exhibits at Bury's trial.

But there were ghosts hovering above this glut of mundaneness as well. The empty portrait frame in the ashes posed the question of whose portrait or photograph had been lodged in it. The obvious answer is that it was of Bury and Ellen, and that he destroyed it to prevent it being used to identify him, had he decided to leave the body behind and flee elsewhere in the UK. But lurking unseen in the shadows alongside this eminently practical reason was its psychological twin: Bury had killed the other person in the frame and then incinerated his own self-image.

This inference is sustained by what the police found loaded in the trunk with the body, packed to secure it, say Lamb and Campbell. In addition to the clothing there were no fewer than 30 books, over a third of which were of a religious nature, including two bibles and the aforementioned *Child of Jesus*. One of the bibles was inscribed 'British & Foreign Bible Society. Courtesy of Sunday Schools 1880'. There is an element of surprise here. One assumed that Bury's religious posturings were meant purely to deceive respectable people like Reverend Gough. But perhaps this is an altogether too one-dimensional view of Bury. Maybe, because he was the man he was, he needed to believe in a higher good, someone, or something, infinitely better than he, who would find it in his heart to forgive him all his terrible sins.

But if that was the case then Bury was symbolically sundering those beliefs. In order to use his bibles and other religious tracts to secure Ellen's corpse he would have needed to unpack them in the first place before replacing them. What he was saying could not be clearer. He had given up any hope of salvation. We can almost see his shoulders slump dejectedly as he piles in the books while Ellen gazes sightlessly up at him. With this crime he had obliterated whatever vestiges of his self-esteem remained after Whitechapel. There was now a new photograph in the portrait frame, one invisible to all bar him – the serial killer at his lowest ebb.

In their own way, just as horrifying as the wounds on Ellen's body was the desecration of her emotions. Littered around her in the trunk were the keepsakes of her dead child. The inventory lists them matter-of-factly, suppressing any private thoughts that the two detectives may have had: 'a bundle of baby's stockings; two pairs of baby's shoes; 8 baby's dresses; and a quantity of baby's underclothing all worn but clean'.

No doubt Ellen had hoped for more children. But a serial killer's sexuality is about the taking of life, not the giving.

Life had barely noticed Ellen Bury. 'A quiet looking woman . . . . neatly dressed' was how Mary Lee depicted her to the *Courier*.[15] Only in death did she cause a flurry of activity. Templeman and Stalker's autopsy was followed by a second carried out on the afternoon of the 14th by two other Dundee physicians, Drs David Lennox and William Kinnear, and the divergent results of their findings were in turn examined by Dr Henry Littlejohn, a prominent Edinburgh surgeon who decided that all should have slaps and endorsed Templeman and Stalker's overall conclusion while criticising the thoroughness of their postmortem. His comments, it should be said, do not materially affect the case against Bury as Jack the Ripper.

Templeman had qualified as a surgeon on the wards of the London Hospital in Whitechapel of all places. He had spent time as a Royal Navy surgeon and practised at the Royal Infirmary in Edinburgh before joining its counterpart in Dundee. His spell in Whitechapel is yet another minor Ripper coincidence. Doubtless he had read of the terrible crimes on his old doorstep; he could never have imagined when he set out for Princes Street on that cold Sunday evening that he would shortly be examining the remains of the killer's latest victim. His private views on the subject are unknown, as are Stalker's. The latter had studied at Edinburgh and Leipzig Universities and had also been a resident physician at Edinburgh infirmary before rejoining Templeman in Dundee.

'The body', they wrote in the autopsy report, was that of a 'well made' woman who had been strangled by a ligature. The two doctors were to be criticised by Dr Littlejohn for 'giving no proper dissections of the front of the neck', although he did not doubt that Ellen had been strangled. They describe the injury as follows:

> There was a mark of constriction around the neck passing in front between the hyoid bone and the larynx and maintaining this level all the way round with the exception of about two inches [5cm] on the left side of the neck where it tended slightly upwards. The whole of the face and neck above this line was congested. There was slight lividity of the lips but no protrusion of the tongue.
>
> From the centre of the neck the first five inches of this

mark to the left was brownish red and hard, and the rest of it was pale in the centre and congested at the edges. It varied in width from an eighth to a third of an inch [0.3–0.8cm]. About an inch and a half [3.8cm] from the middle line on the left side of the neck, was a similar mark joining that above described – three quarters of an inch [2cm] in length and running downwards and outwards. It was at the juncture of these two lines that the first mentioned tended slightly upwards.

About three quarters of an inch above this line, below the angle of the left lower jaw, were two small bruises each half an inch [1.3cm] in length.

In his subsequent statement to the Procurator-Fiscal, Templeman noted that 'the force used in strangling the deceased must have been applied in a direction outwards, downwards and backwards', which, as he confirmed at the trial, meant that Ellen had been strangled from behind. For good measure, he also noted that her fingers were semi-flexed.[16]

The autopsy next details the mutilation of Ellen's body, the injuries that Bury so very evasively did not want associated with Jack the Ripper; so much so in fact that he panicked and lied that he had stabbed the body only once. We shall see that not only was it considerably more than once but that these injuries were, unmistakably, the work of Jack the Ripper. In order to demonstrate this, we will examine Dr Templeman's report on Ellen Bury's mutilations side by side with those inflicted on her predecessors. Where necessary, we will also look at Dr Lennox's findings. A former army surgeon, he credited himself with 'extensive experience' of both treating wounds in the Sudan campaigns and conducting postmortems.[17]

We start with Polly Nichols.

DR LLEWELLYN'S FINDINGS ON NICHOLS, AS GIVEN IN HIS INQUEST TESTIMONY	DRS TEMPLEMAN, STALKER (AND LENNOX) ON ELLEN BURY
'There were no injuries about the body till just about the lower part of the abdomen. Two or three inches [5–7.5cm] from the left side was a wound running in a jagged manner. The wound was a very deep one, and the tissues were cut through. There were several incisions running across the abdomen. There were also three or four similar cuts, running downwards, on the right side, all of which had been caused by a knife which had been used violently and downwards. The injuries were from left to right.'	'There was an incised wound in the centre of the abdomen extending downwards from the umbilicus for four and a half inches [11.5cm]' (to 1½in (3.8cm) above the pubis according to Lennox). 'It penetrated to the abdominal cavity and through it protruded part of the omentum and about a foot of intestine part of which was dry and black from exposure to the air. The cut was ragged towards the lower part' (Lennox specifically notes that this wound had 'penetrated the belly wall'). 'Commencing at the inner end of the fifth right costal cartilage was a cut running downwards and to the left for seven and a half inches [19cm]. This was quite superficial with the exception of the last inch [2.5cm] where it penetrated through the skin into the muscular layer of the abdomen. Half an inch [1.3cm] to the right of this, and running parallel to it, was a similar cut, five inches [12.7cm] in length and superficial throughout. Two inches [5cm] to the right of, and commencing on a level with the umbilicus was an incised wound three quarters of an inch [2cm] in length and penetrating through to the muscular layer. From the lower end of the wound opening into the abdomen, on the left side, were several superficial cuts little more than penetrating the cuticle and running downwards to the pubis . . .'

These two reports could have been of the same autopsy with Templeman and Stalker simply filling in the details! One deep wound and several incisions surrounding it running obliquely downwards.

Turning now to Annie Chapman's and Cathy Eddowes's injuries, we lack detailed knowledge of the former due to Bagster Phillips's reticence. We do not know how many external incisions were made but we do know that there was one major wound to the abdomen, as was the case with Eddowes. So let us compare these two with that very deeply penetrating wound to Ellen Bury's abdomen.

DR BAGSTER PHILLIPS'S FINDINGS ON ANNIE CHAPMAN VIA THE *LANCET*	DR BROWN'S POSTMORTEM REPORT ON CATHARINE EDDOWES	TEMPLEMAN, STALKER AND LENNOX'S POSTMORTEM ON ELLEN BURY
'The abdomen had been entirely laid open and the intestines severed from their mesenteric attachment had been lifted out and placed on the right shoulder of the corpse.'	'We examined the abdomen, the front walls were laid open from the breast bone to the pubis. The cut commenced opposite the ensiform cartilage. The incision went upwards not penetrating the skin that was over the sternum. It then divided the ensiform cartilage. The knife must have cut obliquely at the expense of the front surface of that cartilage . . . The abdominal walls were divided in the middle to within _ of an inch [0.6cm] of the navel, the cut then took a horizontal course for two and a half inches [6.3cm] towards right side. It then divided round the navel on the left side and made a parallel incision to the former leaving the navel on a tongue of skin. Attached to the navel was 2½ inches of the lower part of the rectos muscle on the left side of the abdomen. The incision then took an oblique direction to the right and was shelving. The incision went down the right side of the vagina and rectum for half-an-inch [1.3cm] behind the rectum . . . . the intestines had been detached to a large extent from the mesentery. About 2 feet [61cm] of colon was cut away.'	'There was an incised wound in the centre of the abdomen extending downwards from the umbilicus for four and a half inches [11.5cm]' (to 1½in (3.8cm) above the pubis, according to Lennox). 'It penetrated to the abdominal cavity and through it protruded part of the omentum and about a foot of intestine' (Lennox specifically notes that this wound had 'penetrated the belly wall').

Here again, we seen an identical design between all three attacks, a deep, gaping abdominal wound which left at least 12 inches (30cm) of the intestines either protruding (Bury), partially severed (Eddowes) or detached (Chapman).

Equally clear in all three cases is the sexual nature of the crimes. We remind ourselves that Annie Chapman's pubis had been removed and placed above her left shoulder and that her womb and the upper part of the vagina were cut out and taken away altogether, along with most of the bladder. Having had no medical training, Bury was not able to distinguish which part was which. He knew roughly where the sexual organs were located and scythed away at them accordingly. With Eddowes, he obviously mistook her liver and left kidney for reproductive organs. The latter was removed and taken away, and he inflicted a number of stabs and incisions on the liver. On this occasion, he missed the vagina altogether but got lucky with the womb and cut out and took away most of it. With Ellen he used a different knife. The actual depth of the wounds was similar to those he inflicted on Nichols, and, as with Polly, the incisions to Ellen's private parts were made externally. Templeman and Stalker seem to have been rather prudish about mentioning the focal points of Bury's attack but fortunately Lennox was under no such inhibitions. One incision ran directly across the pubis, another extended to the area between the vulva and the ischium. In addition, two more cuts began just above Ellen's pubis.

Let us now make a number of very direct comparisons between just the murders of Cathy Eddowes and Ellen Bury. First, although there was a considerable difference in their severity, there were identical cuts on the bridge of the nose.[18]

DR BROWN (EDDOWES)	DRS TEMPLEMAN/STALKER
'There was a deep cut over the bridge of the nose extending from the nasal bone down near to the angle of the jaw on the right side of the cheek.'	'Over the bridge of the nose was a small incised wound penetrating the skin only ½ an inch [1.3cm] in length running obliquely downwards from right to left'.

The perineum had been breached in both cases.

DR BROWN (EDDOWES)	DRS TEMPLEMAN/STALKER
'Below this was a cut of 3 inches [7.6cm] going through all tissues making a wound of the perineum'.	'Beginning about an inch [2.5cm] behind the anus was an incised wound running forward and to the left into the perineum dividing the sphincter muscle'.

In both instances the injuries extended down to the thighs.

DR BROWN	DRS TEMPLEMAN/STALKER
'An inch [2.5cm] below the crease of the thigh was a cut extending from the anterior spine of the ilium obliquely down the inner side of the left thigh and separating the left labium . . . there was a flap of skin formed from the right thigh, attaching the right labium and extending up the spine of the ilium.'	'Running downwards from the centre of the pubis to the outer side of the left labium was an incised wound 2½ inches [6.3cm] in length . . . On the inner side of the right labium was a wound 2 inches [5cm] in length . . .'

Both Eddowes's thigh wounds can be seen as extending from the spine of the ilium. In addition to Ellen's thigh injuries, Templeman and Stalker noted two incisions on her in the same region:

> There were other [sic] two cuts on the abdomen. One two inches [5cm] to the inner lid of the right anterior superior

iliac spine and the other at an almost corresponding level on the opposite side. They were each about half an inch [1.3cm] in length running downwards and upwards and penetrating to the muscular layer. These were free from any trace of haemorrhage.

As we shall see, these two cuts are particularly interesting.

There was one main difference between Ellen's murder and those in East London: her throat was not cut. More of that in a moment, because something else that we need to address is the severity of the injuries. Those matched Polly Nichols's but not those of the subsequent victims. As all writers have noted, Jack's ferocity grew with each succeeding murder, ending with the charnel house at Miller's Court. Would we, therefore, not expect to see an even greater holocaust at Princes Street, where Bury was killing not only indoors but also in his own dwelling?

The answer is bound up with the issue that we looked at in the previous chapter, Bury's tiring of this never-ending merry-go-round of butchery. He had reached the stage of inner collapse redolent of so many multicides since. We saw how it influenced him to commit a subconscious form of hara-kiri by going to the police. Its effect was also felt in the severity of the cuts he made on Ellen, a man who could not stop killing but was soul weary and ashamed of what he was driven to do to his victims.

We saw with Long and Heirens previously that this sense of ennui can take many forms. In Ted Bundy's case, he effectively wanted to be stopped, so he fled to the state he was most likely to be executed in and embarked on a feeding frenzy of *disorganised* murder, reflecting how sick of it all he had become. John Christie did much the same. After murdering his wife – like Ellen Bury, she knew too much – Christie embarked on a final killing spree and then wandered around waiting to be caught. Henry Lee Lucas was arrested on a technicality and immediately began to confess. It was, says Brian Marriner, 'a wry recognition of futility and self-disgust. He had reached a point of inner moral collapse.'[19] Ditto Dennis Nilsen, who let it all hang out the moment the police came to call. None could have ceased killing by themselves. Murder is an addictive drug, like alcohol or cocaine, but, like alcoholics and narcotics abusers, they reached a point where they did not want to do it any more.

The nearest to Bury in this respect are Long, obviously, and Kurten, very much a devotee of the Ripper, who abducted his last victim, but then, like Long, let her live. The 'Düsseldorf Vampire' had simply drunk too much blood (literally). After Miller's Court, Bury, too, had had enough. If he did kill Catherine Mylett, then this may, we don't know, have been a factor in his making no attempt to eviscerate her. He didn't want to kill again but he did not want to be captured, either, so he fled to Scotland. But the addictive fantasies were still there and, when Ellen left him with no alternative other than to kill her, he had to give rein to them, although it is unlikely they afforded him any real satisfaction. With the exception of his habitual deep cut to the abdomen, these injuries became progressively more shallow as the sense of futility he felt, the self-disgust and weariness with it all, kicked in and took over. The only reason he eviscerated Ellen's private parts in the first place was that, like our apocryphal scorpion, he had to. But he had had enough and it shows.

We noted earlier the signs of moral breakdown inherent in the crime scene, the final disintegration of his self-image and the way his world was collapsing around him. All of this is reflected in Ellen's murder.

Cutting his victims' throats was not part of Bury's sexual fantasies. It was the ultimate expression of his need to control the women he preyed on. Once it was done he could be sure they were dead and that he would not be splattered by spurting blood. It was a necessity in a darkened street or the victim's hovel, but at Princes Street, his own abode, he had complete command of the situation, winding the ligature around and around Ellen's throat till he was sure she was dead. Cutting her throat was unnecessary. Robert Keppel emphasises the point for us: 'investigators must look for progressive changes in a killer's method of operation from one murder to the next, instead of looking for only those characteristics that were exactly the same'.[20]

The progression here was the elimination of something that, in this instance, was superfluous.

What is crucial in Ellen's murder was the mutilation phase. While the injuries, save one, were not as deep, their motivation and design was exactly similar to those in London. The self-same pattern is repeated.

Despite this, doubters have suggested that Ellen's murder was an imitation crime. This is the first time the murders have been systematically examined one against the other, and they leave no doubt that Ellen died by the same hand as the East End victims. But I will deal with the issue anyway.

There was an imitation murder on 17 July 1889: Alice McKenzie, an occasional prostitute, who was found dead in Castle Alley, Whitechapel. There was a jagged wound to her abdomen and a series of what Bagster Phillips termed 'scorings'. The injury to the stomach had failed to divide the muscle.[21] The impression is of somebody who wanted to make it look like a Ripper murder but was not capable of it. Personally, I suspect that McKenzie's partner, a labourer named John McCormack, knew more about it than he let on.

McKenzie's death was caused by two cuts to her throat, so here we have a case of an imitator trying directly to copy the Ripper. If Bury was also an imitator, then why did he not cut the throat, too?

This, however, is a relatively insignificant question beside strangulation. As we saw in Chapter 9, the only man who was then definitely aware that he first throttled the victims was the murderer himself. So how can Bury imitate something he knows nothing about? The only logical answer is that he was not imitating anybody – he was the murderer.

The final question is, why would he want to imitate the Ripper in the first place? This was an apartment in Dundee, not an alley in the heartland of London's East End. What could it possibly achieve? On the contrary, the mutilations ended up placing him at a grave disadvantage. He carried them out because he had to, end of story.

There was a sting in the tail of the doctors' report, something that clearly mystified those present at Bury's trial because nobody could explain it. Templeman deposed:

> The wounds described in the report as having been inflicted either during life or very shortly after death, while the body still retained its warmth and vital elasticity – must in my opinion have been inflicted within *at most* [my emphasis] ten minutes of the time of death.[22]

An opinion, he felt, that was also borne out by the bloodstained Ulster.

But there was an important qualification to this judgement. The wounds on either side of the iliac spine had not been made at that time. These had definitely been made some time after death, though precisely how long Templeman could not say.[23]

In other words Bury had started to ravage Ellen's remains again some time later.

This has now become standard with sexual murderers when the opportunity is there. Bundy did it, so too 'Warren', Sutcliffe on one occasion, Kurten and Arthur Shawcross. No other form of murderer does this; it is peculiar to sexual multicides. Once again, William Bury was the first.

The link between Ellen Bury and other Ripper victims extends beyond the medical evidence. Two of the rings found in Bury's pockets, Ellen's wedding and eternity rings, had been removed from her finger after death, a point revealed by the *Dundee Advertiser* on the 13th:

> Mrs Smith observed that Mrs Bury was wearing two rings – a wedding ring and a keeper. When the body was taken from the box on Sunday night it was noted that there were no rings on the marriage finger, but when an examination was made of the property found on Bury it included a keeper and two gold rings such as would be worn by a married woman. It is therefore believed that after her death Bury had taken the rings from the woman's finger.

Exactly as he did with Annie Chapman.

The point must of course be made that Bury's interest in Ellen's rings was pecuniary. Robert Ressler observes that serial killers do not usually take expensive jewellery as souvenirs anyway: they prefer knick-knacks, which are going to particularly remind them of their kill.[24] In Ellen's case, the relevance of the issue is that we see the same dark, centripetal force at work that we saw with Chapman: a brutal psychopath callously ransacking his victim for something that in one way or another was going to be of value to him.

Ressler states that keeping personal possessions as trophies is more a trait belonging to organised multicides; disorganised killers keep the body parts.[25] But once again the Ripper straddles the divide and John Douglas has no difficulty in accepting that he could have taken Annie's rings.[26] The point is hammered home by the fact that in both Chapman's and Eddowes's murders the Ripper deliberately cut open their pockets and either examined, or started to examine, their personal possessions. He seemed to know where they would keep them, which in itself makes the point that their killer was a man who knew the ways of homeless people. Bury had himself been a drifter and a vagrant. He had hawked key rings in the street and rubbed shoulders with the type of women he killed in the pubs they frequented. Robert Keppel remarks that in order to operate effectively a multicide must conform to the tone and tenor of the area he preys on.[27] William Bury was invariably drawn to the poorer, eastern quarters of the cities in which he lived.

Earlier, we noted the discovery of two cheap rings, which could have been those taken from Annie Chapman, in Bury's trunk. With the rings were a thimble and two cheap necklets. Speculation is idle, but the interesting point about the thimble is its splendid isolation. One would expect Ellen to have a thimble, especially as she had once been a needleworker. But conspicuous by their absence were pins and needles; even poor Cathy Eddowes had pins and needles to accompany the thimble found on her. But then Cathy still had to darn her clothes; she was not living on an inheritance. One would have expected Annie Chapman to have had a thimble, as she sometimes earned her living from crochet work, but there is no mention of one among her possessions.

Cheap jewellery (as opposed to expensive) and rings are, says Robert Ressler, among the commonest items serial killers take from their victims as souvenirs. The killer 'looks at a necklace hanging in his closet and keeps alive the excitement of his crime'.[28] Keppel endorses this: 'Frequently, family members or acquaintances of the killers unknowingly end up with these items as the killer circulates items among his group to get rid of potential evidence, while at the same time keeping them in sight.'[29]

This is revealing not only as a general point but also about an item found in the fireplace at number 113, a solitary earring discarded by Bury from Ellen's collection. Could this be Catherine Mylett's missing earring, finding its way into Ellen's possession? Had Scotland Yard become involved at the outset we might have been able to answer this question.

One thing for sure is that serial killers cannot keep body parts in a family environment! Which prompts the question of what Bury did with the organs he took away with him. The simple answer is that he probably ate them! Cannibalism is reasonably common among multicides, a way of retaining possession of the victim after death. Arthur Shawcross, for example, claims to have eaten the private parts and a piece of the heart of one of his child victims.[30] However, there is a second possibility: that Bury fed the body parts to his horse as scraps, a symbolic gesture in which his horse feeds on his mother and sister, just as a horse had been responsible for killing and mutilating his father.

Now none of this actually proves that the rings were Annie Chapman's (or the thimble), but it is a strong possibility. We know from the police files that they searched most assiduously for the missing rings without success.[31] Bury himself wore two relatively expensive rings and those in the trunk would appear too downmarket for him. Ellen likewise. She liked flashy jewellery and, as Margaret Corney confirmed to the Procurator-Fiscal on 15 February, she carried it around with her in the little white basket she had shown Margaret in Bow. This was missing when Lamb searched the room, so obviously Bury burned it after pocketing the contents. That the two cheap rings were Chapman's may be speculative, but here it is worth recording an anecdote from the invaluable Robert Keppel. While he and other searchers were combing one of Ted Bundy's crime scenes, they came across a rusty old tyre iron, which all bar Keppel wanted to discard as being unconnected with the murder. Keppel insisted on keeping it. It subsequently turned out to be the murder weapon.[32]

Yet another comparison between Bury and a modern-day serial killer is provided for us by John Douglas. In his book *Journey Into Darkness*, the FBI chief delineates the case of Cleophus Prince, who stabbed six young women to death in the San Diego area between

January and September 1990. Police discovered several knives in Prince's car and a ring in his apartment, which matched one that had belonged to a victim. Again, like Bury, Prince had departed from his normal routine and attempted to clean up the crime scene, likewise covering the body in a sheet. Says Douglas, 'This could have represented a change either in signature or MO, but it could also have been related to the way he felt about this particular victim' (p. 54). Taken in conjunction with the profile that Douglas prepared of the Ripper, the similarities between Cleophus Prince and William Bury are uncanny, an impression not offset by Douglas's comment in *Journey Into Darkness* that 'many sexual sadists are married or in ongoing relationships'.

Finally, Bury's belt. The stains on it were found to precede Ellen's death. However, they certainly could have been the residue of one of his London crimes. As he knelt beside a body, leaning over it to remove an organ, his waist would have come into contact with oozing blood, especially in the darkness. A pity there were no DNA tests then.

The exact series of events leading up to and following the murder of Ellen Bury have never been established with any degree of clarity. The timetable put together both by the prosecution at Bury's trial and Bury himself are so full of holes and improbabilities, and, in the case of the latter, downright lies.

We begin with Bury's version, which was published in the *People's Journal for Dundee* on 27 April, three days after his execution. His story was that he had murdered Ellen on the night of 4 February during a row over money after they had returned home drunk. Next day, he had attempted to cut the body up, intending to dispose of it piecemeal in the River Tay, but found that he was unable to go through with the ghastly chore. Instead, he crammed the corpse into the trunk with the idea of sending it on to London, marked 'to be called for'. However, he then began to fret lest Ellen's absence be noted by the neighbours, and ended up concocting the suicide story.

Concoction does sum the whole thing up very neatly. About the only grain of truth in it is the origin of the quarrel – money – but this was not the actual motive for Ellen's murder. The rest of the story is a mixture of outright falsehoods and theories that had been floated in the Dundee press.

Bury's major lie was his claim that the mutilations were an attempt at dismemberment. Templeman and Stalker were adamant that all bar two of the incisions had been made at the time of death, and I think it safe to add that none of these was by any stretch of the imagination an attempt to dismember Ellen. As for the subsequent minor abdominal cuts, these were near to the iliac spine, a ligament connected to the hip bone, but were no more an attempt to cut the legs off than the symmetrical cuts running off Catharine Eddowes's iliac spine had been. The incisions started out as a clear attempt to reprise these injuries. This in itself portrays with mute eloquence the real purpose of the mutilations – and who their perpetrator was!

The police and prosecution attempted to pinpoint the time of the murder as the early hours of the following day, Tuesday, 5 February. Here, David Duncan, was a key witness. The screams he heard resounded with murder, not the silent passing in the night of a suicide, as Bury claimed. But significantly nobody else heard the screams. Certainly not the Gibsons or the Duffys, who lived between Duncan and number 113.[33] Nor did Duncan impress the trial judge very greatly: 'I do not attach any considerable importance to his evidence,' Lord Young told the jury.

But on the surface Duncan was corroborated by the lack of sightings of Ellen after 4 February. David Walker was the last person to see her alive, on that date when he saw her with Bury, who was wearing a 'tweed' suit, by implication the grey one whose jacket

Lamb had found. The following day Bury was attired in the dark suit and brown overcoat he was wearing when arrested.[34]

Likewise, Mary Lee never saw Ellen again. But on Tuesday afternoon the back blinds were down and remained drawn thereafter, and whenever he went out Bury locked the door after him.[35] Marjory Smith told the police that the last time she had seen Ellen was on Saturday evening, 2 February.[36]

Add to this a statement by the prison doctor, James Miller, that Bury's right wrist and left hand bore scratches approximately four to five days old on the 11th (Bury blamed a cat), and you have a pack of cards neatly stacked in favour of Ellen's having been killed in the early hours of Tuesday the 5th.[37] A *house* of cards, however, is all it is. Walker's statement appears to have been edited to make us assume that Bury continuously wore the dark suit after Monday, and Mary Lee implies that Ellen was no longer around to raise the blinds. But did they remain drawn simply to create the impression that nobody was in? Remember that the letting agent had by then already called twice (without answer) in an attempt to get some rent.[38]

The fact is that Ellen hardly ever went out in Scotland, especially after Marjory Smith told her it was not the done thing for women to go into pubs. On one of the few occasions she did venture forth, Bury humiliated her in front of Janet Martin, and Mary Lee said that, unlike her husband, Ellen had difficulty in making herself understood to Scottish ears. Moreover, there was one person who did originally claim to have set eyes on Ellen after the 4th: 'The last time Mrs Smith saw the deceased was on *Thursday* at breakfast time' (my emphasis).

This was what Marjory Smith told the *Dundee Courier* on 11 February, when her memory was at its freshest. She was very specific about it too: 'at breakfast time'. By the time she made her statement, on the 18th, the police had decided that Ellen was no longer alive by the 7th.

So what does the autopsy report tell us about the time of death? Ostensibly little, but in this instance little may be a lot.

Templeman and Stalker set very wide parameters of three to six days. They were right to do so: Jessica Snyder Sachs in her recent book *Time of Death* makes the point that, if a body has been dead more than 48 hours, it is highly unlikely that the time of death can be determined with any degree of accuracy.[39]

The two doctors noted that there was greenish discoloration on the right side of Ellen's abdomen. This is the first flush of putrefaction. Blood was also trickling from the right side of the mouth, a possible indication of the lungs beginning to decompose.[40]

Professor Knight states that in a temperate climate (which ours is) putrefaction will generally commence three to four days after death, depending on the season, but possibly much earlier – hours, even, on a hot summer's day. Peter Dean says it may start on the second day – subject to temperature again – and Sachs 24–48 hours.[41] In Catharine Eddowes's case, however, the greenish hue was present at autopsy only 13 hours after death, in a room temperature of 55°F.

Its presence on Ellen's abdomen does not suggest a corpse that has been dead six days, even in the middle of winter on the east coast of Scotland. One would expect putrefaction to have advanced beyond the initial stage, but revealingly Templeman and Stalker make no mention of the body being bloated. This occurs from gas forming in the tissues, causing the face, abdomen and breasts to swell. According to Sachs, the cadaver is usually swollen to grotesque proportions after four to five days.[42]

Doubts about the likelihood of 5 February proliferate when we discover that both rigor mortis and postmortem lividity (hypostasis) were still present. In court, Templeman said that rigor mortis could still be observed in the 'head, neck and extremities', while in his report: 'Post-mortem lividity, which was of a bright red colour, was still marked on the back of the trunk and arms.' If the corpse had been dead six days, one would have expected both rigor and hypostasis to be long gone.

There are of course factors that might delay rigor – extreme cold, for instance – and snow had been threatening for days and finally arrived that Sunday evening. However, Ellen's body was not lying exposed to the elements. It was in a room. She was mutilated, possibly naked, but, unlike in the kitchen, the windows were intact and cold air was not blowing in. Moreover, on Sunday evening at least, her corpse was in a trunk swathed in clothes and bed linen and with a fire just a few feet away.

Lack of nourishment can cause rigor to develop more slowly. Templeman and Stalker refer to Ellen as 'poorly nourished' but she had in fact eaten not long before death, and Dr Lennox calls her 'fairly nourished', which indicates a condition actually on the continuum. Overall, Templeman and Stalker describe her as 'well made', meaning she was not frail and debilitated.

Bagster Phillips termed Liz Stride 'fairly nourished' and found that rigor mortis was 'still thoroughly marked' at 3pm on 1 October, 38 hours after her murder. But, even allowing for a difference in room temperature, one would certainly not expect to find a difference of a hundred hours (four days) between the times of death of these two corpses – nowhere near it.

Templeman and Stalker were never asked, either in court or by the Procurator-Fiscal, at which end of their scale death was more likely to have occurred, because, as soon as David Duncan came forward, nobody saw any reason to quarrel with the earlier time of death. It was certainly not in the police's interests, quite the opposite, because they could now use Bury's own statement about it against him. Bury himself had very good reasons to cast Ellen's death as early as Tuesday. It was part of his act, the grieving husband who had sat by his wife's body for days without attempting to escape, frightened to come forward in case the police did not believe him and thought he was the dreaded Whitechapel murderer. The further away the better from the possibility that somebody would look at the *People's Journal* for 9 February and see where the suicide story originated from. Nor did they. Despite the fact that it is in Walker's statement, it was never raised in court. In his 'confessions', Bury saw no advantage in changing the date of Ellen's death. Nothing in them was true, anyway. They were simply designed to show him in the best possible light, and that did not include admitting that he was a sexual serial killer.

On the balance of probabilities presented by the medical evidence, it is more likely that Ellen was slain sometime on Friday evening, 8 February. This ties in more with Dr Miller's estimate of the age of the scratches, 6 or 7 February, than the 4th or 5th. It is also supported by the dishevelled state Bury was in when Marjory Smith saw him on Saturday morning, and the situation Lamb and Campbell found on their arrival at Princes Street: 'there were still little pieces of coal and other articles burning in the fireplace'. They discovered the remnants of the things that Bury had burned in the ashes on the following morning the 11th.[43]

What happened that Friday evening? It is late and Bury has returned home from the pub with a bottle of beer for Ellen. She has already put curlers in in preparation for bed – the autopsy revealed five paper curls in her hair – and she drinks the beer as a nightcap while he swigs from a bottle of whisky. Lamb discovered in a cupboard a tumbler with dregs of beer and an almost empty whisky bottle.

Bury tells her that they are approaching the end financially. Ellen at this point had only £8 left in her bankbook, while he had coins amounting to a mere £0.65 when arrested two days later, and in a bag on the windowsill the police counted a little horde of farthings, 68 in all. Nine pounds, give or take, would probably have lasted Mary Kelly and Joe Barnett around a month and enabled them to pay off their rent arrears, but the Burys, he in particular, have got used to a standard of living well above that. As it is, they will have to move on; they cannot keep ducking the property agent.

The usual subject of work and his getting a job comes up. Tempers begin to rise, dangerously in his case: he has been drinking, the visits to the Magistrates' Court have rekindled memories of lowlife in the East End and it is the end of the first week of the month, when he is psychologically at his most vulnerable. He switches the subject to Ellen's previous jewellery. No ifs, no buts, she will have to hand it over to him so that he can sell it and keep them afloat.

Ellen has seen this coming, knows that the day is close at hand when she will have to deal with it. She has a plan in mind, something to frighten the wits out of him. Or so she imagines, because Ellen has not been gifted with much to think with, and this has not been thought through at all.

She intends to confront him with something visual, something that will bring him up short and make him think twice about taking her jewellery because of what it implies. She puts on her muffler against the cold and, finding a pretext, goes out back, taking a candle to light her way. She is away several minutes. During that time she constructs her little literacy masterstrokes, using a piece of chalk she has found in a corner of the living room. The previous occupant of number 113 was a tailor who used it as a workroom. Writing anything for the poorly educated Ellen is a chore, but she gets the job done. Now to confront him with it.

As she makes her way back into the dingy basement flat – a 'sunk' apartment, the letting clerk termed it – Ellen Bury does not realise that this is her last action on earth. She probably thinks that she is the one person he is never likely to kill, otherwise he would have done so by now. But the accusations she has left, implications that she will unveil to the outside world if necessary, are her legacy to posterity. As for her husband, his luck has just run out, but he doesn't know it yet.

Ellen issues her ultimatum: if he takes her jewellery she will go to the police and tell them everything she knows about him – for example, the times in London when he never came home all night, nights when the Ripper struck. There is a big reward for his capture, even more than the amount he has beaten out of her during her ten months of marriage to him. Suddenly, shockingly, the passive little victim of William Bury's brutal ways has become a major threat to him. What he sees now is an ex-prostitute to whom he has given his name and who now wants to hurt and betray him. Ellen intends to follow this up with her *pièce de résistance*: she is about to tell him to go and look at the messages she has scrawled out back. But she never gets that far.

Bury picks up the poker from the fireplace and commences the sort of blitz attack he launched on his London victims.[44] He fells her with a vicious blow to the temple. The postmortem noted a circular bruise above Ellen's left eyebrow, which Templeman thought had more likely been caused by a poker than a fist.[45]

Bury drops the weapon and picks up the rope he has obtained to tie the packing case. Although half stunned, Ellen struggles. Once again this was confirmed in court by Dr Templeman, who testified that she had bruising on her shoulders. So did Liz Stride, the victim of a similar attack. Here, Bury sustains the scratches reported by Miller. The struggle ends with his garrotting her from behind. Templeman, again, said that the rope had been wound around Ellen's neck 'more than once'.[46] In this fashion, Bury ensured she was dead, obviating any need to cut her throat and make the crime too reminiscent of the Whitechapel murders, should the corpse be discovered. Two livid bruises on Ellen's neck showed where a double knot in the rope had bitten deeply into her flesh as he drew it progressively tighter.[47]

The floodgates were now open and Bury gave way to the demented passions lurking inside of him. It was here that he betrayed who he was. An ordinary murderer would simply have killed, but William Bury was not an ordinary murderer: he killed women whom he hated, then carved his way into their abdomens for sexual pleasure. He had done it in London's East End and now he did it again in the east end of Dundee. For Jack the Ripper not to have been William Bury meant that there were two identically sick ghouls not only at large and living in Britain at the same time, but actually previously resident in the same area at the same time, and using the exact same 'signature', a situation without parallel and as likely as two killers with identical fingerprints. But here in Dundee the mutilations he inflicted on his victim would undo him, because without them he would almost certainly have escaped with a 'not proven' verdict. The scorpion had slain the frog in midstream!

After he finished eviscerating Ellen, Bury was faced with the problem of disposing of her body – as Dennis Nilsen terms it, 'the dirty platter after the feast'. On Saturday night, he brought more matches and candles but went out drinking with David Walker instead. On Sunday afternoon he finally decided what to do. He returned home, washed the corpse, lit the fire and then proceeded to burn the bloodstained apparel and the other unwanted items. It was not a job well done – witness the bloody jacket put into the trunk instead of the fire – but, like a dog standing on its hind legs, the marvel is that it was done at all.

The paper curls still nestling in Ellen's hair gave him the idea of creating a scene of domestic tranquillity shattered by tragedy. Ellen and he had retired to bed as normal; the following day he had found her dead on the floor. To enhance this he dressed her in the chemise. But in the flickering shadows cast by the light from the fire dancing in the background, the corpse, naked but for the chemise, reminded him overwhelmingly of Mary Kelly and his November bloodfest at Miller's Court. Desire momentarily took over and he began mutilating the remains again.

He effectively began where he left off during the first attack on Ellen, making similar incisions to the same areas of the body he had eviscerated during the final stages of Catharine Eddowes's murder, although with nowhere near the same intensity. Then he stopped. Unlike with the other occasions, it was a Sunday and he was not fuelled by drink, a fact confirmed by the police when they interviewed him an hour later – Parr: 'quite sober'; Lamb: 'sane and sober'.[48]

Without alcohol to sustain it, the arousal ebbed away to be replaced by the shame and self-loathing he had felt when he had mutilated Ellen the first time. Perhaps he found himself looking into her eyes, sightlessly accusing him. This was not remorse; the serial killer does not cross the line between feeling sorry for himself and sorrow for the victim. As Keppel points out, shame will afterwards turn to self-justification, the defence mechanism clicking into gear to produce the belief that the victim got what she deserved.[49] We have already seen this self-absorbed self-righteousness with Bury; we shall see it again where Ellen is concerned, even when he is standing in the shadows of the gallows.

Moreover, the more mutilations there were, the harder it would be to explain them to the police.

He arose and put the knife on the windowsill, Ellen's flesh still clinging to the blade. The incisions he had just made would hardly have bled, if at all. Templeman and Stalker found no sign of haemorrhaging around them, and Lamb reported that there was 'little or no blood' on the chemise.[50] Unable to bear the sight of Ellen's ruined corpse any longer, Bury bundled it into the trunk, smashing and breaking her limbs to make them fit in. Then he put on his coat and stepped out into the bitter night to embark on his final journey as a free man.

I cannot vouch for my reconstruction being exactly right in each and every particular. When events take place behind closed doors only the participants know for sure what took place, and even then they may not recall the details with absolute certainty. What I have tried to do is knit together the known facts to form a credible whole.

There are differences of opinion about the 'Jack Ripper' messages. An alternative theory is that Bury wrote them while drunk and forgot they were there. It is unlikely that Bury would have misspelled 'cellar' as 'seller', even when drunk. On the other hand, it is exactly what one would expect from the poorly educated Ellen. Likewise, their syntax also suggests a person of limited attainments. Even so, it cannot be ruled out entirely. We are dealing with a drink-prone multicide at the end of his tether and feeling the need to relieve the pressure on himself, just as another William, Heirens, did when scrawling his message on the apartment wall of one of his victims.

Another question raised is surely that Bury would have seen and expunged the graffiti? Nobody, however, made any mention of seeing him at the rear of the premises during his entire stay at Princes Street, and he would have regarded taking the ashes out as Ellen's job. He spent much of the weekend in David Walker's company, in the pub on Saturday, and either at Walker's lodgings or out walking with him on Sunday before returning home to make his preparations. Obviously he had good reason not to want to be there! When he was, he was somewhat preoccupied with what he was going to do. It is perfectly feasible that he never went out the back.

Whatever the explanation, the fact remains that the messages were there when the police arrived on Sunday night. This is confirmed by the *Dundee Advertiser* of 12 February, a copy of which was preserved in the police files on the case: 'The writing is older than the discovery of the tragedy, and the neighbours were startled and alarmed at the idea that one whom in their terror they associated with the Whitechapel tragedies had been living in their midst.'

Police at the scene suggested that they could have been the work of a boy. This appears to have been based on the handwriting, but, again, it fits Ellen's scholarly attributes perfectly. She had not, said Margaret Corney, had very much schooling and could not write very well.[51]

Plainly, the neighbours did not think one of their kids had written it and the idea is untenable, anyway. For a child to have written the graffiti prior to the discovery of what was, to all intents and purposes, a Ripper crime in that very apartment is simply not credible. There are a great many minor coincidences on display in the Ripper saga – it is one of the fascinations of the case – but this would be one of such gargantuan proportions that it is impossible to swallow.

The wording of the *Advertiser*'s article implies that the police were playing down any connection with the Ripper till Scotland Yard had been heard from. But back at Bell Lane others were jumping the gun and saying what the police really thought. On 12 February, the august *New York Times* subheaded a report entitled London's Great Mystery with the following: 'A wife murder in Dundee connects the husband with the long list of atrocities'.

Bury, said the newspaper, was 'probably "Jack the Ripper" and is subject to fits of unconscious murder mania'. The report continues:

> The theory of the [Dundee] *Police Officials* is that *Bury's wife knew of facts connecting him with the East End atrocities,* and that she took him to Dundee in the hope of preventing a recurrence of the crimes' [my emphasis].

The messages which Ellen chalked at the rear of the wretched apartment in which she ended her life were her indictment of William Bury. For almost a hundred years, they lay as silent and as forgotten as the grave in which she is buried. Today they stand as mute testimony to the real identity of history's most infamous unknown killer.

NOTES

1. David Lamb, statement to Procurator-Fiscal, 18 February 1889.

2. David Lamb, trial evidence, 28 March 1889.

3. Dr Charles Templeman, statement to Procurator-Fiscal, 14 February 1889.

4. The police's special inventory of items found in the fireplace on 11 February lists three brooches and an earring found in the ashes. Obviously, Bury did not consider the brooches as good as the two he pocketed.

5. *Dundee Advertiser*, 13 February 1889.

6. Under Scottish law, the Procurator-Fiscal takes control of a case following the police's initial investigations.

7. According to a journalist friend, the facsimiles would be obtained by reversing the negatives of the photographs.

8. Scottish Record Office reference AD 141891160.

9. Lamb, op. cit.

10. Lamb, statement, 18 February.

11. Margaret Corney, statement to Procurator-Fiscal, 15 February 1889.

12. Police inventory, 12 February 1889.

13. Ibid.

14. Ibid.

15. 12 February 1889.

16. Statement, 14 February.

17. Dr David Lennox, trial evidence, 28 March 1889.

18. Lennox later termed this injury as 'a small bruise and transverse rupture of the skin', but Templeman and Stalker's view that it was an incised wound must be preferred, as they saw the corpse when it was fresher.

19. Brian Marriner, *A Century of Sex Killers* (pbk), p. 260.

20. Robert Keppel, *The Riverman* (hbk), p. 124.

21. Autopsy report, 22 July 1889.

22. Dr Charles Templeman, statement, 14 February.

23. Trial evidence, 28 March.

24. Robert Ressler (with Tom Shachtman), *Whoever Fights Monsters* (pbk), p. 189.

25. Ibid. p. 190.

26. John Douglas and Mark Olshaker, *The Cases that Haunt Us* (hbk), p. 32.

27. Keppel, op. cit., p. 406.

28. Ressler, op. cit., p. 189.

29. Keppel, op. cit., p. 345.

30. Jack Olson, *The Misbegotten Son* (hbk), p. 485.

31. Inspector Abberline, police report, 19 September 1888; Chief Inspector Donald Swanson, police report, 19 October 1888.

32. Keppel, op. cit., pp. 372–3. A rare example of an organised killer leaving the murder weapon behind at the crime scene.

33. Jessie Gibson and Jane Duffy, defence evidence, Bury's trial, 28 March 1889. The

Lees would not have been able to hear anything because of a staircase between their apartment and the Burys'.

34. Statement, 18 February.

35. Statement, 16 February.

36. Statement, 18 February.

37. Dr James Miller, statement, 19 February.

38. *Dundee Advertiser*, 12 February.

39. Jessica Snyder Sachs, *Time of Death* (hbk), pp. 6–7.

40. Professor Bernard Knight (ed.), *Simpson's Forensic Medicine*, 11th edn, p. 28.

41. Ibid., p. 28; W D S McKay (ed.), *Clinical Forensic Medicine*, 2nd edn, p 274–5; Sachs, op cit., p. 20.

42. Sachs, op. cit., p. 21.

43. Lamb, op cit.

44. The presence of the poker is confirmed by Lamb's inventory.

45. Trial evidence, 28 March.

46. Ibid.

47. Ibid.

48. Statements, 13 and 18 February, respectively.

49. Robert D Keppel, *Signature Killers*, pp. 101–3.

50. Statement, 18 February.

51. Trial evidence, 28 March.

CHAPTER TWELVE
THE EXECUTION OF JACK THE RIPPER

Outside of the immediate environs of Princes Street, the first indication that the good Burghers of Dundee might have the London bogeyman under lock and key came when Bury appeared at the Magistrates' Court on Monday morning. Then the ripples began to spread outwards.

If one believed Ellen's death had occurred on the 5th, it was exactly a year since Dundee's last murder, a young woman named Maggie Downs, who had been stabbed to death in the Cowgate district. Rather surprisingly, the culprit, one Dixon, received only an eight-year sentence for culpable homicide, but, as we will see, Dundonians were not exactly enamoured of the death penalty.

The magistrates remanded Bury in custody and that afternoon he was put up before the Sheriff's Court. During the interim, he had had to change from his own clothes into prison attire, with the result that, in the eyes of the *Dundee Courier*'s reporter, he was transformed from being 'a decent-looking man' into one who now appeared 'diminutive', 'insignificant' and 'weak-minded'. The reporter also thought that Bury had 'features somewhat of the Jewish or Semitic type', which was how he had appeared to Elizabeth Long in Hanbury Street.

He stood before Sheriff Campbell Smith for the better part of an hour answering questions calmly enough but occasionally showing signs of agitation. Throughout the session he kept his head down on his chest, avoiding eye contact with anyone. Garbed now in his prison corduroys and wearing the close-fitting, rounded hat then favoured by the penal system, Bury looked like that old racial stereotype, the Chinese coolie.

Chief Constable Dewar telegraphed Scotland Yard with details of the crime and its circumstances. There are two versions of what happened next. The first was offered by James Berry, the executioner who hanged William Bury:

> There was an idea that the London Police were slow to move in the matter, and I am told that they even encouraged the belief that Bury had no connection with the murders.
>
> In spite of this, however, Scotland Yard was working in secret to piece together the antecedents of Bury and satisfy themselves without stepping into the limelight that there would be an end to the flaring headlines in the newspapers of London that Whitechapel had seen yet another mysterious crime . . . Scotland Yard detectives . . . unknown to the Police of Dundee, were visiting every haunt of the prisoner, and submitting to a vigorous cross-examination every one who had known him.[1]

Much the same story was also given to crime historian Norman Hastings, with this addition:

> They [Scotland Yard] kept their own Counsel and when Bury came up for trial it was the common opinion that he was guilty of the Whitechapel crimes and would

make a full confession in the event of his being condemned to death.[2]

All of which I find very unconvincing. The story has all the hallmarks of being devised to cover up an uncomfortable truth, which was that Scotland Yard pooh-poohed the idea that Bury was the Ripper till almost the last minute, when they were suddenly galvanised into action.

If the Met were digging away behind the scenes then they certainly never let on about it to the Dundee Police. As late as 25 April – the day after Bury's execution – their official mouthpiece, the *Dundee Advertiser*, painted a picture of the Met as being slow and uncommunicative. Evidence of this can certainly be gleaned from the fact that, while the press interviewed the Burys' Spanby Road landlord, William Smith, on 12 February, Abberline did not get round to taking a statement from him till the 14th.[3]

And, despite assurances in the *Midland Wednesday News* of 13 February that Abberline and 'other detectives who were engaged in investigating the recent Whitechapel murders have been initiating inquiries among the relatives of the woman Bury', this never seems to have happened. A detective later told Norman Hastings, 'In spite of the organisation at their command Scotland Yard had really failed to trace the complete history of Bury.'[4]

Which explains why there is no statement on file from anyone connected with 11 Blackthorn Street. The Yard never traced them to that address. Yet it was not only known to Margaret Corney, but also the Dundee and Wolverhampton newspapers as early as the 13th (from Bury's business card)! Confirmation of the Yard's lack of interest in Ellen's relatives comes from the treatment meted out to her brother. When George called at his local police station in Bow after reading of his sister's death in London's *Evening Standard*, he was fobbed off with the advice that he should write to the Dundee Police.[5]

There is no evidence that any Met officer visited Dundee prior to 23 April or that Bond or Bagster Phillips was commissioned to go up to Scotland and have a look at the body – or even that Dewar was asked to forward a copy of the autopsy reports. Yet, laughably, one of the reasons given by the Yard for dismissing Bury as the Ripper at that time was that 'the murderer must have some surgical skill, this was entirely wanting in the murder of Mrs Bury'.[6]

Not only had they not seen the body, but the Yard were also contradicting the view of their own expert, Dr Bond, that the Ripper possessed no medical knowledge of any kind, plus those of Drs Brown, Llewellyn, Saunders and Sequeira, none of whom awarded him any surgical skills. They had clearly decided that Dundee and William Bury would be a similar wild-goose chase to the Beetmore episode the previous September.

It gets worse. Even before Abberline had taken statements from Martin, Haynes and Smith, London was dismissing Bury as the Ripper almost with contempt and certainly without adequate investigation as the following gem shows:

> The London authorities are not inclined to believe that prisoner was connected with any of the recent atrocities in Whitechapel, as he was well known in the locality, and *had never been seen out at any untimely hours*' [my emphasis].[7]

Just how extraordinary this statement is we shall see later.

The Met did hold the door very slightly ajar by 'intimating that their investigations would be continued'.[8] However, the following day it was slammed shut. At a press conference, a 'prominent' Scotland Yard investigator – unnamed but almost certainly Donald Swanson – pronounced William Henry Bury whiter than white insofar as the London murders were concerned. Asked whether he affixed any credit to Bury's statement that he was Jack the Ripper, the inspector responded,

'Not for a moment. Were he really the Whitechapel assassin stricken with remorse, we should have a detailed confession of all his crimes. As it is, he merely talks in a rambling, incoherent way about being the author of the London horrors. It is not often that a criminal is so deeply moved by remorse as to make a confession but when that does happen the confession is never made by halves. I have had men when finally driven to the wall break out in a tone at once despairing and relieved – "well, guvnor, I don't mind coming the whole b____ lot." Oh no; you may be quite sure this man Bury is not Jack the Ripper.'[9]

Running throughout this exchange is the unfortunate misunderstanding that Bury had actually confessed to being the Ripper. As we have seen, this was not the case, although it is doubtful whether the true picture would have made a ha'p'orth of difference to Scotland Yard's attitude anyway. According to the *Dundee Advertiser*, 'subsequent communications' to the Dundee Police endorsed their view that 'Bury had no connection with the Whitechapel horrors'.[10]

Robert Keppel stresses how important it is for police forces to work together once serial killers have crossed jurisdictional boundaries.[11] In February 1889, Dundee might as well have been in a time warp as far as London was concerned. Meanwhile, for the next nine weeks – virtually the entire length of time it had taken Bury to commit the 'canonical' murders – Scotland Yard had effectively closed down its investigation into the real Ripper.

For Bury's next court appearance, he was allowed to wear his own clothes again. On Monday, 18 March, he was arraigned to formally enter his plea of 'not guilty'. The *Dundee Advertiser* noted that his appearance was good and his demeanour quiet. During the three-minute hearing, he was dressed in the clothes he had been arrested in. A sketch made of him in the dock silently congratulates the powers of observation of those who saw him in Berner Street, a small, dark man of around 30 clutching a felt hat in his left hand while the right rests on the dock rail. The overall impression is of a clerical worker. The only difference was that he now had a beard and side whiskers, grown since William Marshall and PC Smith had said that Elizabeth Stride's assassin had none.

Bury had acquired the services of a local solicitor, David Tweedie, and a barrister, William Hay, an advocate with a glowing reputation in Dundee.[12] Hay was to be complimented on the quality of Bury's defence by the judge, Lord Young, and his opponent, the advocate deputy, Dill McKechnie. However, Hay and Tweedie might have felt at times as though they were trying to find shards of gold among their client's old sawdust. The main defence plank seemed an improbable one, though Dr Lennox endorsed Bury's story that Ellen had strangled herself. Ironically, it would have mustered more support today; Bernard Knight remarks, 'Self-strangulation by ligature is not uncommon and the victims may be able to wind several turns of rope or wire around their neck and tie multiple knots before dying.'[13]

But, in Dundee in March 1889, Dill McKechnie more or less laughed Lennox and his raw recruit, Dr Kinnear, out of court, advancing his puckish humour from behind the near-impenetrable barrier put up by Templeman, Stalker and the Crown's special adviser, Dr Littlejohn, all of whom emphatically ruled out the possibility of suicide.

Yet behind this confident veneer the Crown had troubles. When it came to the mutilations on Ellen's body, Mr McKechnie could say no more than that they might have been inflicted in a 'mad' or 'playful' manner (!), but that the jury could discount them anyway because the only issue before them was whether Ellen's death was murder or suicide. Hay, wisely, attempted no explanation.

The constraints on the prosecution had actually been imposed by Scotland Yard! The only conceivable reason for the mutilations was that Bury was compelled to do them, and in spring 1889 there was only one man in Britain with the compulsion to eviscerate a woman's private parts. But none of this could be raised against Bury at his trial because Scotland Yard had emphatically ruled him out as that man, meaning that he could now be tried only as a domestic murderer in a Scottish court. There, any mention of the Ripper crimes would be grossly periodical to him. Ironically, the only time that it was raised was his explanation to Parr of why he had not gone to the police earlier. The prosecution could only hope that the jurors would use their common sense. They almost didn't!

It likewise meant that the Crown had no credible motive to put before the jury. The only one they had had originally been canvassed by the Dundee Police on 11 February: Bury had murdered and mutilated Ellen because he feared exposure as the Ripper. But that was now out of the window as well. Bury could not be tried as Jack the Ripper in Scotland if he wasn't Jack the Ripper in London.

Hamstrung by this, McKechnie offered the premise that, having had Ellen's money, Bury had decided to do away with her and dragged her all the way to Scotland to accomplish this: 'Why the prisoner should have come to Scotland was probably because he did not know about the country. He probably thought the people here were still a savage people and that there was no justice in the land.'

McKechnie was flying a kite with the word 'prejudice' writ large on the streamer, and well he knew it. But he hadn't anything else. William Hay's answer was simple and to the point: 'If the prisoner left London and came to Dundee for the purpose of murdering his wife, he would not have advertised his address in Dundee as he had done.'

Bury of course had no need to harm Ellen. All he needed to do was simply walk out of her life. He didn't, because she knew too much!

The trial had pride of place in opening the spring session of the High Court on 28 March, a year to the day of the attack on Ada Wilson.

It was 16 years since anyone had been tried for their life in Dundee – Thomas Scobie, who was convicted of murdering a gamekeeper while poaching – and a huge crowd was anticipated, especially as the man on trial had been linked to the now legendary Jack the Ripper murders.

For this reason, Lord Young decided to dispense with the customary opening ceremonies and sit all day till they got a verdict.

In the event, cold and rain kept the crowd down to several hundred initially. Only those who appeared respectable were allowed inside to sit in the public gallery, mostly women.

The 15-man jury consisted of two farmers, publicans and stationers, a jeweller, an engineer, a labourer, a factory worker, a tea merchant, a joiner, a grocer, a china merchant and an 'assessor' (of what we are not told).

One of the publicans was David Robb. Many years later his great-granddaughter, Eleanor Lynch, wrote to the *Courier* to say that Robb had attributed Bury's behaviour to drink.[14] Doubtless Lynch would have been less than amused by the *People's Journal*'s rather acerbic verdict on her great-grandfather and his colleagues: 'It cannot be said of the Jury that its appearance suggested high intelligence, nor can it be said that one of the verdicts which it returned suggested that the Jury was better than its appearance.'[15]

The first witness was Margaret Corney. Neatly dressed in deep mourning, she gave her evidence clearly and intelligibly despite constantly hovering on the brink of tears. She broke down only once, when the box in which Ellen had been found was brought into court. The *People's Journal* describes her face as 'interesting'; a sketch gives it a faraway look, as if she were wistfully recalling happier childhood days spent with her sister in Southwark.

Margaret was in the witness box an hour and a half before her place was taken by James Martin. A tall, smartly dressed man with dark hair smoothed down on the right and a heavy brown moustache – which made him look older than his late thirties –

Martin impressed the *Journal*'s reporter as a streetwise cockney. His accent at times grated sharply on his Scottish listeners and occasionally drew laughter from the public gallery, but there was nothing remotely funny about the picture he painted of Bury as a drunken wife batterer.

That image was reinforced by Elizabeth Haynes with her evidence of Bury's knife-wielding attack on Ellen shortly after the wedding. The *Journal*'s reporter portrayed Haynes as a traditional Londoner, as cockney as jellied eels and speaking in a dialect 'rarely heard beyond the sound of the "great bell of Bow"'. He would have been surprised to learn that she came from the same Worcestershire area as the man on trial. Middle-aged and grey-haired, in the sketch Mrs Haynes is a matronly-looking woman with somewhat rustic features.

There was little Hay could do about these witnesses, or the picture they were building up of William Bury. When he began to cross-examine Martin about his brothel, Lord Young intervened to point out that this would not show Ellen in a very good light. Bury, meanwhile, hardly glanced at his accusers and seemed entirely unconcerned about what they were saying about him.

The witnesses came and went, little bricks in the prosecution's case being cemented in around the hole that the motive should have occupied. At 1.40, as Margaret Robertson stepped down from the witness box, Lord Young announced the court would recess for lunch. Bury ate a meal of soup and brown bread, seemingly unperturbed by the drama unfolding around him, as though he were a spectator and not the centrepiece. Perhaps somebody should have reminded him that 'brown bread' is cockney rhyming slang for dead.

Bury's apparent indifference continued when the court resumed. He betrayed no emotion as Dill McKechnie and Lord Young dragged David Walker's testimony out of him – the one friend of a friendless man – but suddenly became attentive when Lieutenant Lamb entered the witness box with the opening barrage of the Crown's heavy artillery. Hay's cross-examination was searching and played out against a backcloth of Bury periodically whispering instructions to David Tweedie. When Lamb left the box, he was no doubt reflecting on the drudgery of a policeman's lot: tomorrow, he and Campbell would be back here giving evidence against a local publican accused of receiving stolen goods.

The hub of the Crown's case was the medical evidence. Here, Hay pressed Templeman closely and he could have done without Lord Young taking over to 'clear up some of the phantom difficulties Mr Hay had raised', as the *People's Journal* put it. Dr Littlejohn rounded out the prosecution evidence, after which they rose for supper.

Milk and porridge awaited Bury in the cells below and at last he showed his guards a flash of the real Jack the Ripper, sneering at the porridge: 'This is the kind of thing we give to the pigs in England.' But he steadied himself with the milk and seemed just merely downcast when he said, 'Littlejohn was very hard against me.'

The defence case consisted of only a handful of witnesses, including the Reverend Gough, with Dr Lennox's evidence as its linchpin. McKechnie's jibes at him drew a rebuke from Young during his summing-up, even though the judge had not resisted the temptation to poke fun at Lennox himself.

The shadows of evening had now fallen across the courtroom but Young directed that only a couple of the gas jets be turned on lest the room become too stuffy. To the *Advertiser*, the court now reflected a 'weird and shadowy appearance' as the counsels embarked on their closing speeches. It must have seemed to Bury that he was back in Whitechapel at dusk, but this time he was the one with the cold hands of death stretching out towards him.

McKechnie spoke for only 20 minutes. The famous English advocate Sir Patrick Hastings once told a jury that he could afford to be brief whereas his opponent would need to be four times as long.[16] Implicit in McKechnie's brevity was that same confidence in his case.

Hay, despite the eloquence for which he was commended by Lord Young, required an hour, and the evening was drawing on when the judge took over with his summation. The *Advertiser's* reporter had thought him hostile to the defence, judging by his interventions, and was pleasantly surprised by his impartiality. At 10.05, he sent the jury out to their deliberations.

Back down in the cells again, Bury was cock-a-hoop. 'At six o'clock tomorrow morning I will be back at Princes Street packing up my clothes to start for London.' But he was through with the East End; he would settle down in some new district. He had not long to indulge this particular fantasy: at 10.30 the jury was back: 'We find the prisoner guilty but with a strong recommendation to mercy.'

On the bench Lord Young's features were hooded in darkness, relieved only by a pair of candles flickering in front of him, and his voice had a disembodied effect, as though it came from a long way off, as he spoke demanding to know why they had reached such a verdict.

One of the jurors, not the foreman, answered that it was due to the conflicting medical evidence. That, said the judge, was unacceptable as a basis for mercy; they would have to retire again till they were satisfied about the evidence.

After they had gone out, opinion in the courtroom moved very strongly in favour of a 'not guilty' or 'not proven' verdict. The latter is a verdict peculiar to Scotland, discharging the prisoner but enabling him to be retried at a later date should further evidence come to light.

In fact, the jurors were back after only a few minutes. At 10.40, they pronounced Bury guilty for the second time that evening, this time without the rider. The verdict was unanimous. 'I have been inquiring whether we can dispense with your attendance tomorrow,' said Young, 'and I am informed that we can. So I shall gladly relieve you from further attendance at this circuit.'

The words were polite but the acid in Young's tone would have stripped paint. He was hardly less corrosive as he turned to the man in the dock, the black cap having been placed on his head: 'I am not in a position to say anything which would at all be profitable to you . . . I shrink from prolonging even for a few moments this painful scene with unprofitable and therefore idle remarks of my own.'

Bury listened impassively to the sentence of death. Then he leaned over the dock rail and thanked Tweedie and Hay for their services. Not till he was on his way down to the cells did he falter. Turning to his guards, he said brokenly, 'I will never see you again.' Tears stood in his eyes. But they were entirely for himself of course. His victims could go hang in his stead – except, of course, they were already deep and dead.

Outside, the crowd had grown during the course of the evening to an estimated 5000 people. The *Courier* noted with evident satisfaction that an edition bearing the result had been published within minutes of its being announced and several thousand copies sold. Jack the Ripper was always good business for the newspaper industry.

David Tweedie's work on his client's behalf had not ended with the verdict. Over the weekend, he drafted a petition for Bury's sentence to be commuted to life imprisonment. The document was sent to Lord Lothian, Secretary of State for Scotland, on, ominously, 1 April.

Tweedie cited two grounds for reprieve. The first was that the jury had not been entirely convinced by the medical testimony. The other evidence, said Tweedie, was entirely circumstantial and the jury's recommendation of mercy meant that the Crown had not proven its case with the absolute certainty to justify the death penalty.

It was a strong argument and the solicitor ensured that the text was printed in the *People's Journal* the following Saturday. There was a strong liberal and humanitarian tradition in Dundee and folk there had less than happy memories of capital punishment.

John West (or Watt), the first man to be executed in Dundee, was hanged in 1801 for nothing more serious than a minor burglary. A quarter of a century later, David Balfour symbolically stabbed his serially unfaithful shrew of a wife through the heart and then gave himself up with the words, 'All I wanted was a smile and a kind word.' Balfour was persuaded to plead guilty so that all the extenuating circumstances could be brought out, but they were ignored by the Home Secretary, who refused to commute his sentence. As the noose was fastened around Balfour's neck, people claimed to have heard a series of 'fearful rushing sounds', which led to mass panic and many injuries. The debacle was attributed to God's anger at the execution.

Some idea of how popular capital punishment was in Dundee can be gleaned from the next execution, a rapist named Mark Devlin in 1836. The executioner insisted on wearing a hood in case he was recognised and for many years afterwards a local man named Livingstone, suspected of being the hangman, had to carry about with him a document attesting to his whereabouts elsewhere on the day of the execution. Three years after this, Dundonians were outraged again when Arthur Woods, a once prosperous businessman now fallen on hard times, was hanged for murdering his son in a domestic row. The next case did nothing to quell unease. In 1847, a jury deciding the case of a wife poisoner found him guilty only after several jurors who had favoured 'not proven' accepted a compromise of a recommendation to mercy. Instead, the authorities granted a short stay of execution while the facts of the case were re-examined and then proceeded with the execution.

The upshot was that for the next 42 years nobody was executed in Dundee. Plea bargaining proved an effective way of circumventing the noose, with killers being allowed to plead guilty to crimes – 'a shade less heinous than murder', as the *People's Journal* put it.[17] One beneficiary was Dixon, Maggie Downs's killer, who could probably count himself lucky, although not as fortunate as a man named

Urquhart, who escaped the noose despite having 'smashed his little girl of three into jelly with a poker' while intoxicated.[18] Only in four instances was the capital sentence pronounced and all were reprieved. Bridget Kiernan and Catherine Symon, two destitute single mothers who committed infanticide, and Alexander Hutchinson, convicted of killing his alcoholic wife, were all reprieved on humanitarian grounds, Kiernan after a campaign by the *Advertiser*. The Home Office seems finally to have tacitly understood local feelings. But the fourth recipient of its largesse, the aforementioned Thomas Scobie, was simply not fated to die at the end of a rope. Uniquely for Dundee, the neanderthal Scobie elicited no degree of public sympathy but when the trial judge sentenced him to hang on 'Tuesday, April 29th, next to come' he forgot that April had already commenced and that by the legal definition of his sentence Scobie could not be executed till the next full April in which the 29th fell on a Tuesday! As this was 1879, six years hence, the Home Secretary reluctantly granted a commutation.

Given all these factors, and a general feeling that was beginning to blossom in Dundee that Bury was insane, Tweedie must have been reasonably optimistic that his client's life would be spared.[19] Leaving no stone unturned, he proffered a family history of insanity as his second ground for clemency, listing Mary Jane's incarceration and death in Powick asylum. This, however, cut no ice: a minute in the Scottish Office files notes that her mania was not of the homicidal variety.

Bury, meanwhile, was settling into the grim existence of a condemned man in Dundee Gaol. The death cell was located in the northwest corner of the prison's main block and was continuously lit by gas. The surroundings were otherwise very Spartan: a fireplace, a metal bed, a table, stool and chair. He was guarded day and night by at least one warder.

For the first few days he was withdrawn and taciturn, but as time wore on he began to relax a little, sleeping soundly at night and talking about his chances of a reprieve. He busied himself writing and had the pick of the prison library, reading mainly wildlife books and the Bible. It is a common feature of serial killers that after sentencing their equilibrium begins to return. The awful, crushing burden of their crimes starts to recede and the subconscious death wish fades. Now the objective is to avoid execution and they focus on using others to this end. Here, William Bury was the progenitor of latter-day multicides like Bundy, Lucas and John Wayne Gacy.

His born-again zest for the Bible went hand in glove with his manipulation of the Reverend Gough, who visited him daily. On Sundays he asked for the cell door to be left open so that he could hear the services conducted in the corridor of the south wing by the prison chaplain, the Reverend D R Robertson.

On Wednesday, 10 April, Gough wrote to the Scottish Office in support of Bury's reprieve petition. The clergyman recorded his 'growing conviction that Bury is not guilty of the crime laid to his charge. The man is unquestionably not only sane but very intelligent.'

Intelligent enough, regrettably, to have pulled the wool over the eyes of a decent man who was trying to help him.

No prison story is complete without its bizarre tale, and Bury is no exception. While he was on remand a woman calling herself 'Mrs Handbury' contacted the police with a claim that ten years earlier she had married a man named George Handbury, who hailed from London and hauled sawdust and firewood for a living. They settled in Dundee but the relationship did not prove a success. Handbury became bad-tempered and was very mysterious about his background, at night pulling the bedclothes over his head as though fearful of something in his past. Eventually he became obsessed with another woman and threatened to shoot her if she did not run away with him. Subsequently he had left home and returned to London. From the description given of Bury, his wife thought he may be her errant spouse. She was taken to the prison but failed to identify him.

The suspicion must be that the name 'Handbury' was derived from the Hanbury Street murder and that the woman simply wanted to get a look at the man who might be Jack the Ripper? If so, then she succeeded.

As the execution date approached, Bury began to show signs of anxiety. When Reverend Gough called on him on the 19th, Bury greeted him with the news that he had murdered Ellen and now wished to set the record straight. [20]

Gough's reaction can only have been one of sadness at Bury's duplicity, but the gentle clergyman was to stay by his side to the end. According to the *Dundee Advertiser* of 25 April, Bury reiterated his confession in writing. The document was apparently deposited with David Tweedie. The *People's Journal*, which published the details two days later (see the previous chapter), does not give its source, merely remarking that Bury had also confessed to 'others' besides Gough. However, the *Midland Weekly News* of the same date was rather less reticent and named the source as Bury's 'legal agent', i.e. David Tweedie.

Gough, though, did ask Bury to 'also commit to writing the simple fact of his guilt', aside from the confession, which the condemned man did on the 22nd. [21] That morning, Tweedie brought news as cold as the death it foretold. The reprieve had failed and Bury would hang two days hence, Wednesday, 24 April. For those who believe in portents, as one monster busied himself with preparations to leave this world, another with an infinitely greater capacity for evil had just made his entry into it, Adolf Hitler, born on Saturday, 20 April 1889.

There is nothing in the Scottish Office files to explain, specifically, why Bury's reprieve was not granted, beyond the dismissive comments about the nature of his mother's illness. Obviously, Lord Lothian entertained no doubts about his guilt, and, while there was a feeling in some quarters that Bury was insane, equally there was anger that he should bring his violence to Dundee and mar its inauguration as a City.

The crime had also unleashed the darker forces lurking inside one Dundonian. Two days after Bury was sentenced to death, Joseph Redmond, a grocer, fatally stabbed his wife in the back at their shop. Redmond's mental balance had been precarious for some time and he was swiftly incarcerated in the city's Westgreen lunatic asylum. It was said that he had become obsessed with the Bury case and that the verdict had tipped him over the edge.[22]

Above all else, the spectre of Jack the Ripper hovered over Dundee Gaol. Even as Lothian reached his decision, two gentlemen from Scotland Yard were at long last making preparations to travel north.

Bury was unaware of this. After hearing Tweedie's news in silence, he sat down and penned the written statement he had promised Gough, adding the proviso that the clergyman would release it only after the execution.

> I admit that it was by my own hands that my wife Ellen Bury met with her death. On Feb 4th in the house 113 Princes Street, Dundee by strangulation.
>
> But I solemnly state before God as a dying man that I had no intention of doing so before the deed was done.
>
> I have communicated to you my motive for the crime but as it concerns so closely the character of my wife I do not wish you to make it known publicly.
>
> And for this act of mine I ask the pardon of Almighty God trusting in his mercy to grant me that pardon which he is ever willing to give to those who are deeply sorry and truly penitent for their sins.
>
> I declare that as a dying man that this is the absolute truth.[23]

The confession, was addressed to Gough and witnessed by the prison governor, William Geddes, and a warder, John Robertson.

Paragraph three might stand as the definitive example of what Robert Keppel says about the serial killer reverting to the self-justifying belief that the victim deserved what she got. This, in subtle words, is what Bury is saying: it was all Ellen's fault; she was no good and asked for it.

It would be hard to imagine a more cowardly and despicable attack, but then Jack the Ripper was a cowardly and despicable man.

The implication in Bury's words – 'it concerns so closely the character of my wife' – needs to be read in conjunction with what appeared in the *People's Journal* about his stated motive: 'A quarrel occurred on account of certain suggestions made by his Wife with the view of his earning some money. The proposals were of such nature that Bury became furious . . .'

One interpretation of this is that Bury was saying that Ellen had suggested returning to her old profession with him taking on the role of minder or procurer.

If that were true, then Jack the Ripper's discovery that his wife wanted to prostitute herself would indeed have been likely to trigger off a homicidal rage, but Bury's feigned shock does not ring true. He knew Ellen was a working prostitute when he met her, and he lived in the brothel in which she serviced her clients. She had married him to escape that life, and like other Victorian women, expected her husband to provide for her. Instead, his idea of moral values was to lie, cheat and steal from her, drink away her nest egg, which he had got his hands on by battering her from pillar to post, infect her with venereal disease and finally add her to his list of victims when she threatened to expose him as the satanic murderer he was. Now, in true multicidal fashion, he was blaming the victim.

His deviousness may have extended beyond what he told Gough and Tweedie. There have always been rumours of a second written statement, a document that roused Scotland Yard from its prolonged torpor and forced it to take him seriously as the Ripper. Something did.

The *Scots Black Kalendar* mentions the possible existence of either a second statement or an addendum to his written confession, but this would seem to be the 'long written statement' referred to by several evening newspapers on 24 April, which, as Reverend Gough makes clear in a letter published the following morning in the *Dundee Courier*, is the broader confession made on the 19th. Unless part of the contents were withheld by David Tweedie and relayed secretly to London, it contains nothing about the Ripper murders.

That aside, there is an interesting letter to the Scottish Office in 1908 written by a journalist named Ernest Parr in which he claims to have seen a newspaper report stating that Bury 'made a full confession of the ripper crimes; which document was forwarded to the Secretary for Scotland'.[24]

Although here Parr's newspaper account may have been confusing Bury's admission to Ellen's murder with a Ripper confession in general. But unless one accepts the official Scotland Yard assurance of their continuing interest in Bury from his arrest – and the evidence is decidedly against it – then something suddenly galvanised them into action. Bury, we recall, did a lot of writing while he was in the death cell and in the days leading up to his execution became very anxious about the reprieve. We have seen how serial killers do make use of their crimes as a means of staving off execution.

Bundy and Lucas have used confessions as bargaining chips, not good for the soul but for the neck. Precisely what Bury wrote we cannot know without the input of his Scotland Yard file, which we do not have, but, if my assessment is correct, it was enough to put him fairly and squarely in the frame as Jack the Ripper. That the police did have access to Bury's prison writings was confirmed by the man who executed him, James Berry:

> The rest of the time he spent in writing, and his handwriting was submitted to the closest scrutiny. The

detectives who came from London saw it . . . it settled the matter beyond doubt for the handwriting of Jack the Ripper was known at Scotland Yard.[25]

How Bury's handwriting came to be 'known' at Scotland Yard was never explained to the hangman. He later came to believe that they were referring to a series of letters purportedly written by the murderer to the eminent Victorian doctor and alienist Lyttleton Forbes Winslow, although Berry is quick to add that he has no confirmation of this. In fact, the letters concerned were never passed to Scotland Yard.

So we can only speculate as to precisely what the detectives were referring to. Berry obviously assumed that they had examined Bury's handwriting at the prison, but it is equally possible that what they actually meant is that they had already seen it at the Yard, because Bury's jottings had been sent there for analysis. This would explain the Met's sudden interest.

If they were under the impression that Bury had written a Ripper letter, or letters, then this illusion was doubtless swiftly dashed by the Home Office expert's return to normal duties from the Parnell Inquiry, then in progress, because Norman Hastings's sources made no mention of handwriting links to Bury.

Perhaps, though, it is all very simple. Inspector Henry Moore is believed to have taken over Abberline's role in March 1889. Possibly, Moore did not share the latter's negative view of Bury and decided to investigate him more thoroughly. Something, or someone, picked up on Bury – take your pick.

By 1889, James Berry had held the office of public executioner for the better part of five years. His had been a colourful career, which was no stranger to controversy. On one occasion, questions had been asked in the House of Commons after Berry was paid £10 by a baronet to assist him in an execution. On another, in Ireland, he refused to attend the formal inquest on the man he had hanged, with the result that it was adjourned *sine die* and Phillip Cross remains officially alive to this day! Rather less humourlessly, two men whom Berry hanged did actually stay alive for several minutes, slowly suffocating to death, and he went to the other extreme with a prisoner named Goodale in Norwich, tearing his head off his shoulders.

Eclipsing all these, however, was the hanging – or rather attempted hanging – of 'Babbacombe' John Lee at Exeter. Three times the trapdoor failed to open, after which Lee's sentence was formally commuted and he became famous as 'the man they could not hang'. In fairness, the fiasco was not Berry's fault: the scaffold worked perfectly when Lee was not on it and the generally accepted explanation is that the timber joints were warped!

By 1888, the erosive drip, drip, drip of miscreants consigned to oblivion was beginning to tell on Berry. He changed from being a teetotaller to a heavy drinker and suffered a nervous breakdown after a triple hanging in Ireland. He developed a particular dread of hanging women, having become convinced that his first, Mary Leffey at Lincoln, was innocent.[26] His peace of mind cannot have been helped by the fact that he had actually danced with one of his victims, another namesake, called Elizabeth Berry, who was executed in 1887 for poisoning her little girl, although it is unlikely that he had any qualms about Mrs Berry's guilt: there is little doubt that she also murdered her mother and possibly her husband and son too.[27]

James Berry had of course heard of Jack the Ripper. As he travelled to Dundee that Monday, he had no idea that he was going to hang him. He left Dundee convinced that he had.

For what had been happening in London in the days leading up to Bury's execution, we turn to crime reporter Norman Hastings. I approached Hastings's writings on the Ripper with some degree of caution, finding some minor inaccuracies in his 1929 *Weekly News* series – the victims' ages for instance. On Bury, he regurgitates the myth of his blurting out that he was the Ripper when he gave himself up. But this is a mistake made by most previous writers and Hastings's objectivity is demonstrated by the fact that, minus the full range of facts assembled here, he stops short of endorsing Bury as the murderer. His potted account of the crimes are highly accurate and, impressively, he was the first historian to draw attention to a number of aspects of the case: Sarah Colwell's story and the Beetmore distraction for example, which nobody else mentioned till 1987 (Martin Fido)[28] and 1996 (Peter Turnbull),[29] respectively. Intriguingly, Hastings is specific about the number of incisions to Chapman's body (three) and does not repeat the canard that a pair of farthings were found at her feet, a common fallacy till the 1980s. Although it was published by the same newspaper, Hastings does not appear to have read and been influenced by James Berry's account, and his contacts can only have come from inside Scotland Yard. In effect, Hastings was giving a summary of what was in Bury's file there.

The Yard, he states, assigned a dozen detectives to check on Bury. They established that he was the same height and build as the suspect seen 'after [sic] two of the murders', and that he 'was in the habit of walking about very quietly and had often frightened people by his silent approach'.

Which recalls the slippers Mary Lee saw Bury go out in in the mornings:

> The knife that the terror [Hastings's term for the Ripper] used was probably just such a one as that carried about by Bury, and on one occasion when he was definitely known to be staying in the East End at the time of a Ripper Crime he had absented himself from the house for that night in the most suspicious manner.

Frustratingly, we do not know which of the murders Hastings is referring to here. It could be any of the 1888 crimes bar Chapman and Kelly.

At this point an old bugbear rears its head: 'Against that was the fact that he did not look much like a foreigner.'

Seen briefly in the darkness, Bury's dark features were easily mistaken for a foreigner's, and the *Dundee Courier* had noted the hint of Jewishness about him. Had Scotland Yard sent an officer to Dundee at the outset they would have known this.

The objection was, anyway, overcome by a new discovery. At the time of Annie Chapman's murder: 'Bury had kept away from his home and his manner on his return the next afternoon suggested a madman.'

This was buttressed by similar findings for the night of 8/9 November:

> '[T]he Police established that he was missing from his lodgings on the night Marie Kelly was done to death and that he was in the habit of carrying that knife around with him.
>
> His description was very like that of the man who had been speaking to Kelly on the night of the crime.'[30]

Here, the man Bury most resembled was the individual seen with Kelly by Caroline Maxwell.

Scotland Yard now found themselves up against Bury's execution date. It was decided that two officers should travel up to Dundee in secret. Who they were we do not know. Hastings mentions only the visit and its outcome, and it is at this point that James Berry takes up the story.

Berry's biographer, Justin Atholl, sets the scene for us:

> On one occasion he [Berry] was asked by a Scotland
> Yard detective to try and get something out of the
> condemned man. The prisoner was twenty-nine-year-
> old William Henry Bury, who was hanged in Dundee
> prison in 1889 for the murder of his Wife . . . the special
> interest of Berry and the Police lay in the suggestion
> that Bury was in fact the mysterious Jack the Ripper
> whose crimes had terrorised the East End.[31]

Berry was to try to get a confession out of his namesake while the
two London detectives hovered nearby. It has hitherto been assumed
that Bury was unaware of who they were, but Berry does not
confirm this and it would have made little sense for them to have
travelled all that way and not interviewed Bury themselves.[32]
Norman Hastings, who makes no mention of the hangman's story,
implies that an interview did take place in which Bury simply
stonewalled. Logically, it was after this that the two officers asked
James Berry to make a final attempt, as last-minute confessions were
quite common.

Wednesday, 24 April 1889. Bury rose at 5.20. On this, the last day
of his life, he was allowed to change into his own clothes again. He
breakfasted on poached eggs, bread and butter and tea and then read
the scriptures for a while before being permitted to smoke his pipe.
Having lit it, he remarked, 'This is my last morning on earth; I freely
forgive all who gave false evidence against me at my trial' – a little
whiff of hypocrisy to flavour an assassin's final hours – before adding
that he hoped God would forgive him.

Reverend Gough arrived at 6.30 according to the *Courier* – the
Advertiser had it three-quarters of an hour later – and at 7.30
Reverend Robertson added his ministrations. Meanwhile, the prison
bell tolled mournfully to announce the arrival of the two magistrates
who were to preside formally over this harrowing scene. In almost

every other execution there is a deep sense of sadness over a person's last living moments. You wonder what it is like to know you are about to die when the hands of a clock reach a certain position. Would you spin out every moment trying to make them last as long as possible, or sigh in weary resignation and want it to be over? What terror goes through the mind knowing that shortly you will never again speak to another person on earth, or that you will not again in life see friends and family, share joys and triumphs, do all the everyday things that are bound up with the living?

But none of these thoughts touches the heart with William Bury. Instead, we call to mind those whose lives and little happiness were curtailed to bring him fleeting morsels of perversion and the appalling photographs of Cathy Eddowes and Mary Kelly, broken on the wheel of his hatred.

By 7.45, the magistrates were in place; so too were those representatives of the press permitted to attend. In Scottish executions, two magistrates were seated behind a desk in the corridor facing the door of the death cell. Between them and the cell itself stood six warders, a burly phalanx to guard against the evil-doer inside.

At 7.53, Governor Geddes entered the cell and told Bury that it was time to make his final preparations. Stepping outside again, he sent a warder to fetch James Berry, who arrived clutching his pinioning belts. It is to him that we are indebted for what happened next:

> When I walked into the Cell Bury looked at me almost defiantly, and then he tussled his face up into a sneer.
>
> 'I suppose you think you are clever to hang me?'
>
> Now, there isn't much in that question when you see it in cold print, but had you heard it spoken you would have thought as I did at the time.

The man about to die laid particular emphasis on the last word he spoke. He talked as if he thought himself to be one who stood head and shoulders above every other criminal who had passed through my hands.

Meanwhile the detectives had drawn near, and were straining their ears to catch any word which might fall from his lips.

I looked at him and waited.

'I suppose you think you are clever because you are going to hang me,' he repeated. 'But because you are to hang me you are not to get anything out of me.'

Berry then manoeuvred him into a corner to pinion his arms. At first Bury glared but then held out his arms and, according to press reports, said, 'You have a very disagreeable task to perform,' to which Berry responded that he would make it as painless as possible. Neither was aware of the irony of coincidence that newspaper accounts of Bury's father's death had originally called him 'James Berry', and that Berry the hangman had himself once been the victim of a recalcitrant horse, bearing the scar from its kick on his cheek till his dying day.

Berry had the condemned man take off a pair of white linen cuffs and himself removed Bury's collar. After the execution he noted that the sleeve links discarded with the cuffs bore the Masonic insignia.

As he pinioned Bury, the executioner tried again, whispering in his ear, 'Now, if you have anything to say it will be as well for you to say it. When I get you on the scaffold I will not give you time to unburden yourself. It is your last chance.'

But William Bury never spoke to another living man again.

Out in the corridor sat the twin crows. It was before them, Magistrates Craig and Stephenson, that Bury was now paraded, ashen-faced, as Governor Geddes intoned the death warrant. Then it was placed on the table for them to sign. It was at this point that the *Courier*'s reporter saw one of Bury's eyes twitch distinctly. Simultaneously, his colleague on the *Advertiser* noted Bury's face 'pale and flush by turn'.

Bury's final destination was no more than 40 yards (37 metres) away and the death party moved off towards it in a tight, boxlike formation, led by two warders and followed by Geddes, Robertson and Gough, the last reading aloud the prayer for the dying, after which came Bury, flanked by more warders, with James Berry bringing up the rear.

A step behind them were a posse of dignitaries, including Chief Constable Dewar, Drs Miller, Templeman and Stalker, quite literally in at the kill, and those reporters privileged to have been granted access to Dundee's first hanging for nearly half a century and the last they would ever see for there were to be no more executions in the city after William Bury.

They passed through a small porch and came to a shed, which housed the scaffold, hastily erected, as the scene would otherwise have been visible to staff working in a public building in Loskee Road that overlooked the gaol. Public executions were banned in 1868 – they encouraged imitators!

The procession halted momentarily, the scaffold itself still not quite visible, and Berry darted forward and placed a white hood over the prisoner's head. Just another few steps and they stood before the scaffold where 'a smart looking young fellow', Scott, Berry's assistant, was waiting with the rope in his hand.[33]

Once Bury was on the scaffold, the rope was placed around his neck. Gough's peroration reached its climax. Inside the hood it must have seemed like a crescendo, jangling incandescently and incoherently with all manner of jumbled thoughts – terrors closing in on Bury – although how can we know what a condemned man thinks and feels in those few seconds? Reporters heard him respond with 'Amen', and then he cried out, 'Lord Jesus have mercy on me, Lord Jesus receive my soul.' And it was finally over as Berry pulled the level and launched the man who was Jack the Ripper into eternity. That afternoon's *Midland Evening News* provided him with a fitting epitaph: 'Justice has been vindicated, and an evil and vicious life terminated by an ignominious and shameful death.'

As Berry operated the lever, the two Scotland Yard men unobtrusively joined the knot of people standing before the scaffold. Theirs had been a secret journey known only to those who needed to know; seemingly not even Chief Constable Dewar was aware of who they were – if he actually noticed them there. Their only conversation was with the hangman.

> 'Well Mr Berry, will you tell us what opinion you have about him?'
>
> 'Did you hear him make that statement?' I asked.
>
> 'Oh yes, but unfortunately you could construe it two or three ways. It is nothing definite to go on. What do you think yourself?'
>
> 'I think it is him right enough.'
>
> 'And we agree with you,' replied one of the detectives.
>
> 'We know all about his movements in the past, and we are quite satisfied that you have hanged "Jack the Ripper". There will be no more Whitechapel crimes.'[34]

And, of course, there never were. The key phrase 'I suppose you think you are clever to hang *me*' (my emphasis) has often made its way into print but the most vital part has always been omitted. That is, '*because you are to hang me you are not to get anything out of me*' (my emphasis). Bury was telling his executioner that, because he was hanging him, he – and by extension the state, which employed him – would not get a confession out of him. Almost a century later, Ted Bundy said the same thing: 'If you bring the full weight of the State [execution] on them . . . you're a goner.'[35]

Bury's plan would appear to have been that he would clear up the London murders in return for which he would gain a reprieve and spend the rest of his life in gaol for the crime he had already been convicted of, Ellen's murder. The likes of Lucas and Bundy have thought the same way since. Scotland Yard and the Home Office were obviously not attuned to his wavelength.

James Berry, and later Norman Hastings, never revealed and probably didn't know the names of the two detectives. Their visit was known only to those who needed to know and probably that did not include even Dundee Police.

Donald Swanson would have delegated the task to a trusted subordinate, obviously somebody of Abberline's status, and, if he was now on other duties, his replacement, Moore, although another possibility is Inspector Roots, who had gone up to Durham to look into the Beetmore case the previous September. Roots is known to have been involved in the Ripper investigation as late as December 1888. Moore is the likelier of the two, however. His one and only newspaper interview sheds no light on it, but, then, nor does it on any aspect of the case.[36]

James Berry was resolute to his dying day that he had hanged Jack the Ripper. In 1908, he was interviewed by the aforementioned Ernest Parr, who in his letter to the Scottish Office states that Berry *'told me explicitly that Bury was known to have been Jack the Ripper'* (my emphasis).[37]

In 1892, Berry resigned after executing a man named Conway at Kirkdale Gaol, Liverpool, during the cause of which he had a row with the prison authorities. He became an evangelist but subsequently tried to get himself reappointed as hangman, destroying all the unsold copies of his autobiography in order to ingratiate himself with the Home Office. He is also said to have withdrawn a newspaper article about Bury's execution, deferring publication of his account of the Yard's visit to Dundee till after his death.[38] It was all to no avail, as he was never reinstated, and died in October 1913 at the age of 61.

He was unaware of the fact that the Met's enquiries into William Bury did not cease till his execution. We return to Norman Hastings:

> Scotland Yard concentrated on the personal details given to them. At first the facts they gathered pointed more and more clearly to Bury . . . but it was a slow task entailing months of work and they had been ordered to make nothing public.
>
> They established where he had been staying on the nights of three other of the Whitechapel murders, and from the recollections of those who lived nearby it was quite possible that he had the opportunity to commit them. In addition he had periodical outbursts of almost maniacal anger in which he cruelly ill treated his wife and threatened to use the knife on her. At such times he was very strange in his behaviour and people were afraid to approach him.
>
> All the evidence was entirely circumstantial with opinion at the Yard sharply divided as to whether Bury was the guilty man or not. Such information as was available never reached the public . . . Those in authority were quite content that this should be so, for it is a notable fact that at this period there were no more outrages and alarms throughout the kingdom, as though the execution of the Dundee murderer had removed the long period of terror in which the people had lived.[39]

Had William Bury's crimes occurred today, he could have been tried both in Scotland and then England, with his conviction for Ellen's murder used against him for the London murders. This is because it would have constituted evidence of 'system'. Established in 1915 by the 'Brides in the Bath' murders committed by George Joseph Smith, 'system' is evidence of a method of operation unique to one individual, or group of individuals. Like Smith's crimes, Ellen's murder was so identical to those of Nichols, Chapman and Eddowes that, in my view, it is *prima facie* evidence of system. More recently, system has unconsciously broadened into 'signature'. In 1966, despite their crimes differing from murder to murder, Ian Brady and Myra Hindley were convicted of the three the Crown then had evidence of on the grounds that killing children and burying them on the Moors was their signature. Bury's signature, his hate-filled sexual lust, can be seen as clearly in Ellen's murder as it was in London.

When he went to the gallows, the long shadow Jack the Ripper had cast over the East End was lifted.[40] That speaks as eloquently of Bury's guilt as do the glistening array of hard facts that we have examined. Ellen was the unwitting heroine of this blood-soaked saga. She died trying to say what she knew and now it has been said.

At the top of where Quickett Street used to be there is now just a desolate piece of waste ground. The surrounding area has been completely rebuilt, leaving this wild patch of land standing on its own as though developers fear to tamper with evil spirits that may lurk there. Fittingly, it is almost next door to Tower Hamlets Cemetery.

It was an early October afternoon in 1998, a bleak overcast day turning towards being cold with the wind growling and the clouds giving way to sudden squalls of rain. Standing on this derelict piece of ground I had the feeling that Jack the Ripper was grinding his teeth at me and I was comforted by the presence of a solitary police officer exercising his horse there. Even so, he could not dispel William Bury's benighted presence and it made comparisons with the blasted heath from *Macbeth* inevitable:

Fair is foul and foul is fair:
Lower through the fog and filthy air.

Here, in this street, it had all begun. William Bury met Ellen Elliott and laid the foundations for the marriage made in hell. There was something else, too. Here not only was the myth of Jack the Ripper created, but the seeds of a genre came to fruition, one etched in blood against the most repulsive canvas human wickedness can devise, and nourished by what Shakespeare has Banquo term the 'insane root which holds reason prisoner'. Today, all we can do is lop the heads off the hydra as they show themselves.

One of them belonged to Frederick Walter Stephen West, whom we British have turned into a modern-day Sweeney Todd – never mind the evil, enjoy the story. The Ripper, too, has become such a creature of the entertainment industry that we might as well award him an Equity card. But the reality is that Fred West and Jack the Ripper were twin scavengers meeting on the cusp of hell.

They go well together. West was Bury reinvented. Both were born in rural poverty; both were thieves. Bury peddled sawdust from a horse and cart; West once drove an ice-cream van. Bury married a prostitute from the house in which he dwelt; Rose West serviced clients at the home she shared with Fred. But the most startling comparison is that Fred West's first wife was also a prostitute before they married, and, like the Burys', their relationship was marked by his violence towards her, which culminated in his strangling her to avoid exposure for previous murders.

Fred West had never heard of William Bury, yet he imitated him, because he was imitating Jack the Ripper. So, too, did Kurten, Christie, Lucas, Sutcliffe, 'Warren', Bundy and all the other grossly inadequate perverted deviants, gnarled and twisted with hatred, whose horrors have leaped out at us from every page of this book.

During the final stages of writing it, I chanced upon a Sunday-morning religious programme. It had nothing to do with the subject of this work, yet in a way it had everything to do with it because one of the participants made this simple but far-reaching declaration about the way in which we treat children in our society: 'If adults think children are worthwhile they'll believe they're worthwhile themselves.'[41]

If we are to overcome the terrible threat posed by the serial offender, then this is the lesson we must learn.

NOTES

1. *Weekly News*, 12 February 1927.
2. Ibid., 26 October 1929.
3. *Dundee Courier*, 14 February 1889.
4. *Weekly News*, 26 October 1929.
5. *Dundee Courier*, 14 February 1889, which records George as living at 84 Ford Road, Bow. Irritatingly, it appears to be the one address missing from the road in the 1891 Census.
6. *Dundee Advertiser*, 25 April 1889.
7. *Dundee Courier*, 14 February 1889.
8. *Dundee Advertiser*, 25 April 1889.
9. *Dundee Courier*, 15 February 1889, quoting answers given to the *New York Herald*'s reporter.
10. As reported in the newspaper on 25 April.
11. Robert Keppel, *The Riverman* (hbk), p. 165.
12. *Dundee Advertiser*, 19 March 1889.
13. Professor Bernard Knight (ed.), *Simpson's Forensic Medicine*, 11th edn, p. 77.
14. Letter in *Dundee Courier*, 2 December 1977.
15. 30 March 1889.
16. *Laski v. the Newark Advertiser*, 1945.
17. 27 April 1889.
18. Ibid.
19. Ibid. The newspaper describes Bury as 'irresponsibly insane'.
20. Gough, in a subsequent letter to the *Courier*, merely says 'last week', but the *Advertiser* (25 April) is more specific in stating 'Friday last'.
21. Reverend Gough, letter to *Dundee Courier*, 24 April 1889.
22. *People's Journal for Dundee*, 30 March 1889.
23. Scottish Public Records office ref. HH16/69.
24. Ernest Parr, letter, 28 March 1908.
25. *Weekly News*, 12 February 1927.

26. Brian Bailey, *Hangmen of England*, pp. 89–104.

27. Berry was her married name; she was born Elizabeth Welsh and later used her stepfather's name, Finlay.

28. Martin Fido, *The Crimes, Detection and Death of Jack the Ripper*.

29. *The Killer Who Never Was*, published in 1996.

30. *Weekly News*, 26 October 1929.

31. Justin Atholl, *The Reluctant Hangman*, p. 71.

32. Justin Atholl says that Berry 'claimed to have questioned Bury with hidden detectives listening'. His book, however, was published over 40 years after James Berry's death and this seems to have been a misinterpretation of Berry's own account published in 1927. It is also difficult to see how the detectives could in some way have remained hidden from view in a prison cell.

33. *Dundee Advertiser*, 25 April.

34. *Weekly News*, 12 February 1927.

35. Keppel, op. cit., p. 280.

36. Stewart Evans and Keith Skinner, *The Ultimate Jack the Ripper Sourcebook* (hbk), pp. 675 and 678.

37. Letter, 28 March 1908. Parr subsequently wrote again saying that, since his last letter, 'further details to hand certainly point to the criminal referred to having had something to do with the crimes attributed to the Ripper'. Unfortunately, Parr does not enlighten us as to what these were.

38. Private information given to the author. The source is impeccable.

39. *Weekly News*, 26 October 1929.

40. There were a number of Ripper 'scares' over the next few years as well as Alice MacKenzie, Elizabeth Jackson mid-1889, the Pinchin Street torso in September of that year, and, finally, Frances Coles (February 1891). None is given credence as a Ripper murder.

41. *Who is this Jesus?*, ITV1, 10 March 2002.

BIBLIOGRAPHY

JACK THE RIPPER

Begg, Paul, *Jack The Ripper: The Uncensored Facts*, Robson Books, 1988.

Begg, Paul, Fido, Martin, and Skinner, Keith, *The Jack the Ripper A to Z*, 1st, 2nd, 3rd edns, Headline Books, 1992, 1994, 1996.

Connell, Nick, and Evans, Stewart, *The Man Who Hunted Jack The Ripper*, Rupert Books, 2000.

Evans, Stewart, and Skinner, Keith, *The Ultimate Jack The Ripper Sourcebook*, Robinson Books, 2000.

Fido, Martin, *The Crimes, Detection and Death of Jack the Ripper*, Weidenfeld, 1987.

Hinton, Bob, *From Hell . . . The Jack the Ripper Mystery*, Old Bakehouse Publications, 1998.

Macpherson, Euan, *The Trial of Jack the Ripper*, Mainstream Publishing, 2005.

Odell, Robin, *Jack the Ripper in Fact and Fiction*, Harrap, 1965.

Paley, Bruce, *Jack the Ripper, The Simple Truth*, Headline Books, 1995.

Smithkey, John C III, *Jack The Ripper: The Inquest of the Final Victim Mary Kelly*, Key Publications, 1998.

Sugden, Philip, *The Complete History of Jack the Ripper*, Robinson Books, 1994.

Turnbull, Peter, *The Killer Who Never Was*, Clark Lawrence, 1996.

SERIAL KILLERS

Birnes, William J, and Keppel, Robert D, *The Riverman*, Constable, 1995.

——, *Signature Killers*, Arrow Books, 1998

Burgess, Ann, Douglas, John, and Ressler, Robert, *Sexual Homicide, Patterns and Motives*, Lexington Books, 1988.

Douglas, John, and Olshaker, Mark, *The Anatomy of Motive*, Pocket Books, 2001.

——, *The Cases that Haunt Us*, Simon & Schuster, 2000.

——, *Journey Into Darkness*, Arrow Books, 1998.

——, *Mindhunter*, Arrow Books, 1997

Gregg, Wilfred, and Lane, Brian, *The Encyclopedia of Serial Killers*, Headline Books, 1992.

Larsen, Richard W, Bundy, *The Deliberate Stranger*, Pocket Books, 1986.

Marriner, Brian, *A Century of Sex Killers*, Forum Press, 1992.

Norris, Joel (Dr), *Serial Killers: The Growing Menace*, Arrow Books, 1990.

Olsen, Jack, *The Misbegotten Son*, Headline Books, 1993.

Ressler, Robert, and Shachtman, Tom, *Whoever Fights Monsters*, Pocket Books, 1993.

Seaman, Donald, and Wilson, Colin, *The Serial Killers*, W H Allen, 1990.

MEDICAL WORKS

Cummins, Richard (Dr), Payne, Fiona (Dr), and Williams, Francis (Dr) (eds), *The Visual Dictionary of the Human Body*, Dorling Kindersley, 1991.

Erzinglioglu, Zakaria (Dr), *Forensic True Crime Investigations*, Carlton Books, 2000.

Joseph, Christopher, *Pocket Anatomy*, Silverdale Books, 2006.

Knight, Bernard (Prof.) (ed.), *Simpson's Forensic Medicine* (11th edn), Arnold, 1997.

Lechtenberg, Richard (Dr), *Epilepsy and the Family* (2nd edn), Harvard University Press, 1999.

McLay, W D S (Dr) (ed.), *Clinical Forensic Medicine* (2nd edn), Greenwich Medical Media, 1996.

Sachs, Jessica Snyder, *Time of Death*, William Heinemann, 2002.

Youngson, Robert (Dr) (ed.), and the Royal Society of Medicine, *Encyclopedia of Family Health*, Bloomsbury Publishing, 1995.

GENERAL WORKS

Abnett, Kathryn, Rhodes, Linda, and Shelden, Lee, *The Dagenham Murder*, Barking & Dagenham Libraries, 2005.

Anderson, Robert, *The Lighter Side of my Official Life*, 1910.

Atholl, Justin, *The Reluctant Hangman*, John Long, 1956.

Browne, Douglas, and Straus, Ralph, *The Rise of Scotland Yard*, 1956.

Bailey, Brian, *Hangmen of England*, The Leisure Circle Limited, 1989.

Barber, Richard, and Camps, Francis E (Prof.), *The Investigation of Murder*, Michael Joseph, 1966.

Britton, Paul, *The Jigsaw Man*, Corgi Books, 1998.

Canter, David (Prof.), *Criminal Shadows*, Harper Collins, 1994.

Carey, John (ed.), *The Faber Book of Reportage*, Faber & Faber, 1987.

Critchley, T A, and James, P D, *The Maul & The Pear Tree*, Constable, 1971.

Dew, Walter, *I Caught Crippen*, Blackie & Son, 1938.

Fishman, William (Prof.), *East End 1888*, Duckworth, 1988.

Foster, R F, *Lord Randolph Churchill, A Political Life*, Clarendon Press, 1981.

Friedland, Martin L, *The Trials of Israel Lipski*, Macmillan, 1984.

Knight, Stephen, and Taylor, Bernard, *Perfect Murder*, Grafton Books, 1987.

London, Jack, *The People of the Abyss*, Journeyman Press, 1977.

Smith, Sir Henry, *From Constable to Commissioner*, Chatto & Windus, 1910.

Wilson, Colin, *The Criminal History of Mankind*, Granada, 1984.

——, *The Mammoth Book of Murder*, Constable, 2000.

VIDEO/TV DOCUMENTARIES

Secret History: 'The Whitechapel Murders', Channel 4.

The Secret Identity of Jack the Ripper, Cosgrove-Muerer Productions, video.

Serial Killers – Ted Bundy, Channel Five, 1999.

——, 'John Wayne Gacy'.

——, 'Richard Ramirez'.

NEWSPAPERS AND PERIODICALS

Advertiser, Brierly Hill & Stourbridge Gazette

Bournemouth Guardian

Bristol Evening News

Daily Chronicle

Daily Mail

Daily News

Daily Telegraph

Dundee Advertiser

Dundee Courier & Argos

Dundee Weekly News

East Anglian Daily Times

Eastern Post & City Chronicle

East London Advertiser

East London Observer

Evening Express & Star

Globe

Halfpenny Weekly

Illustrated Police News

Lloyd's Weekly News

London Evening News

BIBLIOGRAPHY

London Evening Standard
Manchester Guardian
Midland Counties Express
Midland Evening News
Midland Wednesday News
Midland Weekly News
Morning Advertiser
Newcastle Chronicle
Newcastle Daily Journal
New York Times
Northern Daily Telegraph
Pall Mall Gazette
People's Journal for Dundee
Philadelphia Times
Ripperana
Ripperologist
Scotsman Magazine
Southampton Observer
Southend Observer
Star
Times
Weekly News
Western Mail
Worcester Chronicle
Yorkshire Post